Cambridge Studies in Management

The process of technological change

Cambridge Studies in Management

Formerly Management and Industrial Relations series

Editors
WILLIAM BROWN, *University of Cambridge*
ANTHONY HOPWOOD, *London School of Economics*
and PAUL WILLMAN, *London Business School*

The series focuses on the human and organisational aspects of management. It covers the areas of organisation theory and behaviour, strategy and business policy, the organisational and social aspects of accounting, personnel and human resource management, industrial relations and industrial sociology.

The series aims for high standards of scholarship and seeks to publish the best among original theoretical and empirical research; innovative contributions to advancing understanding in the area; books which synthesize and/or review the best of current research, and aim to make the work published in specialist journals more widely accessible; and texts for upper-level undergraduates, for graduates and for vocational courses such as MBA programmes. Edited collections may be accepted where they maintain a high and consistent standard and are on a coherent, clearly-defined, and relevant theme.

The books are intended for an international audience among specialists in universities and business schools, undergraduate, graduate and MBA students, and also for a wider readership among business practitioners and trade unionists.

The process of technological change

New technology and social choice in the workplace

JON CLARK

Senior Lecturer in Industrial Relations, Department of Sociology and Social Policy, University of Southampton

IAN McLOUGHLIN

Senior Lecturer in Industrial Relations, Kingston Business School, Kingston Polytechnic

HOWARD ROSE

Research Fellow, New Technology Research Group, University of Southampton

and

ROBIN KING

Senior Lecturer in Communications, School of Electrical Engineering and Computer Science, University of New South Wales, Australia

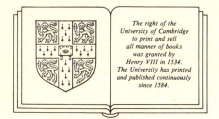

The right of the
University of Cambridge
to print and sell
all manner of books
was granted by
Henry VIII in 1534.
The University has printed
and published continuously
since 1584.

CAMBRIDGE UNIVERSITY PRESS

Cambridge
New York   New Rochelle   Melbourne   Sydney

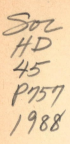

Published by the Press Syndicate of the University of Cambridge
The Pitt Building, Trumpington Street, Cambridge CB2 1RP
32 East 57th Street, New York, NY 10022, USA
10 Stamford Road, Oakleigh, Melbourne 3166, Australia

First published 1988

Printed in Great Britain at The University Press, Cambridge

British Library cataloguing in publication data
The process of technological change: new technology and social
choice in the workplace. – (Cambridge Studies in Management).
1. British Telecom 2. Industrial relations–Great Britain 3.
Telecommunications–Great Britain–Technological innovations
I. Clark, Jon II. Series
331'.04138406541   HE8100.B7

Library of Congress cataloguing in publication data
The process of technological change.
(Cambridge Studies in Management)
Bibliography.
Includes index.
1. Technological innovations – Management.
2. Industrial relations – Effect of technological
innovations on.
I. Clark, Jon, Dr.Phil. II. Series.
HD45.P757 1988   658.5'14   87-6641

ISBN 0 521 32303 7

CE

Contents

Contents

Contents

Illustrations

List of illustrations

Tables

Acknowledgements

This book could not have been written without the support of a large number of people. First and foremost we would like to thank British Telecom for allowing us to carry out the research discussed in this book, and all the staff in BT, the National Communications Union (NCU) and the Society of Telecom Executives (STE) who gave us so much of their time over such a long period. We would particularly like to thank Ray Bluett, Brian Haigh, Bernard Stewart, John Tippler, David Barfoot, Alan Kelly, Deryck Rogers, Les Burridge, Ron Noakes, John Brooks, John Lashmar, Howard Marchant, Ted Webb, John Starmer, Alan Webb, Mike Henson, John Ellis, Bill Harvey, Phil Roberts, Steve Webb and the ubiquitous Melvin Johnson. We would like to stress, though, that the views expressed in this book are exclusively those of the authors and do not necessarily reflect the opinion of British Telecom, the NCU or the STE.

Major sections of the book are based on fieldwork conducted over four years by the four named authors, and our report of 150 pages presented to BT, the NCU and the STE in the spring of 1985. We owe a special debt of gratitude to other members of the New Technology Research Group at the University of Southampton who assisted in setting up and carrying out the research, in particular Bob Smith, John Smith, Hazel Downing, Ruth Carr, Gordon Causer and Heather Rolfe. We would also like to acknowledge the support of the Joint Committee of the SERC and ESRC, who funded the research programme of which our studies in British Telecom were a part.

Special thanks are due to Julie Zillwood, who cheerfully and efficiently typed more versions of this book (and the report which preceded it) than she would probably care to remember, and to all the members of the academic and clerical staff in the Department of Sociology and Social Policy and the Department of Electronics for their forbearance and assistance throughout the research and the production of this book.

In the early phases of our work we were particularly fortunate to enjoy the support and encouragement of Dorothy Wedderburn and Harold

Acknowledgements

Palmer. The manuscript was read in its final stages by Deryck Rogers and Alan Kelly (British Telecom), Paul Willman (London Business School) and Rod Martin (Imperial College), and we are most grateful to them for comments which have enabled us to correct some of the weaknesses and highlight some of the strengths in our argument.

Photographs are reproduced by kind permission of British Telecom plc. Special thanks are due in this connection to David McMillan and Sue Hunt of the British Telecom Photographic Unit, London.

Finally, thanks to Georgiana for being such a good companion throughout the whole project.

Southampton
October, 1986

JON CLARK
IAN MCLOUGHLIN
HOWARD ROSE
ROBIN KING

Abbreviations

AEE	Assistant Executive Engineer
BIS	Brought Into Service
BT(HQ)	British Telecom (Headquarters)
BTTC	British Telecom (Technical) Training College
CNC	Computer Numerical Control
COMFORTE	Computerisation of Maintenance for TXE4 Exchanges
EE	Executive Engineer
ETG	Engineering Technician Grade
FPO	(Teleprinter) Fault Print-Out
GEC	General Electric Company
GM	General Manager
GSC	Group Switching Centre
ISDN	Integrated Services Digital Network
LCS	Local Communications Services
LES	Local Exchange Services/Systems
MAC	Measurement and Analysis Centre
MCU	Main Control Unit
MUMPS	Multi-User Microprocessor System
NC	Numerical Control
NCU	National Communications Union (until 1985 the POEU)
NN	National Networks
OMC	Operations and Maintenance Centre
OMU	Operations and Maintenance Unit
PATE-4	Print-Out Analysis for TXE4 (computer analysis of FPO)
PABX	Private Automatic Branch Exchange
PBX	Private Branch Exchange
PCB	Printed Circuit Board
POEEJ	*Post Office Electrical Engineers Journal*

POEU	Post Office Engineering Union (renamed NCU in 1985)
RSC	Repair Service Control
SCPS	Society of Civil and Public Servants
SFI	Special Faults Investigation (Unit)
SPOE	Society of Post Office Executives (renamed STE in 1983)
SPU	Supervisory Processing Unit
STC	Standard Telephones and Cables
STE	Society of Telecom Executives (until 1983 the SPOE)
THQ	Telecommunications Headquarters
TI	Telecommunications Instruction
TO	Technical Officer
TOA	Technical Officer with Allowance
TOIT	Technical Officer in Training
TTA	Trainee Technician Apprentice
T2A	Technician 2A
TXD	Telephone Exchange Digital (e.g. System X)
TXE4(RD)	Telephone Exchange Electronic-4 (Rectory Design)
TXE4A	Advanced Form of TXE4(RD)
TXK	Telephone Exchange Crossbar
TXS	Telephone Exchange Strowger
UAX	Unit Automatic Exchange (usually unattended)

Introduction

Origins and objectives

This book is concerned with the way managers, trade union representatives and workgroups shape the processes and outcomes of technological change in the workplace. Like many academic researchers, our interest in this issue was stimulated by the public debate over the likely impact of micro-electronics on work and employment. In particular we were dissatisfied with the macro-level and futuristic orientation of much of the discussion in the late 1970s. Whilst making for dramatic headlines and book titles, it seemed to reveal very little about the day-to-day realities of technological change in the workplace. One objective we therefore set ourselves was to attempt to study processes of change as they actually occur in the workplace and to capture the experiences of the people involved in them. By choosing to focus on micro-processes of technological change we knew we would be limiting our research to specific cases. As such our findings are not likely to establish once and for all answers to questions such as whether new technology creates unemployment or whether it leads to a general de-skilling of work. On the other hand, we felt that by looking in detail at micro-processes, rather than simply attempting to assess macro-impacts, we would be able to provide empirical material which might perhaps be of more immediate relevance to practitioners involved in the introduction of new technology.

However, we did not see our objectives as confined to producing interesting and useful reading matter for practitioners and policy-makers. We also felt considerable dissatisfaction with the way social scientists and engineers approached the issues raised by the introduction of new technology into the workplace. The main focus of our discontent was the analysis, or rather lack of it, traditionally devoted to technology by social scientists. The reasons for our particular interest in this question derived directly from the context in which we set out to conduct our research. This was an inter-disciplinary group of social scientists and engineers at the University of Southampton, whose founding members

1

began collaboration on teaching programmes in 1978 and by 1979 had found sufficient common ground to form the New Technology Research Group to carry out case-study research into technological change at workplace level. The principal project which we conducted, a study of telephone exchange modernisation in British Telecom, is the empirical focus of this book.

Our initial discussions revealed to us that the social scientists' standard criticism of engineers – that they do not take enough account of the social implications of their work – could equally be applied in reverse. Indeed, it became apparent very early on in our collaboration that pious references to the need to avoid 'technological determinism',[1] which are ritually made by social scientists when confronted with technology or technologists, simply did not get us very far. We decided, therefore, that we should not only be concerned with the role of managers, trade union representatives and workgroups, but also with the influence of the technology itself in shaping outcomes of technological change.

Book structure

The structure of this book reflects these concerns. Chapter 1 outlines the conceptual framework which informs the analysis contained in the rest of the book. At the heart of this framework lies the conceptualisation of technology as 'engineering system'. This concept is first presented in general form and then illustrated by reference to the two telephone exchange systems which were the focus of our empirical investigation. We also elaborate a model of the process of technological change as a series of analytically distinct stages. During these various stages we suggest that there are a range of points or 'critical junctures' at which organisational actors can intervene, within the constraints and opportunities presented, among other things, by technology, to influence the nature and organisation of work.

In chapter 2 we examine the national background to exchange modernisation, with particular emphasis on the replacement of electromechanical (Strowger) by semi-electronic (TXE4) exchanges. We also discuss the relationship between corporate exchange modernisation strategy and the implementation sub-strategies developed by operating managers in three telephone areas in the south of England. In chapter 3 we look at the nature of the exchange maintenance workforce prior to TXE4 modernisation, the national industrial-relations framework for change and the character and policies of the two main telecommunications trade unions. We also examine how this framework was applied and how the unions responded at local level. In chapter 4 we use the concept of engineering system to examine the links between the Strowger and TXE4 exchange systems and the work tasks and skills of exchange maintenance technicians. We also look at the technicians' experience of re-training and the ways in which new maintenance skills were acquired at various stages during the exchange modernisation process. In chapter 5 we turn our attention to the maintenance supervisors. We look at the factors which shaped the changes in their role as a result of the introduction of TXE4 and also at their experience of modernisation. Chapter 6 examines the emergence of new forms of work organisation and control at various stages in the process of change. In chapter 7 we discuss the implications for maintenance work and supervision of the next generation of exchange systems, particularly British Telecom's digital 'System X'. Chapter 8 draws together the arguments of the book and discusses the wider applicability of our findings.

Research rationale

The choice of telephone exchange modernisation as the focus of our empirical investigation was, in part, for pragmatic reasons. Two of the founder members of the New Technology Research Group (NTRG) had good contacts with engineering managers and trade unions in what was then the nationalised Post Office Telecommunications business. The choice was also based, however, on the wider significance of the exchange modernisation programme for the debate about workplace technological change. First, it represented an extremely large-scale investment in terms of time, money, manpower and machinery. Second, it was concerned with a central aspect of the telecommunications infrastructure – the telephone exchange network – whose modernisation is generally regarded as an essential prerequisite for the full exploitation of information technology (see Gershuny and Miles, 1983). Third, since the switching and control of calls through telephone exchanges was already fully automated in Britain by 1976 it represented an example of an already high level of automation.[2] Fourth, the research allowed us to study two occupational groups which have been widely regarded as problem areas in British industry: maintenance workers and supervisors. While supervisors have recently been referred to as 'lost managers' (Child and Partridge, 1982; see also Thurley and Wirdenius, 1973), an investigation of automated process systems in the chemical industry found a 'fairly wide consensus' amongst managers and workers that 'maintenance was the British managerial problem' (Gallie, 1978: 110). This view was confirmed by a more recent study, which showed that automated systems not only still require maintenance but often enhance

3

its importance, concluding 'British managements are reluctant to face up to the possibility that the use of more complex automated production systems will result in the need for highly trained maintenance people with multiple skills' (Senker, 1984: 142). Maintenance technicians and supervisors are the main subjects of this book.

In short, we believe that the type of technological change involved, the large-scale nature of the investment, the strategic importance of the telephone exchange network for the full exploitation of information technology in Britain, the already high level of automation in exchange switching and control, and its implications for maintenance technicians and supervisors, all point to the wider significance of our chosen material.

Research design

The overall design of the research project was strongly influenced by the basic objectives of the New Technology Research Group (NTRG) and its emphasis on inter-disciplinary studies of processes of technological change in the workplace.[3] However, the eventual research design was also the product of extensive discussions with senior telecommunications managers and national trade union officers. In fact, members of the Group spent around eighteen months prior to the commencement of field work gathering information about exchange modernisation from BT Headquarters staff (in eight different departments) and from representatives of the two main BT engineering unions, the NCU and the STE (at the time called POEU and SPOE respectively).

It quickly became clear that the original intention, to study the introduction of fully electronic digital exchanges, would be impossible as the System X modernisation programme was still in its early stages (see chapters 2 and 7). On the other hand the programme of introducing medium-sized semi-electronic (TXE4) exchanges as a replacement for electro-mechanical (Strowger) local exchanges was in full swing, and so it was soon agreed that the modernisation from Strowger to TXE4 would be the focus of the study. In the autumn of 1980 BT gave approval to the project in principle and on this basis the four founding directors of the NTRG applied for and were awarded a three-year research grant by the Joint Committee of the Science and Engineering Research Council and the Social Science Research Council.

Having collected a large amount of data and visited a number of telephone exchanges, the NTRG presented an outline research programme to British Telecom in late 1981. This formed the basis of a protocol, signed in February 1982, which outlined the main areas of the project and gave formal approval for the fieldwork to commence. The research design envisaged an in-depth longitudinal study of the process of exchange modernisation in two exchanges in two different telephone regions. The intention was to monitor these 'conversion' exchanges and the experience of their staff and supervisors for a period commencing approximately three months prior to the start of exchange installation through to a point approximately three months after the new exchanges were brought into service. To help our understanding of the conversion process, it was also agreed that we should study one Strowger exchange not immediately scheduled for conversion, as well as two established TXE4 units. These exchanges were to form, so to speak, the bookends of the conversion studies. The main themes to be investigated were work tasks and skills, training and selection for training, industrial relations, work organisation, supervision and the management of change at local level.

Prior to the main investigation, a pilot study was carried out in April and May 1981 in three exchanges: one small Strowger, one large Strowger and one TXE4. Altogether twenty-two staff were studied (the research methods are discussed in more detail below and in Appendix B). In the light of the pilot study, and after further discussions with BT and the trade unions at national and regional levels, we decided that it was unlikely that we would find two conversion exchanges which would meet the criteria outlined and the time constraints imposed by our research grant. It was therefore agreed that we should study a number of exchanges at different stages of the conversion process, which together would satisfy as near as possible our original objectives.

Study sample

In the event we studied eight exchanges in two BT regions and three separate BT telephone areas in the south of England (for details of BT structure see 2.3 below). One was a very large Strowger unit not immediately scheduled for conversion: we have called this unit Strowger A. A second, much smaller Strowger exchange was due for conversion within the timescale of our project, but in the event the changeover was delayed so that we were only able to study it as a Strowger unit. We have called this exchange Strowger B. We studied four further medium to large Strowger exchanges, all of which were converted to TXE4 during the course of our research. We have called them Conversions A, B, C and D. We were able to study all but one of these units (the exception was Conversion D) before, during and after conversion. Finally, we studied two units which had converted to TXE4 prior to the commencement of our fieldwork: we have called them TXE4 A[4] and TXE4 B.

We have called the three telephone areas in which our exchanges were located Town, Coast and Metro, since these names broadly reflect the character of the areas concerned. Town Area included a number of semi-rural communities, but was dominated by a large town with a population of around 130,000. A number of commercial companies were based there and the town's numerous telephone exchanges (including the two studied, Strowger A and TXE4 A) served predominantly business traffic but also a significant number of residential customers. Coast Area included one medium-sized town (population around 80,000) on the south coast of England, a number of smaller towns and a spread of semi-rural communities. The three exchanges studied in this area (Strowger B and Conversions A and B) were all located in small coastal towns, and carried a mix of commercial (mainly small business) and residential customers. Metro Area, in contrast, was situated in London and covered a geographical area best described as an urban sprawl with a touch of green-belt suburbia. All three exchanges studied here (Conversions C and D and TXE4 B) served predominantly business customers, some of which were extremely large commercial organisations. All seven supervisors (one supervisor was in charge of two of the units studied) and all thirty-seven senior technicians in the eight chosen exchanges were approached, and only three senior technicians declined to participate in our study.[5] All ten junior technicians approached agreed to co-operate.[6] The study sample is summarised in Table A.

Research methods

A variety of research methods were used to collect data during the study. These included self-report diaries, semi-structured interviews, personal questionnaires, observation of work, background 'informant interviews', and documentation. Each of these different methods was important in opening up particular areas of investigation. The self-report diaries enabled us to collect quantitative data on the work tasks and job content of individual technicians and the amount of collaborative working between them. This data was backed up by our own observation and by semi-structured interviews. The interviews themselves were the main source of data on the perceptions and attitudes of technicians and supervisors towards their work, while personal questionnaires assisted us in gaining a broad profile of their main personal characteristics (age, education and training, and so on) and career paths. Our understanding of the different exchange systems and their influence on maintenance

Table A *Summary of study sample*

Area	Exchange	Exchange connections	Period of study	Senior technicians	Junior technicians	Supervisors
Town	Strowger A	24,000	1 month	8	5	1
	TXE4 A	12,000	1 month: 12 months after changeover	3	1	1
Coast	Conversion A	11,000	13 months: 4 months before changeover to 9 months after	4	0	1
	Conversion B	9,000	17 months: 15 months before changeover to 2 months after	3	0	
	Strowger B	10,000	1 month; with monitoring visits over 13 months	3	0	1
Metro	TXE4 B	14,000	1 month: $5\frac{1}{2}$ years after changeover	4	0	1
	Conversion C	12,000	14 months: 6 months before changeover to 8 months after	6	3	1
	Conversion D	15,000	2 × 1 month (3 and 11 months after changeover)	3	1	1
				34	10	7

work was based on many lengthy periods of observation of technicians in a number of exchanges. During these periods of observation the technicians would explain to us in detail what they were doing, and in one or two cases they would locate and diagnose 'simulated' faults in order to help us understand the function of particular pieces of exchange equipment and each discrete step in the faulting process. This intensive observation was supported by reading background literature and BT documentation on the different exchange systems, in particular technical articles contained in the journal of the Institution of British Telecommunications Engineers, *British Telecommunications Engineering* (formerly *The Post Office Electrical Engineers' Journal*). In addition, verbatim transcripts were made of particular sections of the interviews, especially those passages where the technicians were asked to describe in detail how they would go about different types of maintenance task.

Six-monthly review meetings with a senior British Telecom Liaison Team were also held throughout the duration of our research. At these meetings we received comments and suggestions about our preliminary findings as they emerged. These two-way discussions with senior managers, plus regular meetings with union officials, provided an important additional source of data for our work. When our report to BT was completed in 1985, we made oral presentations to senior BT management, the Network Committee of the NCU and the Executive Council of the STE, middle-managers and union representatives in the telephone areas, and supervisors and technicians in the case-study exchanges, all of whom gave us additional feedback.

In short, various methods of collecting data proved to be important for some areas of our investigation and not so important for others. However, when taken together they acted as multiple points of reference, as checks and balances to ensure as far as possible that we had accurately captured the workplace reality it was our aim to understand (see Appendix B for a more detailed discussion of research methods). These processes of data collection were of course followed by many days and weeks of data analysis, and continual internal debate about whether we had got it right. These internal discussions were crucially important in our attempt to develop a precise yet flexible concept of technology. This eventually emerged out of five years of inter-disciplinary debate between the authors, three social scientists and one electronics engineer. The outcome of this debate is presented in chapter 1.

1
Understanding technological change in the workplace

1.1 Introduction

Most discussions of technological change conducted by social scientists tend to avoid analysing in any detail the nature of technology and its influence upon work and organisation. In this first chapter we will confront this issue directly. Our intention is to provide a definition of technology which is accurate in engineering terms and concrete and flexible enough to be applied in the analysis of technological change at workplace level. The key to our approach lies in conceptualising technologies as 'engineering systems'. The central part of this chapter is devoted to developing this idea and to showing how the concept can be applied to the two types of telephone exchange systems which were the focus of the empirical research discussed later in the book. Towards the end of the chapter, we will also outline a model of the main stages in the process of technological change in the workplace. Conceptualising the introduction of new technology as a process is central to our argument that technology can have an independent influence on outcomes of change. We will begin the chapter, however, with a brief consideration of the treatment given to technology in recent research.

1.2 Beyond technological determinism

It has become customary in social science discussions to preface one's remarks with a statement rejecting the idea that the outcomes of technological change are determined by the technical capabilities of a given technology (see e.g. Buchanan and Boddy, 1983: 20; Child, 1984: 247; Wilkinson, 1983: Preface). In part this is a reaction to the work of industrial sociologists such as Joan Woodward, who in the 1950s and 1960s accorded technology a high status in explaining forms of work and organisational structure. Woodward had wanted to find out whether certain types of organisation structure (which she defined as control systems) were best suited to certain types of technology (which she defined as production systems). Her basic hypothesis was that technology was a contingent factor of industrial organisation, creating a set of constraints or situational demands with which organisations were forced to come to terms. Her broad conclusion was that 'the existence of the link between technology and social structure . . . can be demonstrated empirically . . . There is a particular form of organisation most appropriate to each technical situation' (Woodward, 1980: 50, 72).

Woodward's work has often been held up as a prime example of 'technological determinism'. In our view, however, it is unhelpful and inaccurate to describe it in this way. In her classic book of 1965, for example, she also stressed the importance of the history and background of an organisation and the personalities of its founders and senior managers in shaping organisation structure (1980: 50). She argued, too, that more research was needed to identify the range of variables other than technology on which organisational behaviour depends. In the context of the argument presented in this book, though, the distinguishing feature of Woodward's work was her treatment of technology as 'a primary, independent, explanatory variable' (Wilkinson, 1983: 11). Although we do not accept her particular definition of technology, we do regard the general principle that technology can act as a significant explanatory variable as an important insight. Indeed, it is one that has guided this study.

To this extent our argument goes against the grain of much of the work that has developed following the publication of Braverman's highly influential book *Labor and Monopoly Capital* (1974). Braverman's thesis is well known and we do not intend to review it or the many subsequent criticisms that have emerged in the 'labour process' debate (for this see Wood, 1982; Thompson, 1983; Knights, Willmott and Collinson, 1985). However, it is useful to contrast Braverman's concept of technology with that of Woodward. In fact, although he offers no formal definition of technology, he does devote some space to the analysis of 'machinery' and the 'scientific technical revolution'. For Braverman machines have two main functions. Their technical function is to increase the productivity of labour, something which 'would mark machinery under any social system' (1974: 193). In a capitalist society, however, machines also function as an integral part of management's wider drive to de-skill work and to wrest control of the labour process from the worker. According to Braverman, then, the capabilities of technology are dependent on and explained by the objectives of capitalist management. There is, apparently, no analytical space for the idea that technology can have an influence on work independent of management's intention to control the labour process.

Nearly all recent research, whether sympathetic to Braverman and the labour process debate or not, has tended in similar fashion to downplay the independent influence of technology. Instead, emphasis has been placed on the importance of social variables in shaping forms of work and organisation structure. Wilkinson is typical in this respect:

> Previous analyses have tended to treat new technology as if it had 'impacts' on work organisation – especially skills – which are inevitable in particular technical and economic circumstances. It is in opposition to this view that technical change is here treated as a matter for social choice and political negotiation, the various interested parties to the change being shown to attempt to incorporate their own interests into the technical and social organisation of work. (1983: Preface)

Similarly, Buchanan and Boddy have argued:

> The changes to structure that accompany technological change reflect strongly and directly the expectations and objectives of management, and weakly and indirectly the characteristics of the technology. (1983: 24)

While agreeing that particular technologies do not have inevitable impacts, it is our view that serious analytical flaws follow from adopting an approach which openly rejects the idea that technology can be regarded as a significant independent explanatory variable. In some ways, the unwillingness to subject technology to serious analysis reflects the social scientist's traditional belief that technical things do not matter (see Winner, 1977, 1985). Yet common sense should indicate that in the context of technological change technology should be of something more than just a residual interest. As Winner puts it, 'if [technology] were not determining, it would be of no use and certainly of little interest' (1977: 75). The problem with recent research has been that an obsession with technological determinism has obscured the need to include an analysis of technology as one of the many factors which shape the outcomes of technological change. Put another way, the technology baby has all too often been discarded with the determinist bath water.

Our view is confirmed by the fact, that despite more general disclaimers to the contrary, recent empirical studies do often make passing references to particular influences that given technologies have had on the outcomes of the technological changes under investigation. Consider, for example, Gallie's observation that advanced automated process technologies are 'conducive to a certain degree of team

11

autonomy' (1978: 221), or Buchanan and Boddy's assertion that 'when technology changes, the tasks that have to be performed change' (1983: 244). Each implies some kind of significant relationship between technology and a form of work organisation or work tasks. Even Child, who tends to relegate technology to a relatively minor place as a derivative of strategic choices by organisational actors, comments that 'a given technological configuration (equipment, knowledge of techniques etc.) may exhibit short-term rigidities and perhaps indivisibilities, and will to that extent act as a constraint upon the adoption of new workplans' (Child, 1972: 6).

We should stress that we are not arguing for a reinstatement of technological determinism, rather that pronouncements on the need to avoid it often miss the point. What is required is a detailed analysis of the precise form and nature of the relationship between social and technical variables. To accomplish this task using existing conceptual tools would be difficult (see Rose *et al.*, 1986). Indeed, there is considerable confusion amongst social scientists surrounding the very definition of technology. Our intention in the following sections is to provide a definition of technology which will enable us to open up the 'black box' usually constituted by technology in social-scientific research. We will then be in a position to test one of the principal hypotheses guiding our research, that technology can act as an independent variable influencing the way the outcomes of technological change in the workplace are socially chosen and negotiated.

1.3 Defining technology as engineering system

There is probably no other issue which causes greater confusion amongst social scientists than the significance of technology in shaping workplace behaviour. As Bedeian concluded in a critical review of thirty-three published studies: 'the research dealing with the influence of technology on structure is not only conflicting, but in extensive disarray' (Bedeian, 1980: 234). One of the major sources of this conflict is the lack of a clear definition of what is meant by technology. Despite this, most definitions do recognise that the concept has a number of different elements or levels. Common to all is some concept of technology as 'equipment' (Rice, 1958: 4; Pugh and Hickson, 1976: 93), 'apparatus' (Thompson, 1983: 9) or 'hardware' (Child, 1984). Many then go on to define technology at a second level in terms of 'process lay-out' (Winner, 1977), 'workflow process' (Woodward, 1980: 36) or 'pattern of operations' (Winner, 1977), while some see it in much more comprehensive terms as 'organisation' (Rice, 1958: 4), 'the work done in organisations' (Pugh and Hickson, 1976: 93) or 'the body of ideas which express the goals of the work' (Perrow, 1967: 194).

We have much sympathy with those writers who see technology as more than simply equipment but we feel that they often extend the definition so widely that it becomes virtually impossible to assess its independent influence on work and organisation. Our definition, in contrast, begins from the basic assumption that all 'technologies' are *engineering systems*.[1] In other words, they are not just pieces of hardware and software, but also systems based on certain engineering principles and composed of elements which are functionally arranged (configured) in certain specific ways. On our definition, therefore, all engineering systems have three primary elements: system principles, an overall system configuration and a system implementation or physical realisation in a given technology. In the discussion which follows we will call the first two elements the *architecture* and the third the *technology* (embracing both hardware and software). In the design of an engineering system, architecture and technology cannot be totally separated. However, as we will show below, several 'implementations' of a given basic architecture are possible. Conversely, standardised implementations of certain functions in electronics-based hardware and software are found in a wide variety of system architectures.

Engineering systems are also characterised by two further elements. These are secondary to the extent that they are shaped by the three primary elements outlined above. However, they are analytically distinct in that they can and do exert an independent influence on various aspects of work and organisation. First, a given system is normally dimensioned to suit a particular workplace or user application. For example, while computer-aided design systems can be regarded as a basic type of engineering system, the specific hardware and software configuration to a given work setting (e.g. the number of work stations and the customising of the applications software used) is a matter of detailed design, or what we call system *dimensioning*. Choices made by engineers and planners about the specific dimensioning of a particular engineering system can exert significant influences on the nature and experience of work. In addition, an engineering system in its physical implementation possesses visual and audible characteristics. These will certainly depend on the technological implementation and dimensioning and may be a direct result of the system architecture, but they may also be shaped by ergonomic and aesthetic considerations (see Ashford, 1969). We shall see in later chapters that system *appearance* can have a significant bearing on the content and experience of work where there is a change from mechanical to electronics-based systems.

13

```
┌─────────────────────────────────────────────────────────┐
│                   PRIMARY ELEMENTS                         │
│                                                            │
│      Architecture                        Technology        │
│     system principles                     hardware         │
│   overall system configuration            software        │
├─────────────────────────────────────────────────────────┤
│                  SECONDARY ELEMENTS                        │
│                                                            │
│                    Dimensioning                            │
│            detailed design for a particular                │
│                organisational setting                      │
│                                                            │
│                     Appearance                             │
│            audible and visual characteristics              │
│                     ergonomics                             │
│                     aesthetics                             │
└─────────────────────────────────────────────────────────┘
```

Figure 1.1 The concept of engineering system

Our concept of engineering system is represented schematically in Figure 1.1.

Our treatment of the technical variable in terms of the concept of engineering system is related to, but distinct from, other approaches. It incorporates a narrow definition of technology as equipment or apparatus, but also includes the overall system configuration and the system principles. It includes the pattern of operations or work flow only in so far as they are directly embodied in the engineering system itself. It excludes factors such as organisation and the work done in organisations, which are part of more all-embracing but analytically less useful definitions of technology. It also excludes the overall objectives of the work organisations, sometimes called the 'primary task'.[2] Factors such as these are discrete and independent variables in work organisation and thus require separate analysis.

The utility of our concept of engineering system in explaining the relation between technical and social factors in work organisations will be put to the empirical test in the analysis of our case-study material later in the book. The next section of this chapter will seek to demonstrate the applicability of the concept by presenting a description of the principal features of the Strowger and TXE4 exchange systems which formed the basis of our study. Our concern will be to outline the architecture underlying the two exchange types and the technology used in their physical implementation. We will also be concerned with the appearance

14

of the two exchange systems. At this stage the detailed design or dimensioning of exchanges will not be considered in detail, as this is only of relevance to specific settings.

1.4 Telephone exchanges as engineering systems

The function of a telephone exchange is to connect calls between parties with access to a telephone line. In the early stages of the development of exchange systems, the connection was performed manually by a human operator by means of a plug and socket (see photographs 1 and 2). Over the past seventy-five years, however, all exchanges in Britain have been converted from manual to automatic switching systems, thereby eliminating the need for human operators to switch calls. Automated exchange systems are able to recognise that a customer wishes to make a call, interpret the destination instructions and establish the necessary connection – the switch – to the required destination. Exchange systems thus have two main functions: *switching*, that is, physically to connect callers, and *control*, that is to initiate and control the necessary actions such as setting up, maintaining and terminating the required connection (see Ward, 1974: 7). The importance of the distinction between switching and control will be elaborated further below.

In order to make a call all telephone subscribers must be connected into the exchange network, normally via a line into a 'local' exchange. During this century local exchanges have gradually been linked together into a hierarchical network comprising local, junction, national ('trunk') and international exchanges. The sending of messages via the connections made in the exchanges is the function of the *transmission* system. The transmission of calls has traditionally been effected by a system of telegraph wires and copper co-axial cables providing lines (including those of individual customers) into, out of and between exchanges. Each exchange building has a cable chamber in the basement and the connections made by these cables form some of the main 'peripheral circuits' into the exchange system proper. Access to cables and wires located outside the exchange buildings can be gained via holes in the ground and telegraph poles above ground (the staff carrying out external maintenance of the transmission lines are known colloquially as 'holes and poles'). Recent advances in electronics – fibre optics, satellite links and so on – enhance greatly the capabilities of transmission systems and are crucial to the full exploitation of digital exchange systems (see chapter 7).

1. An early example of an operator-controlled manual switchboard (*circa* 1893)

The Strowger exchange system

The first commercial telephone service began in the USA in 1877, and the first 'proper'[3] exchange came into operation in January 1878 in New Haven, Connecticut (see Brooks, 1975: 59–65). The British telephone exchange system was inaugurated one year later in 1879 by the Edison Telephone Company of London (one of whose first employees was George Bernard Shaw). In these early exchanges, as we have seen, callers were connected manually by switchboard operators. It was not

2. Direct supervision of manual switchboard operators (*circa* 1926)

until 1912 that the first automatic exchange was opened in Britain at Epsom in Surrey. This exchange utilised a mechanical system invented in America in 1889 and patented in 1891. The system in question had been developed by Almon Brown Strowger, a Kansas City undertaker. Strowger is believed to have been motivated to find a way of eliminating the human element in the switching of telephone calls by his concern that corrupt local operators 'deliberately gave busy signals or wrong numbers when potential customers called him, thus depriving him of business' (Brooks, 1975: 100; see also Povey, 1979: 35). There is an apparently

17

apocryphal story that the wife of his main competitor in Kansas City was a switchboard operator and that she systematically switched business calls meant for Mr Strowger to her husband! The Strowger system was first installed in a public exchange in the USA in 1891. In 1922 the system was adopted by the British Post Office as its standard for automatic telephone exchanges. Until the mid-1960s development and refinement of the Strowger system was the principal means by which the switching of calls in Britain was automated.[4] In 1983, fifty-six per cent of exchange connections were still served by Strowger exchanges (see table 2.6 below).

The system invented by Strowger was based on a 'step-by-step' architecture, implemented using electro-mechanical technology. The essential features of Strowger exchange architecture can best be described by considering the setting-up of a call being made by one party to another connected to the same local exchange. When the telephone handset is lifted, an electrical circuit is completed between the phone and the exchange; the exchange responds by connecting the calling line to a component known as a selector. This connects 'dial tone' to the circuit and thus gives audible instruction to the caller that dialling can proceed. Figure 1.2 shows what happens as the digits are dialled by the caller. Dialling the first digit of the wanted number causes the selector to move the switching contacts so that a connection is made to a second selector. Dialling the second digit results in a connection to a third selector and so on. Once dialling is complete, and if the sequence corresponds to a valid number, the process finishes by the connection of the caller to the called party. A ringing signal is then connected to the line (or an engaged signal if the party is busy) and, when answered, the ringing stops and the connection is completed ready for conversation to commence.

The description of the switching principle involved in this operation as step-by-step is a literal reference to the incremental fashion in which a connection between two parties is made. An important feature of this process is that each step of setting-up is controlled directly by the dialling procedure, that is by the electrical dial pulses which activate control circuits in each individual selector or switch. Thus, in terms of the configuration of functional elements, control and switching are co-located. Control itself is based on relatively simple electrical principles which enable successive links in the setting-up process to be established and held. The time to set up a connection in this way takes a few seconds. As we shall see, the setting-up of a call in a Strowger exchange differs in many important respects from the way calls are set up in other exchange systems.

The architecture of the Strowger system involves a succession of switching stages. The switches for each stage are usually arranged in

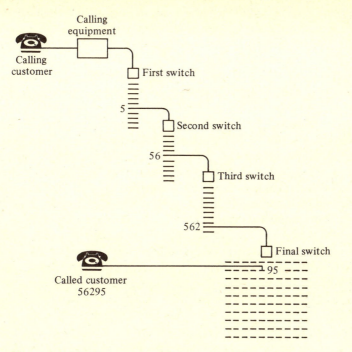

Figure 1.2 The Strowger step-by-step switching system

successive racks in the exchange to minimise the length of interconnect-ing wiring. The selectors deal at each stage with one or two digits of the dialled number and allow succeeding digits to be passed to the later switching stages. In principle, therefore, this particular form of system configuration makes it possible to follow – or trace – the electrical path of a call through the successive stages of the switching equipment. As we shall see this has important implications for the location of faults by maintenance technicians.

Strowger exchange architecture is implemented in electro-mechanical form. The key component is again the selector or Strowger switch. The selector is a switching device which enables a contact arm to be moved over a series of electrical contacts which offer potential connections to other selectors. There are two types of selectors: uniselectors and two-motion selectors. The uniselector is the simpler type since it can only move in a rotary mode. In contrast the contact arm on a two-motion selector can rotate and also move vertically, allowing access to a larger number of potential outlets on a bank of contacts. The movement of the contact arm is controlled by means of electro-magnetic relays, responding in part to the electrical pulses generated by dialling. As we will show in chapter 4, this combination of electrical contact and mechanical movement (thus the designation electro-mechanical) gives rise to particular kinds of maintenance problems.

The final point to consider in relation to the Strowger exchange system is its appearance. What is most likely to strike any visitor on an initial visit to a Strowger exchange is the staccato rattle made by hundreds of switches as their selector mechanisms move up and down and rotate. At the busiest times of day the noise created can be unpleasantly loud to the unaccustomed ear. A Strowger exchange is laid out in numerous rows of floor to ceiling racks upon which the individual selectors are mounted. Closer inspection reveals the movement of the selector mechanisms as calls are being set-up or terminated. The switching process therefore has both audible and visual expressions. As we shall see, these are significant elements in shaping both the skills required in the maintenance of the system and the subjective experience of maintenance work itself. The importance of the appearance of the Strowger system will become clearer when we consider the TXE4 exchange system.

The TXE4 exchange system

It is only since the mid-1960s that exchange systems other than Strowger have been introduced into the British public telecommunications network. The main development between then and the mid-1980s involved the gradual replacement of local Strowger exchanges with a range of semi-electronic exchanges (known as TXE2, TXE4 and TXE4A). These systems were developed as an intermediate step pending the development of a fully electronic exchange system (for further details see chapter 2). Our focus in this section will be on the TXE4 system, which was developed as a replacement for medium to large local Strowger exchanges.

TXE4 utilises an architecture which combines common control and matrix switching principles. The control function is implemented using electronic technology and the switching function using electro-mechanical technology – hence the designation semi-electronic. In describing the principal characteristics of the TXE4 system we will first outline the architecture and technology of the common control function and second the architecture and technology of the switching function.

Unlike Strowger exchanges, where each selector combines the switching mechanism with control circuits, common control exchanges remove the control elements from the switches and concentrate them in one part of the exchange.[5] This equipment is then shared by other functional areas of the exchange – hence the term common control. The common control area of a TXE4 exchange is similar in its overall configuration to a standard computer, comprising processing, storage and input/output devices. It operates by constantly cycling through a program which enables it to respond to information coming from, and to generate instructions to, other functional areas. It is in effect a specialised stored program-control (SPC) system.

The TXE4 program is implemented in the form of miniature threaded-wire units (see Goodman and Phillips, 1976). In fact, most of the common control functions of TXE4 exchanges are carried out by electronic circuitry and components (transistors, resistors and diodes) mounted on plug-in units (PIUs), which are themselves mounted in floor-to-ceiling racks. The PIUs can of course be taken out of the racks and the electronic components changed but this technology is not as flexible or technically advanced as the software-controlled technologies which lie at the heart of the TXE4A and System X exchange systems.

TXE4 exchange architecture also utilises a separate 'matrix switching' principle. In its simplest form this means that a call is set up by operating a cross-point, or switch, at a point on a matrix to connect calling and called parties (see figure 1.3). In fact, in TXE4 exchanges a series of matrices are linked together, so that the connection of a call requires the activation of several cross-points (see figure 1.4). The matrices are inter-related in a way which enables access to the whole switching network from any connection. The matrix cross-points are implemented using electro-mechanical reed-relays. The basic reed-relay unit consists of two nickel-iron reeds sealed in a glass tube.[6] These devices are considerably smaller than the Strowger switching mechanism and, because they contain far fewer moving parts, are less liable to failure. They are also mounted on PIUs, which are much heavier than those in the common control area.

The connection of a call in a TXE4 exchange is fundamentally different from Strowger. In the TXE4 system the lines terminating in the exchange are constantly scanned by part of the control equipment at a rate of about six times per second to determine whether they are free, busy or calling (see Goodman and Phillips, 1976: 201ff). When a customer lifts a handset to make a call, the raising of the handset is recognised by the scanning equipment and signalled to the Main Control Unit (MCU) (see Appendix A, TXE4 Block Diagram). The MCU identifies the calling customer and, following dialling, the identity of the called party.[7]

If the dialled number is valid and not engaged, the task for the MCU is to find a free path through the switching matrices to connect the call.

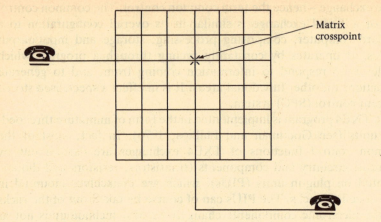

Figure 1.3 The matrix switching principle

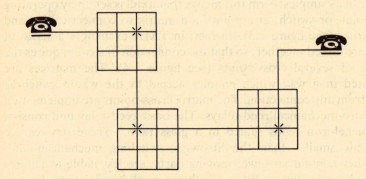

Figure 1.4 TXE4 matrix switching

Once this is accomplished, the connection is made and ringing tone provided ready for conversation to commence when the call is answered. If the called customer is interconnected via other semi-electronic or electronic exchanges without having to pass through an electro-mechanical exchange, then the connection ringing tone can be achieved almost immediately, that is, much less than a second after the last number is dialled.

One of the most distinctive features of this system compared with Strowger is that at various times during the setting up of a call, the paths are checked automatically to ensure that they have been correctly established. If not, a repeat attempt facility (sometimes called second-attempt facility) automatically comes into operation and chooses a different path through the network. This happens so quickly that it cannot be perceived by the person making the call. It is one of the main features that makes TXE4 exchanges inherently more reliable for the customer.

The appearance of TXE4 also provides a vivid contrast to that of Strowger. The system is extremely quiet in operation. The only significant audible sound is a soft click made by a few mechanical components. In the control area of the exchange there is virtually no sound at all except for the periodic chatter of teleprinters which provide information on faults. Visually the exchange also offers a striking contrast. A TXE4 exchange is normally smaller than a Strowger exchange, requiring only around seventy per cent of the space needed for Strowger equipment. Almost all that can be seen of a TXE4 exchange is, as one of our respondents put it, 'rows of cream coloured covers' (see photograph 3). Finally, whilst in Strowger a relatively dust-free environment is required, this is even more essential in TXE4.[8] The electronic equipment in TXE4 exchanges also requires a stable temperature and, hence, air-conditioning plant is installed.

One final and important point which needs to be made about the TXE4 exchange system is that it has a high degree of 'system security'. In other words, it is capable of maintaining a high quality of service to the customer despite significant degrees of equipment or component failure (see Huggins, Mills and Patel, 1977: 12). This is partly a result of its repeat attempt facility and inbuilt automatic maintenance features. In addition, the control part of the exchange has a distributed and modular form. Essentially each functional area of control equipment is split into a number of identical pieces – or modules – so that, in the event of failure in one module, a back-up is automatically provided. In this sense TXE4 is a more fault-tolerant and secure system than Strowger.[9]

However, because common control architecture involves a much greater functional interdependence between parts of the exchange, the risk of a failure of one call or one part of the system having repercussions for other calls and other parts of the system is greater than with Strowger, where an equipment fault normally affects only one connection. Such system failures – known at the time of our research as 'major service failures' – refer not only to the rare event of a complete failure or isolation of an exchange, but also to situations where service is lost to a significant number of customers. As we shall see in subsequent chapters, these features of the TXE4 system have direct implications for maintenance skills and the experience of maintenance work and supervision.

3. A view of the equipment layout in a TXE4 exchange

The automation of exchange maintenance

Fully automated systems for switching telephone calls have been available since the invention of the Strowger system at the end of the nineteenth century. The technological developments that have been described therefore represent different systems for achieving the same end, namely the automation of the switching process. In contrast the process of maintaining these different systems has been, and still is, dependent on human intervention. To see how far the changes in switching systems have brought about the automation of maintenance, we have to shift our focus to the maintenance process itself. (We will examine the management strategy behind these developments in chapter 2.)

In general terms the maintenance process involves the routine servicing of equipment (broadly preventive maintenance) and the correcting of faults after they have occurred (broadly corrective maintenance). In telephone exchanges, corrective maintenance is usually synonymous with 'faulting'. The faulting process comprises four linked but discrete stages: *identifying* the existence of a fault condition; *locating* it – or tracing it down – to a particular area or particular piece of equipment; *diagnosing* the cause of the fault; and carrying out the necessary *repair* action.

In electro-mechanical switching systems such as Strowger, the automation of the maintenance process has proceeded slowly and consists largely of bolted-on equipment to aid the identification of fault conditions. However, such equipment can also aid fault location and, in some cases, fault diagnosis too. In semi-electronic switching systems, such as TXE4, some fault-identification facilities have been designed into the system and, more recently, there have been significant advances in the development of bolt-on fault location and diagnosis equipment. The more comprehensive automation of maintenance is likely to come about with the sophisticated fault-diagnosis facilities designed into digital exchange systems such as System X.

To illustrate these points further, it is worth taking a brief excursion through the development of automated maintenance features associated with the different exchange systems. It must be stressed that the concern here is to describe the broad form of automation of the maintenance process which is achieved by particular technical means. A more complete account is given in chapters 4 and 6, when we examine in detail the organisation and execution of maintenance tasks in our case-study exchanges.

The provision of exchange 'alarms' represented the first step in the

25

automatic identification of fault conditions. They were first introduced in the 1930s and have since become a design feature of all exchange systems. Faults identified in this way bring up an audible alarm, which rings continuously and also causes a lamp to be lit up over the rack of equipment in which the fault condition is located. Strowger alarms are divided into two classifications, prompt (needing immediate attention) and deferred (needing attention when staff are available). In this way the attention of maintenance technicians is directed to a particular area of equipment. The degree of priority to be given to the alarm is also identified automatically.

Since the 1950s, new systems have been introduced which extend the automation of the faulting process. In the late 1950s automatic 'routiners' were introduced which enable the periodic testing of the equipment to which they are connected. They are normally used during periods of light traffic, particularly at night. For this reason they are often called night routiners. The programme of tests, which is carried out to high technical standards, is started and stopped automatically by a pre-set time-switch. The aim is to expose potential equipment weaknesses and identify fault conditions in advance in order to prevent them from affecting customer service.[10] In Strowger exchanges the whole of the switching system is subject to regular testing by automatic night routiners. If a switch fails a particular test or is busy when tested, the routiner prints the identity of the switch and either 'busy' or the sequence number of the failed test onto an individual fault docket. These are then checked by the technicians the following morning.

In the 1960s Call Failure Detection Equipment (CFDE) and Artificial Traffic Equipment (ATE) were introduced to monitor exchange performance and generate artificial test calls. More recently, in the 1970s, centralised monitoring facilities called Measurement and Analysis Centres (MAC) have been added to the network. These use computer-controlled call sending and testing techniques which provide immediate reports to exchanges on 'MAC failures' and summary reports (normally on a monthly basis) on the overall performance of individual units.[11] The automatic test and monitoring equipment described above has been bolted on in one way or another to electro-mechanical exchange systems but still leaves a significant amount of fault location and diagnosis untouched by automation.

Like electro-mechanical exchange systems, the TXE4 system is provided with alarms, classified as catastrophic (the equivalent of prompt alarms in Strowger) and deferred. However, the priorities for the different alarms depend more than in Strowger upon the relative functional importance of particular pieces of equipment to the exchange's overall operation, that is, upon its system configuration and dimensioning. Night routiners, too, are also a source of fault identification in TXE4 exchanges, although information about faulty or busy items is printed out onto a 'routiner teleprinter' located on the exchange floor rather than onto individual fault dockets as in Strowger. Unlike Strowger, too, night routiners are not applied to the whole of the switching system (see Huggins, Mills and Patel, 1977: 17–18). This is because the architecture and technology of TXE4 exchanges allows for a repeat attempt facility and the incorporation into the system of automatic fault identification equipment unknown in electro-mechanical systems. This prints out fault information on teleprinters at a central location in the exchange and is operational twenty-four hours a day. The significance of the Fault Print-Out (FPO) for both customer service and maintenance can best be illustrated by a comparison with Strowger.

If a fault occurs during the setting-up of a call through a Strowger exchange, this results in a failed call being experienced by the caller. However, a similar fault occurring in a TXE4 exchange is recorded on the fault print-out teleprinter but is not normally experienced by the caller due to the repeat attempt facility. The teleprinter, therefore, provides an important source of maintenance information about fault conditions within the exchange system before they become service-affecting. The fault information is provided in a standard format message on the teleprinter, which includes a seven-digit exchange identity code and other coded data from which the items of equipment involved and the broad type of fault condition can be identified. The FPO teleprinter is quite distinct from the night routiner teleprinter, although both are normally located close to each other on the exchange floor.

Although TXE4's centralised fault print-out facility is clearly an advance on what is available in electro-mechanical exchanges, it is still relatively unsophisticated so far as the automation of maintenance is concerned. Whilst the print-out allows the identification of the type of fault condition and the items of equipment involved in a fault, it is not normally possible to identify the actual piece of faulty equipment from a single line of print-out. Similarly, although the print-out contains data which assist in diagnosing the cause of a fault, the teleprinter itself does not actually automate diagnosis. This still requires, as we will see, analysis and interpretation on the part of maintenance technicians, and sometimes the use of a diagnostic manual which recommends procedures for dealing with information from alarms and the fault print-out.

Since the 1970s, however, software systems have been developed which automate the analysis of FPO data and, more importantly, bring the possibility of automated fault diagnosis closer to the exchange floor.

In the early days of TXE4, the FPO teleprinter produced simultaneously a punched paper tape which was periodically sent away for computer analysis. The results would come back some time later, by which time the concealed faults would normally have been discovered by other means. A software package called PATE-4 (Print-Out Analysis for TXE4) was then developed by BTHQ to carry out this analysis on a micro-computer. One way of dealing with the problem of delay was for the exchange to have both a punch-tape reader and micro-computer on site so that detailed print-out analysis could be carried out by exchange staff. If several exchanges in a locality shared the facility at one exchange, relatively efficient use of resources was possible. While this development was an improvement, it was still inconvenient for those exchanges without a facility on site. It also continued to use the slow paper-tape method of data input to the computer.

A later development was to use exchange teleprinters which outputted the fault data onto magnetic tape. Exchanges were provided with a VDU, printer and modem link to a central mini-computer (one such system was called a Multi-User Microprocessor System or MUMPS), thereby making available a much more flexible method of print-out analysis. BT also engaged in the development of a more comprehensive computerisation of maintenance for TXE4 exchanges called COM-FORTE, which aimed to 'bring together under one system a collection of exchange management and faulting aids' (BT, 1983b: 40). The significant point about these developments was that they anticipated to some extent the centralised fault detection and diagnosis facilities integral to digital exchange systems design. It should be emphasised that computerised print-out analysis was not at the front-line of fault location and diagnosis in our case-study exchanges. Instead it tended to provide a specialised back-up facility for identifying concealed or intermittent fault conditions, particularly when fault levels were high.

One final aspect of the automation of maintenance should be mentioned before concluding this section: the availability of discrete equipment maintenance aids to assist staff in locating, diagnosing and repairing faults. In the electro-mechanical Strowger system, electrical faults can be identified by use of simple devices to test the current in a particular switch connection. The (night) routiners can also be operated manually to test particular sections of equipment and feeler gauges are often used to check tolerances on individual switches. In TXE4, on the other hand, more complex test equipment is required and available, including storage oscilloscopes to detect electrical pulses at particular test points, and bench-mounted diagnostic testers to pinpoint faulty components on plug-in-units or faulty reed relays on matrix switches. At the time of our research more comprehensive programmable test equipment was normally located in a centralised repair facility, which dealt with the more difficult PIU faults. In chapter 4 we will examine the significance of these maintenance aids for the maintenance process as a whole.

1.5 The process of technological change

We argued above that social science studies of technological change have tended to neglect a detailed analysis of the independent influence of technology. In order to facilitate such an analysis we have outlined the concept of 'engineering system' and used it to analyse the nature of the Strowger and TXE4 telephone exchange systems. In chapters 4, 5 and 6 we will explore the influence of these engineering systems on various aspects of maintenance work and organisation. One obvious criticism of our line of argument so far, however, is that we have failed to take account of the view that economic and political objectives are built into particular technologies during the design process and that therefore the choice of a particular technology is itself the outcome of socially constructed decisions and the reflection of particular social values. According to this view, technology is not an independent variable, as we have suggested, but a dependent variable in the analysis and explanation of organisational behaviour.

A number of comments need to be made in this connection. First, it is not our intention to develop a theory or paradigm in which technology (however defined) is the only independent variable explaining all aspects of technological change. Even if we wanted to, neither our data nor that of any previous research would support such an approach. What we are attempting to do is to show how specific aspects of engineering systems can influence specific aspects of work, both constraining and extending the range of choices available to managers, workgroups and trade unions in the workplace.

Second, the argument that technology embodies certain socially constructed choices and values is either stating the obvious (it makes little sense to deny that technology is socially constructed) or suggesting certain specific causal connections which require detailed analysis and proof (as, for example, the contention of many labour process theorists that technologies embody capitalist or managerial objectives). As to the latter suggestion, there is clear empirical evidence to suggest that specific design choices can have significant implications for job content, skills and work organisation. This has been shown convincingly in studies of NC and CNC machine tools (see Wilkinson, 1983: 87–9; also Noble, 1984).

However, to assert, as Braverman and some of his followers seem to do (for example, CSE, 1980; Albury and Schwartz, 1982), that because a technology is developed and introduced within a capitalist mode of production it is necessarily impregnated with capitalist imperatives, is not a view that we can accept *a priori*. We would suggest that no such direct or necessary link exists between choices made in design and work tasks, supervision and the organisation of work.

Third, even if technology can be regarded as a dependent variable in the sense that its design embodies social choices (although even here technology can still be expected to have an independent influence on the range of choices available, see Mackenzie and Wajcman, 1985), this does not divest us of the need to examine its operation and influence in practice. Even if we can show that certain strategies and values are embodied in a particular technology, this does not automatically mean that it will have the intended effects on all aspects of work when introduced. Whatever our view of the social nature of technology, it is still both legitimate and necessary to analyse and explain how technologies, *once chosen*, shape the nature of work and organisation in practice. More specifically, it is important to explore the relation between particular technologies and particular aspects of work and organisation.

This brings us to our fourth and perhaps most fundamental point. Technological change, by which we mean in the context of this book a 'radical' rather than 'incremental' innovation,[12] needs to be seen as a process. Here we would agree with those labour process theorists who have argued that writers such as Woodward tend to see technology in a static fashion as having 'impacts' or 'imposing itself' on organisational behaviour. Such an approach neglects the processes through which new technologies are implemented and operated and outcomes of change established and modified. It is therefore essential to incorporate into analyses of the influence of technology what Elger calls the 'processual viewpoint' (quoted in Dawson and Wedderburn, 1980: xxx). This point is also recognised by Wilkinson, who suggests that the process of introducing a new technology into the workplace can be broken down into a number of stages, including design, choice, and implementation and debugging. It is from the design stage onwards, he suggests, that technology can act as an independent variable influencing the way the outcomes of change in the workplace are chosen and negotiated:

> Within *adopting* organisations . . . constraints on possible
> work organisations may already have been *inbuilt* during the
> design process, which could have been carried on largely

externally . . . In this sense technology *can* have 'impacts' on work organisation and skills. (1983: 21; original italics)

The primary focus of Wilkinson's analysis, however, is not on the 'impacts' of technology but on how managers, trade unionists and workgroups contest and make choices about skills and work organisation at particular 'junctures' (*ibid.*) during the process of change. In this book we will be charting a broadly similar course. We will, though, also be examining the ways in which the capabilities of given engineering systems can help define the discretion or room for manoeuvre – what Bessant calls the 'design space' (1983: 26) – available to organisational actors in their attempts to shape the outcomes of change.

Our particular framework for analysing the process of change is a modified and extended form of that suggested by Wilkinson and has three main elements: *stages* of technological change; *issues* arising during change; and *critical junctures* in the process of change. On the basis of previous research (see Buchanan and Boddy, 1983; Wilkinson, 1983; Hage, 1980; McLoughlin, Rose and Clark, 1985) we believe that the process of introducing new technology can be broken down for analytical purposes into five main stages each with its own dynamics and significance. We have termed these: initiation; decision to adopt; system selection; implementation; and routine operation. By initiation we mean the process by which organisational actors identify a need or pursue an opportunity for the adoption of a new system. By decision to adopt we mean the process leading up to a decision to invest appropriate resources to buy and implement a new system, while system selection denotes the process of system design, development or choice leading to the placing of an order or manufacture. The fourth stage, implementation, encompasses the whole process of introducing a new system into the workplace, including the negotiations and sub-strategies relating to its introduction, while routine operation denotes a point at which a new system has settled down and the staff directly involved with the system have established a stable pattern of working.

This model of analytically distinct stages aims to capture the temporal element of technological change. However, in any process of change a number of substantive issues arise which require decisions to be made by actors, either by conscious choice and negotiation or by omission (non-decision). These include not only traditional collective bargaining issues such as pay and grading, staffing levels, and the selection and training of staff, but also 'control' issues such as skills, job design, supervision, and the organisation and control of work. The relative importance of particular issues at particular stages is likely to vary

31

significantly from case to case and therefore needs to be specified empirically. Critical junctures, the last main element in our framework, are points at which temporal stages and substantive issues intersect. They are points at particular stages of technological change where organisational actors are able or seek to intervene to influence a particular issue or outcome. In their timing and significance, critical junctures are likely to be unique to a particular organisation and innovation.

To summarise: we are suggesting that, within a design space defined amongst other things by the capabilities of the technology being introduced, critical junctures arise at various stages during any process of technological change at which organisational actors are able or seek to intervene to influence particular substantive issues. In the following chapters we will be using this framework to analyse and explain the process of TXE4 modernisation in our chosen case-study workplaces.

1.6 Conclusion

We began this chapter by expressing our dissatisfaction with the treatment given to technology in recent social science research on technological change. We suggested an alternative approach based on the conceptualisation of technology as 'engineering system'. Our intention was to provide an analytical tool with which we could test the hypothesis that technology can have an independent influence on the way outcomes of technological change are socially chosen and negotiated. In order to substantiate this proposition we argued that it was essential to see technological change in processual terms as a series of stages and critical junctures at which issues and outcomes of change are shaped by organisational actors. We have also argued that once the stages leading to the choice of a particular system are accomplished, then social choices become frozen in a given technology. It is particularly from this point onwards that technology can be regarded as having an independent influence on issues such as skills, supervision and work organisation. In the remainder of this book we hope to show that an analysis of the independent influence of technology is not a replacement but a complement to the analysis of social variables in understanding technological change in the workplace.

2

Management strategies and the modernisation of the telephone exchange network

2.1 Introduction

The first three stages in the process of technological change have been defined in the previous chapter as initiation, decision to adopt and system selection. In this chapter we will discuss these three stages in British Telecom's TXE4 modernisation programme. Our major concern will be to examine BT's corporate business strategy and its relationship to the strategy to modernise the telephone exchange network. The 'strategic choices' (Child, 1972) that lay behind senior management's decisions to introduce new exchange systems will be seen as 'corporate steering devices' (Child, 1985) influencing the 'design space' (Bessant, 1983) of organisational actors at subsequent stages in the process of change.

This chapter raises two important conceptual and practical questions: First, to what extent is the behaviour of managers at operating levels influenced by corporate strategies? Second, and perhaps more fundamentally, to what extent is it useful or even accurate to use the term 'strategy' to characterise managerial actions? Some writers have argued that strong links between corporate and line-management behaviour cannot necessarily be assumed to exist or be proven empirically and that the concept of strategy itself may therefore be inappropriate (Wood and Kelly, 1982; Rose and Jones, 1985). With a somewhat different emphasis, Child (1985: 109) has suggested that the potential discontinuity between different levels of managerial action is best conceived in terms of an 'attenuation' between corporate policy and its implementation. Child's framework thus allows scope for 'variability' in the 'tightness of coupling' (*ibid.*: 112) between senior management intentions and line-management practices.

Previous research by the present authors has shown that some notion of strategy is inherent in managerial actions concerning processes of technological change in work organisations (see McLoughlin, Rose and Clark, 1985). However, we have argued the case for a more dynamic and flexible notion of strategy, suggesting that decisions and choices made by operating managers might best be conceived as sub-strategies developed at different stages in the process of change. Adopting Child's terminology, we would expect there to be scope for attenuation between the exchange modernisation strategy of BT corporate management and the sub-strategies developed by local management to implement the new systems in the workplace. We would also expect that the sub-strategies developed at local level would demonstrate the independent influences and interests of the operating managers charged with implementing change (see Batstone, Ferner and Terry, 1984: chapter 1). In addition, omissions and errors both in corporate strategies and local management sub-strategies, which have often been referred to as the unanticipated or unintended consequences of action (see Merton, 1936; Burns, 1977: 272; Giddens, 1977), also need to be considered in analysing the outcomes of change.

The structure of this chapter reflects this general approach. In the first four sections we will examine recent technological changes in the British telephone exchange network and their relation to wider business strategy. In particular we will discuss the process leading to the decision to launch the TXE4 modernisation programme in 1973. In the fifth section we will begin our examination of the main critical junctures in the implementation of TXE4 modernisation in the workplace. Our concern here will be to outline the different implementation 'sub-strategies' developed by local managers in our three telephone areas. We will hope to show that these were critically important factors in explaining the different degree of influence exerted by management on the process and outcomes of change in the workplace.

2.2 The telecommunications infrastructure in Britain

The telecommunications industry in Britain is engaged in two distinct but inter-related activities, the provision of a 'basic infrastructural service' (Batstone *et al.*, 1984: 45) and the manufacture of telecommunications equipment. In this book we are concerned with the basic infrastructural service. The main milestones in its recent commercial development are shown in table 2.1. The significance of a commercial organisation's place in the economy of any advanced industrial society can be measured in a variety of ways: its turnover; profit; fixed assets; investment in equipment and R and D; the size of its workforce; and its contribution to Gross National Product. On all these counts BT was one of the leading commercial organisations in the UK at the time of our study. In the year April 1983 to March 1984, for example, its turnover was £6,876 million,

Table 2.1 *Developments in the commercial structure of the UK telecommunications infrastructure industry (1969–84)*

1969	The General Post Office (GPO) ceases to be part of the civil service, is renamed the Post Office and becomes a public corporation with greater formal independence from government. It is split into a number of semi-autonomous businesses, including posts, telecommunications and Girobank.
1981	The Post Office is split formally into two separate and independent public corporations, the Post Office – henceforth confined to the postal and banking services – and British Telecom – with responsibility for the telecommunications business. The 1981 Telecommunications Act also ushers in the 'liberalisation' of telecommunications in the UK, breaking British Telecom's monopoly and opening up competition in the provision of some services and equipment.
1984	The 1984 Telecommunications Act prepares the way for the 'privatisation' of British Telecom. In November 1984 51 per cent of BT shares are sold by the government to private investors and BT becomes a public limited company.

profit before tax £990 million, fixed assets £8,840 million, net expenditure on fixed assets £1,533 million, investments in research and development £179 million, and its workforce just under 250,000.

BT's primary activity involves the provision of a national network of telephone exchanges and transmission lines to both business and residential customers. For business organisations, this infrastructure is a basic necessity, as crucial to commercial prosperity and communications as the rail, road and shipping networks were in the eighteenth and nineteenth centuries. Since the 1950s, too, an increasing number of private (residential) customers have been connected to the network, so that by the mid-1980s, over eighty per cent of households in Britain possessed a telephone line. The growth in the UK telephone network between 1960 and 1983 is shown in table 2.2.

The switching element of the telecommunications network, the main focus of our research, comprises a hierarchy of telephone exchanges. At the lowest level are the local exchanges connecting customers to the network (the TXE4 modernisation programme was concentrated at this level). Local exchanges within a particular geographical area are directly connected to each other via the junction network. Connections between exchanges in different areas are made via the trunk (or national)

Table 2.2 *The growth of the UK telephone network (1960–83)*

Year	Telephones (million)	Exchange connections (million)	Telephones per 100 population	Total inland calls (billion)	Inland trunk calls (billion)
1960	7.9	4.8	15.0	4.3	0.4
1965	10.0	6.0	18.3	6.3	0.7
1970	14.0	8.6	25.1	9.6	1.4
1975	20.4	12.7	36.4	14.3	2.3
1978	23.3	15.1	41.5	17.3	2.7
1981	27.9	18.4	49.8	20.2	3.3
1983	28.6	19.5	52.4	21.4	3.6

Source: Telecommunications Statistics.

network, where access to international telecommunications is also made.

Maintenance is an essential activity within the automated switching network. If calls are to be switched effectively, the equipment which effects the switching must be kept in satisfactory working order. However, as we will see, the balance that is struck between the conflicting requirements of cost and quality of service for different exchange systems has a crucial bearing on corporate policies towards exchange modernisation and the operational control of maintenance. Before we look at these policies, we will first trace recent developments in BT's overall corporate business strategy and how they were reflected in changes in its organisation structure.

2.3 Corporate business strategy and organisation structure

The idea of 'strategic choice' points to the primary role played by management in shaping organisation structure and technological change through processes of choice (see Child, 1972, 1985). Our concern in this section is to examine the strategic choices made by Post Office management at corporate level in response to changes in its business environment. It was against this background that plans were initiated and decisions taken to modernise the telephone exchange network. As we will see, the changes in corporate business strategy and organisation structure which have taken place since the 1960s can be considered significant enough to constitute a 'paradigm shift' (Batstone *et al.*, 1984: 26). It is important to appreciate, however, that the changes took place over a relatively long period of time and at different rates but with an ever increasing pace in recent years.

There has been a long and continuing debate about the merits of the postal and telecommunications services being run by the public sector or private sector (see *ibid.*: chapter 2). Pressure for privatisation is not new and led in the inter-war years to a compromise whereby the Post Office remained a part of the Civil Service but was partially re-organised and given a degree of financial autonomy. An important feature of the ensuing organisation structure was a sharper differentiation of postal and telephone management. It was in the 1960s that the pressures leading to the paradigm shift began to be exerted. This started with the requirement, introduced in 1961, for the Post Office to operate in accordance with the rules for other nationalised industries. This can best be summarised as requiring that they operate at 'arm's length' from government, and act '*as if* they were a private company, according to a series of market proxies' (*ibid.*: 27).

Thus, from the early 1960s, the Post Office management was under an obligation to adopt a more commercial orientation. This process was carried a stage further by the Post Office Act 1969, under which it became a public corporation and its senior personnel changed from being civil service administrators to being public corporation directors and managers. As a result of these changes, a system of semi-autonomous businesses was adopted within the Post Office, separate regional structures for posts and telecommunications were introduced, and a separate corporate identity began to be developed for Post Office Telecommunications.

Despite these attempts to infuse a more commercial approach, the results were not altogether encouraging. To a significant extent this was because governments continued to interfere in commercial judgements (*ibid.*: 30–3). In fact, what Batstone and his colleagues have called the 'political contingency' (*ibid.*: 10) – the range of forces acting on state enterprises which include ministerial intervention, the policies of political parties, public opinion and the activities of various pressure groups – was one of the most important factors shaping corporate business strategy in the Post Office up to and including the period of our study. The political problems which inhibited the development of a more commercial approach in the Post Office were compounded by its traditional organisation structure and style of management. The Carter Committee, for example, which was set up to review the role of the Post Office, noted in 1977 that 'within the Post Office the management style has been to try to operate with minimum risk and criticism by laying down a rigid centrally determined framework' (Carter, 1977: 57).

This traditional model of corporate management had a number of features with important implications for our analysis. First, within the context of the philosophy of providing a universal public service, there was the dominance in strategic decision-making of the 'priorities and ethos' of the engineering function (Batstone *et al.*, 1984: 51). Associated with this was the close relationship with the major equipment manufacturers and a tendency to become fascinated 'with the techniques of electronic *switching* . . . [and] . . . the neglect of computer techniques for organising and controlling the work of the exchange' (*ibid.*). As a result, it is claimed, Britain was not only backward in exchange systems, particularly in terms of exploiting advances in electronic control technology, but was also poorly placed to exploit the growing convergence of telecommunications and computing.

Second, technological developments within the telecommunications infrastructure industry tended to be regarded by management as evolutionary rather than revolutionary, with the emphasis on continuity and incremental change rather than discontinuity and radical change. In short, technological change was driven largely from within a conservative engineering culture. Third, management practices reflected a bureaucratic civil service response to the public corporation requirements of commercial operation. This was based on a heavily centralised approach to planning and control, embodied in nationally formulated Telecommunications Instructions (TIs) which laid down detailed guidelines for many aspects of work in exchanges, from tensions for springs in electro-mechanical switches to triennial programmes for the routine servicing of parts of equipment. Under this system, managerial discretion and initiative in local areas and exchanges were not encouraged. Finally, under the traditional model there was a tendency to reward seniority rather than individual performance in pay, grading and promotion.

By contrast, under the emergent new model corporate business strategy became increasingly dominated by a new ethos of commercialism, with its stress on change and competitiveness (*ibid.*: 63ff). The strategy was designed to make the organisation more market-led, to redirect its capital investment programme towards the needs of business customers, and to reduce costs. Although national management continued to establish broad 'decision rules', wider discretion was given to junior and middle management to take detailed decisions and exercise initiative. The underlying theme was the redefinition of the notion of service, away from the idea of a universal public service towards a more direct response to customers' needs and requirements. Indeed, it is symptomatic of this change that during this period the term 'customer' supplanted the traditional term 'subscriber'. Within the organisation itself there was an increasing stress on productivity and efficiency, flexibility of labour, and merit rather than seniority.

It is important to emphasise that this change from a traditional to a commercial orientation in overall business strategy was not a smooth and swift transition. The attempts to bring marketing and finance to a dominant position were not only resisted by some parts of the engineering function but were also inconsistent in some respects with the requirements of the exchange modernisation programme. Such changes were made even more difficult by the fact that decision rules established nationally had to percolate down through an extremely hierarchical and often cumbersome organisation structure. The result was that 'changes in managerial practice often lagged some way behind ideological shifts and formal organisational changes' (*ibid.*: 71). There was therefore considerable scope for the attenuation of corporate policy at lower levels within the organisation.

Under the Post Office Act of 1969 the Post Office Telecommunications business had been divided into a three-tier structure comprising Telecommunications Headquarters (THQ), ten telecommunications regions and sixty-one telephone areas. In 1983 about ten per cent of the total BT staff of 245,000 worked in the mainly London-based THQ (the BT Research Centre in East Anglia and the factories were counted as part of THQ). Another five per cent were employed in the headquarters of the Regions, and the remaining eighty-five per cent in the telephone areas. Reflecting the transition towards the commercial paradigm, THQ in particular underwent a number of re-organisations after 1979. Prior to then it was organised into functional departments comprising Research, Development, Network, Planning, System Strategy, Finance, and Personnel. The engineering bias was evident and marketing and sales had a comparatively low profile. For a brief period from 1979 to 1981, THQ was re-organised around a task-oriented structure comprising seven executives (Technology, Network, Marketing, International, Procurement, Finance and Management Services, Personnel) each under a Senior Director. This represented a clear shift in emphasis away from engineering towards non-engineering functions, particularly in the recognition of marketing as an increasingly important corporate activity. Following the Telecommunications Act 1981, BT was again re-organised, this time into four main market-oriented operating divisions; BT Inland, BT International, BT Enterprises and Major Systems (the latter division was renamed Development and Procurement in 1983). The post-1981 structure of THQ, and of BT more generally, therefore reflected more closely a commercial orientation and an emphasis on serving particular markets.

The largest of the new divisions, BT Inland, was broadly responsible for the provision of the local and national switching and transmission network. Subsequently it was split into two independent profit account-able business units, Local Communications Services (LCS) and National Networks (NN). National Networks became responsible for the long-distance trunk network and advanced network services for business customers, while LCS became responsible for the local switching and transmission network and was thus the first point of contact for BT's twenty million customers. In 1983–4 LCS employed nearly ninety per cent of all BT staff.

However, as indicated above, these changes at national level were not always reflected immediately in the management structure at lower levels within the organisation. It was not until 1983, in fact, that telephone areas were re-organised in conformity with the new commercial paradigm. BT explained the 1983 change as follows:

> The present organisation . . . was created to serve the requirements of a monopoly and give uniformity . . . Its key point is that staff are grouped together because of what they do rather than why they do it . . . The key to the re-organisation . . . was to look at why each member of staff in an area was doing his or her job from the customer viewpoint. (BT, 1983a: 2)

Under the old structure managers and staff had been organised because of their common responsibility or work tasks (maintenance, installation, planning), whereas under the new structure they were organised into a number of groups each dealing with particular types of customer require-ments (business systems, customer products, local network services). Exchange maintenance staff were thus no longer part of a separate maintenance organisation and hierarchy, but incorporated into 'local exchange services'.

The implications of these changes for maintenance work and the implementation of exchange modernisation will be touched on at various points below. For the present we should note that the decision to launch the TXE4 modernisation programme in 1973 was made at a relatively early stage in the emergence of the new commercial paradigm, while a large part of the implementation programme occurred between 1978 and 1985 during a period of rapid change in both organisation and phil-osophy. As we will see, however, the 'attenuation' of corporate level strategy meant that at telephone area and exchange level the traditional paradigm still exerted a considerable influence on management organi-sation and practice.

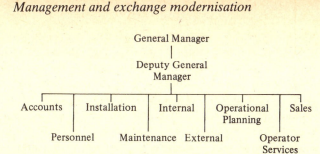

Figure 2.1 Typical telephone area organisation before April 1983

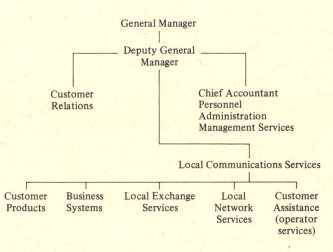

Figure 2.2 Typical telephone area organisation after April 1983

2.4 TXE4 modernisation strategy and the development of the exchange network

Buchanan and Boddy (1983) have argued that managements often have a mixture of objectives in deciding to introduce new technology: 'strategic' objectives concerned with external economic, market, and customer-oriented goals; 'operating' objectives concerned with internal technical goals and overall system performance; and 'control' objectives concerned with operational performance, including human performance, in the workplace. In the next two sections we will examine the strategic, operating and control objectives behind the corporate decision to select the TXE4 exchange system and to invest in a major programme of TXE4 modernisation, relating these to the changes in overall corporate business strategy discussed above.

In order to appreciate the full significance of the TXE4 modernisation strategy, it is necessary to place it in the context of the broader historical development of the exchange network in Britain. Seen in this context, it is possible to identify a number of key dates in the modernisation of the British telephone network. Although the first telephone exchange owned by the British Post Office (at that time a government department) was opened in 1881 in Swansea, probably the most significant date in the early history of the UK exchange network was 1912. In this year the BPO took all public exchanges under its monopoly control and opened the first automatic Strowger exchange in Epsom in Surrey. By the 1920s the BPO had adopted the Strowger system for all its automatic local exchanges. It then embarked on a long-term programme to introduce automatic switching into all its local exchanges. Between 1930 and 1970 the proportion of automatic Strowger exchanges rose from seven per cent to ninety-nine per cent of the local exchange network.

In 1958 the programme was extended to include the switching of long-distance trunk calls by the gradual introduction of Subscriber Trunk Dialling (STD). This meant that long-distance calls within the UK could be switched by automatic direct dialling through trunk exchanges rather than connected through an operator. Since that time, direct dialling (which is what automatic exchange switching means for the customer) has been extended to the international telephone network, so that by the mid-1980s it was possible to dial direct to a large number of countries in the world. It should be noted, however, that the vast majority of BT's exchanges are local exchanges (over 6,000 in 1983 compared with around 100 trunk and 20 international). The main impetus of the exchange modernisation programme since the early 1970s has therefore been concentrated on these exchanges. Because of this, and also because our study focused on local exchanges, we will concentrate largely on this aspect of the exchange modernisation programme.

By the time the last manual local exchange on the Isle of Skye was replaced by automatic switching in 1976, Strowger exchanges dominated the local network. It should be stressed that these were substantially updated systems compared with the 1920s, with a number of semi-electronic and electronic elements, particularly in the 'peripheral area' of the exchange. However, by 1976 the absolute dominance of Strowger was being challenged by more modern exchange types and a programme of exchange modernisation was already in full swing. It is to an examination of this programme, and the reasons behind it, that we now turn.

The BPO's local exchange modernisation strategy in the 1960s, leading up to the decision to invest in the TXE4 modernisation programme in 1973, must be seen to a large extent as a reaction to its failed attempt to develop a viable all-electronic exchange system. A watershed in this development was reached in December 1962, when the first electronic exchange in the world was opened at Highgate Wood in London and then immediately withdrawn as unviable and too complex (see Broadhurst, 1963; Lawrence and Harris, 1966: 208; Harris, 1966: 214; Povey, 1979: 90). Contrary to the traditional paradigm of corporate management so characteristic of the Post Office at the time, this attempt to introduce an all-electronic exchange system had been a bold and innovative step technically and managerially. It had been initiated by the research and engineering divisions of the business in collaboration with the five principal British exchange equipment manufacturers. The strategy behind it was therefore not primarily market or customer driven (although of course its success would have improved the quality and range of customer service) but 'technology' driven, underpinned of course by the commercial objectives of the equipment manufacturing companies.

At the time when this experiment failed and was referred back for further research, the Post Office was coming under considerable pressure from government and other sources to expand the exchange network, mainly because of growing 'traffic' congestion and the need to meet the increasing demand for telephone services. On top of this, the equipment manufacturers were applying pressure for new orders as the programme of replacing operator-controlled exchanges by automatic Strowger exchanges was slowing down (for detailed discussions of the economic and political pressures surrounding the exchange modernisation programme, see Harlow, 1977: chapter 4; Carter, 1977: chapter 12; Batstone *et al.*, 1984: chapter 3). The response of Post Office management was two-fold. First it decided in 1963 to develop a semi-electronic reed-relay exchange type in two designs, one for small exchanges and the other for medium and larger units. Second, as a stop-gap prior to the development of the larger semi-electronic exchange type (which eventually became TXE4), it decided to introduce a number of Crossbar exchanges, a design first patented in the USA in 1916 but substantially updated in the 1940s and 1950s. Crossbar was chosen because it was available and already operating successfully in a number of countries, involved less equipment than Strowger, had improved call-routing, and was more reliable – in other words, it gave better quality of service and required less maintenance. Thus, by the mid-1960s, under external pressure from government, customer demand and the equipment suppliers, and against the background of the failure of the Highgate Wood experiment, the Post Office's exchange modernisation strategy had assumed a hybrid character, involving the adoption of several exchange types in tandem pending the ultimate development of a reliable fully electronic digital exchange system.

In 1964 a Reed Electronic Project Executive Board was set up to oversee the development for production of semi-electronic reed-relay systems. Prototype systems for small exchanges had already been designed, built and tested in 1963 and these were then developed into experimental systems for public field trials from mid-1965. Following the field trials the BPO took the decision in 1966 to go ahead with the manufacture of the small exchange design, known as TXE2. In making that decision, it also decided that no further orders for electro-mechanical systems would be made for future small and medium exchanges. By the mid-1960s, therefore, the Post Office was committed in its modernisation strategy to a form of electronic switching technology.

The first production TXE2 exchange was opened at Ambergate, Derbyshire, in December 1966. The numbers increased in subsequent years so that by 1983 there were nearly 1,500 in operation. In contrast, the development of the TXE4 system was subject to considerable delay. Following the decision to develop larger reed-relay exchange systems, the design work on the prototype (called TXE1) began in 1964 and it was confidently expected that the first exchange would open in 1965 at Leighton Buzzard. However, field trials did not begin until 1967 and it did not go into public service until 1968. Despite the considerable delay the TXE1 system proved to be a satisfactory design. Nevertheless work soon began on an improved and cheaper TXE3 system. As with TXE1, the design work was carried out in collaboration between the Post Office and the five main equipment manufacturers under the Joint Electronic Research Agreement (JERA), which had been signed in 1956 in order to promote joint research on a fully electronic exchange system.

After the Post Office became a public corporation in 1969, the JERA terminated, and it was then agreed that one of the manufacturers, Standard Telephones and Cables (STC), should pursue the development of a cost-reduced version of TXE3, called TXE4. Field trials were carried out on a test-bed exchange from 1969 to 1972, and in 1971 a contract was placed with STC to produce a production-engineered version of the TXE4 system. By 1972, therefore, having initiated the development of a range of different exchange system designs, the Post Office Board was faced with a major decision concerning the replacement of medium-size Strowger local exchanges: the choice was between Crossbar and the new TXE4 system.

In the event, the Board decided to defer making a major commitment to either system until the end of 1972, whilst continuing to monitor the progress of TXE4. In January 1973, however, it came to the decision that:

the Telecommunications Business should proceed with the modernisation of its local network and eliminate Strowger step-by-step equipment from large local telephone exchanges before the end of this century. The new large electronic exchange (TXE4) is to be used alongside Crossbar equipment which is already being applied in increasing quantities. (Harris and Budgen, 1974: 11).

This was a firm commitment to adopt TXE4, supplemented by Crossbar, to meet immediate needs. What were the main reasons behind the choice of TXE4 in 1973? We have already noted a range of external pressures in the 1960s to expand the telephone network – to that extent the TXE4 modernisation strategy had 'strategic' objectives in terms of external economic, political and customer-oriented goals. In particular, TXE4 promised improved quality of service to customers in comparison to both Strowger and Crossbar (see *ibid.*).

However, these strategic objectives alone do not fully explain the choice of TXE4. For this, we need to look at the Post Office Board's own consideration of internal 'operating' objectives prior to the 1973 decision. Already in 1969 Post Office Telecommunications management had initiated a series of detailed economic studies of the operating costs of the various exchange systems, and it was the result of these studies (which used computer modelling techniques) that proved to be a decisive factor in the choice of TXE4. This is confirmed by J. S. Whyte, who had overall responsibility as Director of Operational Programming for the development of the local exchange strategy within the organisation:

Although the evolution of policy is a continuous process . . . decisions of a magnitude comparable to this one are taken by telecommunications administrations very infrequently. Perhaps only the change from manual to automatic switching and the introduction of STD were of comparable significance. Both of these decisions were, however, taken at a time when the system was much smaller, and, in consequence, the capital implications were of a different order of magnitude. Recognizing not only the economic significance of the decisions they would have to take, but also their commercial, industrial, and service importance, the BPO Board insisted that the issues involved be subjected to the most detailed scrutiny. The investigations covered a range and depth greater than for any previous decision taken by the BPO. Of the many studies that were undertaken, those concerned with the economic consequences

of alternative strategies were of particular importance.
(Whyte, 1974: 130)

Although the economic studies considered in detail the capital expenditure costs associated with modernising or updating the exchange network, it was the promise of reduced maintenance, the 'main operating cost', which was identified as a critical factor in the eventual decision to select the TXE4 system:

> The assessments showed that, after an initial settling-down period, Crossbar exchanges are likely to require about half the maintenance attention of Strowger exchanges, and that, in turn, the requirements of TXE4 exchanges should approach half those of Crossbar exchanges . . . Maintenance savings with modern systems [were] one of the main arguments in favour of replacing Strowger equipment. (Benson, 1974: 133)

The economic studies also found that other operating costs apart from maintenance 'had little influence on comparative results' (*ibid.*). This was important since it had often been argued that electronic exchanges had high running costs because they needed to use power continuously, whereas electro-mechanical systems such as Strowger only used power intermittently when activated by customer calls (on this, see Braun and MacDonald, 1978: 179). In addition, it was discovered that TXE4 systems required only seventy per cent of the space needed by Strowger units with the same level of traffic and number of exchange connections. Thus, in terms of 'operating' objectives, reduced maintenance costs were a decisive factor in the decision to adopt TXE4.

The installation of the first public TXE4 exchange at Birmingham Rectory commenced in 1974 and it was finally brought into service in 1976. The overall development period for the larger reed-relay exchange system was therefore twelve years. During the period in which the system was being developed, however, further opportunities for cost reduction became apparent, particularly through the use of integrated circuits in exchange design. Following a feasibility study, Post Office Telecommunications management therefore placed a contract in 1975 to develop an improved TXE4 system, which came to be known as TXE4A. The original version of TXE4 was then designated TXE4(RD), or Rectory Design, after the first exchange in which it had been installed.

By the mid-1970s, the exchange modernisation strategy was firmly based on a programme for replacing small and medium local Strowger exchanges by the TXE2 and TXE4 systems. Table 2.3 shows the development of the overall programme from 1967 until 1986. Although the first TXE4 installation took place in 1976, the initial stages were slow,

Table 2.3 *The development of local automatic exchanges according to exchange type (1967–86)*

At 31 March	Strowger No.	Strowger % of total	Crossbar No.	Crossbar % of total	TXE No.	TXE % of total	Overall total
1967	5,833	100.0	1	0.0	1	0.0	5,835
1970	5,991	99.3	11	0.2	31	0.5	6,033
1974	5,489	88.3	234	3.8	492	7.9	6,215
1976	5,206	83.2	359	5.7	668	10.7	6,260
1980	4,542	72.6	514	8.2	1137	18.2	6,260
1983	3,830	61.4	565	9.1	1748	28.0	6,235
1984	3,274	57.1	557	9.7	1852	32.3	5,733
1985	3,251	55.9	552	9.5	1957	33.6	5,819
1986	3,218	53.9	553	9.3	2066	34.6	5,965

Source: Telecommunications Statistics and British Telecom. Mixed exchange types, such as Strowger/Crossbar and Strowger/TXE4, and digital exchanges are included in the overall totals where appropriate, but are not listed separately.

partly because of prolonged industrial action by the POEU in 1978 over a shorter working week, and partly because the first exchanges proved to have a number of technical problems, particularly with defective transistors in plug-in units. By January 1979 only eight TXE4(RD) units were in operation. However, the programme accelerated from then on and was completed on 16 February 1985 when the 342nd TXE4(RD) exchange was brought into service (see table 2.4).

The initial capacity of TXE4 units in operation by the end of March 1983 ranged from under 5,000 to over 18,000 lines (see table 2.5). However, over thirty of the very small TXE4 units were not discrete exchange units of the kind investigated in our study, providing direct dialling-in facilities only. In fact eight of these units had under 300 lines. If only discrete stand-alone units are considered, then the average size of a TXE4 exchange in 1983 in terms of exchange connections was between 9,000 and 10,000 lines.[1]

Finally, if we look at the number of exchange connections served by each exchange type, we can appreciate better the strategic importance of the TXE4/4A range for the telephone exchange system as a whole in the mid-1980s. As table 2.6 shows, by 31 March 1983 the 308 TXE4/4A units[2] served 2.3 million customers or just over one-tenth of all exchange connections. By 31 March 1985, these figures had more than doubled to 4.8 million or nearly one-quarter of all exchange connections.

47

Table 2.4 *The development of local TXE exchanges (1976–86)*

At 31 March	TXE2	TXE4	TXE4A
1976	667	2	—
1980	1,085	51	—
1983	1,440	269	3
1986	1,582	342	145

Source: British Telecom. The figures for 1983 and 1986 exclude those small TXE4 systems connected to direct dialling-in facilities. In 1983 these numbered 36 in total.

Table 2.5 *Breakdown of TXE4/4A exchanges by number of exchange connections (31 March 1983)*

No. of exchange connections	No. of exchanges
Under 5,000	92
5,000–6,000	9
6,000–7,000	26
7,000–8,000	32
8,000–9,000	40
9,000–10,000	46
10,000–12,000	23
12,000–14,000	17
14,000–16,000	10
16,000–18,000	4
Over 18,000	9

Source: British Telecom.

Table 2.6 *Exchange connections served by exchange type (31 March 1983)*

Exchange type	No. of exchanges	No. of exchange connections	% of total exchange connections
Strowger	3,830	10,900,000	55.9
Crossbar	565	3,000,000	15.4
TXE2	1,440	2,100,000	10.8
TXE4/4A	308	2,200,000	11.3
Mixed and digital	92	1,300,000	6.6

Source: British Telecom.

2.5 Corporate strategy towards the operational management of TXE4 maintenance

We have seen how the choice of the TXE4 exchange systems was strongly influenced by 'operating' objectives concerned with the reduction in the costs of exchange maintenance. In this section we will examine corporate management's 'control' objectives, in particular the extent to which corporate management strategy also included a policy for the operational management of TXE4 maintenance at area and exchange levels.

In the internal economic studies which played such a crucial role in the development of the exchange modernisation strategy in the early 1970s, the productivity of the maintenance workforce was identified as one of the two main reasons in favour of replacing Strowger with TXE4 exchanges (the other reason was the cost of the maintenance workforce). At a general level, therefore, the efficient use of labour was a clear objective behind the choice of TXE4 (see Benson, 1974: 134). A closer examination of this objective, however, reveals a relative absence of specific national guidance as to how it was to be achieved. To a certain extent, of course, the development of automated routiner equipment and exchange monitoring systems since the 1950s had enabled local managements to gain more accurate information about the performance of individual exchanges (whether Strowger, Crossbar or TXE4) and to reduce the amount of labour-intensive routine servicing of equipment. In addition, national as well as regional and area performance targets for different exchange types did provide local managers with indicators by which to judge the performance of the units under their control. But these developments, which tended to shift the emphasis away from direct supervision of work towards more administrative and technical forms of management control (see chapter 5), still left open the question of how national guidelines and targets were to be achieved in practice and how the new monitoring facilities were to be exploited.

In the early and middle phases of the national TXE4 modernisation programme, no training courses were devised by corporate headquarters specifically geared towards the management of TXE4 maintenance operations. Until 1983, when, as we shall see in chapter 5, a two-week course in TXE4 exchange management for supervisors was instituted at national level, the only TXE4 training available for supervisors consisted of two short, largely technical, system 'appreciation' courses. It must therefore be assumed that BT corporate management did not initially envisage any major change in supervisory skill requirements or procedures, despite their belief that the introduction of TXE4 would lead to significant increases in labour productivity. In this sense the 'Strowger culture' still dominated corporate thinking. In the absence of clear national guidelines, area managements within BT thus had extensive 'design space' to define and implement their own 'control' objectives for TXE4 modernisation and in particular to construct a role for the maintenance supervisor during and following implementation. The sub-strategies developed on these and other questions by managements in Metro, Coast and Town Areas are discussed in the next section.

2.6 TXE4 implementation: management sub-strategies in Metro, Coast and Town Areas

There are three main issues which are of interest in this examination of management implementation sub-strategies: the co-ordination of area TXE4 modernisation programmes (most telephone areas had a number of TXE4 exchanges due for conversion); the management of individual exchange conversions; and the role of maintenance supervisors in the implementation process and in the operational control of maintenance following conversion. As these questions require an understanding of the area management of exchange maintenance in BT, this will be outlined briefly.

Formal responsibility for the area management of exchange maintenance at the beginning of our research in Autumn 1982 was typically as represented in table 2.7. The General Manager, assisted by a Deputy General Manager, had ultimate overall responsibility in the telephone area. In practice, though, operational responsibility for maintenance and maintenance policy lay with the Head of Maintenance. Below the Head of Maintenance the Executive Engineer (EE), as the job title suggests,

Table 2.7 *Area management of exchange maintenance prior to reorganisation (1983)*

Job title	Main responsibilities in the area
General Manager (GM)	General management of all BT area operations
Deputy General Manager (DGM)	Two DGMs, one with responsibility for the general management of all engineering activities
Head of Maintenance	Operational management responsibility for area exchange maintenance
Executive Engineer (EE)	Operational management responsibility for sub-area of exchange maintenance
Assistant Executive Engineer (AEE)	First-line maintenance supervisor with direct operational responsibility for maintenance of individual exchanges

carried out executive engineering management duties, with responsibility normally for between four and five first-line supervisors and between 100 and 130 technicians. The job involved co-ordinating and planning telephone operations over a wide geographical area, including anything from ten to twenty exchanges. In contrast the Assistant Executive Engineer (AEE), or maintenance supervisor, had direct operational responsibility for individual exchanges and their maintenance staff. They were directly accountable for the control of maintenance operations in the workplace, thus carrying out a 'pure' type of formally defined supervisory role (see chapter 5; also Dawson and McLoughlin, 1986).

One of the most immediate differences in management implementation sub-strategies in our three telephone areas concerned the question of line-management continuity and responsibility for the area co-ordination of the exchange modernisation programme. In Town Area, which was divided into a number of 'sub-areas' for administrative purposes, one EE was given overall responsibility by the Head of Maintenance for co-ordinating all aspects of modernisation in his sub-area. He acted as the management focus for all technical staff, and developed, almost single-handedly, a clear sub-strategy for staff selection, training and post-course experience in the three Strowger-TXE4 conversion exchanges under his control (including TXE4 A).

In Coast Area we found no one member of line management with similar overall responsibilities. In the sub-area in which our exchanges were located, though, one maintenance supervisor was appointed by the Head of Maintenance to plan and co-ordinate the re-training courses for all technical staff. Decisions about selection of staff for re-training were taken jointly by maintenance supervisors and EEs within the guidelines agreed between the Head of Maintenance and the local branch of the POEU (see chapter 3). In Metro Area, selection for training and the organisation of training courses were co-ordinated by one EE in collaboration with the relevant maintenance supervisors, also within local guidelines agreed between the Head of Maintenance and the local branch of the POEU.

In summary, in each of our three telephone areas the co-ordination of the local TXE4 modernisation programme was devolved to junior middle management (EE) or first-line supervisory (AEE) levels, but only in Town Area was there line management continuity and a clear line of management responsibility throughout the programme. As we shall see, this affected many issues arising during the implementation process as well as the attitudes of technicians towards their local management's handling of modernisation.

Different approaches with wide-ranging implications were also adopted towards the management of the conversion of individual exchanges. Of particular importance here was the relation between the managers responsible for installing the new equipment (BT installation staff) and those responsible for maintaining it after conversion (BT maintenance staff). In fact, in all three telephone areas studied, the day-to-day management of the implementation process from the beginning of exchange installation to changeover was in the hands of BT installation staff, usually at first-line supervisory level. Day-to-day management in this context involved co-ordinating the technical testing and preparation of the new equipment once it had been installed and allocating duties to both installation and maintenance technicians prior to conversion. However, the role of maintenance managers and supervisors during this period differed significantly from area to area and exchange to exchange. In exchanges Conversion A (Coast Area) and Conversion C (Metro Area), the maintenance EEs were both within one year of retirement and had virtually no on-site involvement throughout the implementation process. In Conversion B (Coast Area), in contrast, the maintenance EE, although only a few years from retirement, took overall responsibility for conversion in the weeks prior to changeover and made regular visits to the exchange floor. In exchange TXE4 A (Town Area), however, maintenance managers at EE and AEE level were directly involved in all aspects of the implementation process, developing a close working relationship with installation managers throughout the whole area TXE4 modernisation programme. This was facilitated by the fact that the maintenance EE, the overall co-ordinator of exchange modernisation in his sub-area, had previously worked as an installation supervisor himself, and also by his decision to select the future maintenance supervisor and involve him in the implementation process at an early stage. This was in direct contrast to our exchanges in Coast and Metro Areas, where the future TXE4 maintenance supervisors were hardly involved in the conversion process at all prior to changeover.

It is apparent from the above discussion that the philosophy, style and personality of the middle manager in Town Area exerted a significant influence on the management of change in the exchanges under his control. In direct contrast, the relative absence of a 'promoter of change' (Buchanan and Boddy, 1983: 24) in Metro Area led to a lack of co-ordination and certainly a lack of continuity in the management of the implementation process. In Coast Area, there was a lack of management continuity and co-ordination in Conversion A but a greater co-ordination, if still a lack of continuity, in Conversion B.

At least part of the difference in the way the three telephone areas set about the management of change can also be explained in terms of their differing approaches towards the role of the maintenance supervisor, both in the implementation process as such and in the eventual management of maintenance operations. The full implications of the different approaches they adopted towards the operational control of maintenance will be discussed in chapter 5. However, we can note here that the co-ordinating EE in Town Area took a conscious decision to select and system-train one maintenance supervisor and to place all three TXE4 units in the sub-area under his responsibility. Consistent with this policy, the 'specialist' supervisor was fully involved at an early stage in the implementation process. Not only was he encouraged to spend a great deal of time in the exchange during the installation and de-bugging of the new unit and to assist the installation supervisor in the management of the changeover, he also spent some time prior to changeover working alongside the maintenance technicians on the exchange equipment and discussing with them the way the new units would be maintained.

In neither Coast nor Metro Areas was such a clear and consistent policy developed. In Coast Area, the initial policy decision on this matter, taken by the Head of Maintenance, was to appoint a 'semi-specialist' TXE4 supervisor, who would be in charge of all TXE4 units but would not be system-trained. However, this policy was subsequently set aside, as we will see, due to the priority demands of area reorganisation. As a result, the maintenance supervisors were considerably confused about what their superiors expected them to do during and following implementation. In Metro Area, too, there was no clear policy concerning the role of the TXE4 supervisor or the operational control of TXE4 maintenance. In Conversion C the 'sitting tenant' Strowger supervisor was eventually given responsibility for the new TXE4 unit, apparently by default rather than by any positive decision, and he was given no guidance by area management on his future role.

In the absence of clear national guidelines on exchange implementation or the operational management of TXE4 maintenance, what we found in Coast and Metro Areas was not so much an 'attenuation' of corporate strategy as a failure to exploit the 'design space' available to area managements to define their own detailed 'control' objectives and in particular to devise a new role for the maintenance supervisor. In essence Coast and Metro Area managements made the tacit assumption that the role of the maintenance supervisor would be broadly the same in TXE4 as it was in Strowger. The implications of this approach for the role of the maintenance supervisor in the conversion process and in the day-to-day control of maintenance operations will be discussed in more detail in chapters 5 and 6.

2.7 Conclusion

Although not the primary focus of the research reported in this book, we have outlined in this chapter the development of corporate strategy towards exchange modernisation and the operational management of maintenance which lay behind the initiation, decision to adopt and selection of the TXE4 system. We have also examined the relationship between corporate strategy, control objectives and area implementation sub-strategies. On the basis of this analysis we see little point in questioning whether or not corporate BT management had a strategy in relation to exchange modernisation and operational control. Clearly they did in the sense that there was a 'rational consideration of alternatives and the articulation of coherent rationales for decisions' (see Child, 1985: 108). Nevertheless, we would agree with Child that corporate strategies, although having implications for the organisation and control of work, do not of necessity contain precise articulations to this effect. Indeed we have seen that there was an absence of detailed corporate guidelines on operational management and implementation at workplace level, the consequences of which have been touched upon in the last section and will be a critical component in our analysis below.

This highlights the importance of our notion of sub-strategy in the analysis of middle and supervisory management influence over technological change. Our data from the three telephone areas studied revealed contrasting responses to the design space left by the absence of detailed national guidelines. In all three areas responsibility for managing the introduction of TXE4 was delegated to junior middle management. In Town Areas a promoter of change emerged who assumed overall responsibility and developed a clear and coherent sub-strategy towards TXE4. One consequence of this was to create line management continuity throughout the process of TXE4 modernisation. In contrast, in neither Metro nor Coast Areas did such a promoter of change emerge. In consequence there was an absence of continuity and a less clear definition of responsibilities. This difference of approach was also reflected in management policies on the role of the TXE4 supervisor. The effect of these different implementation sub-strategies on the outcomes of TXE4 modernisation in individual exchanges will be a major theme of subsequent chapters.

3
Industrial relations and the negotiation of change

3.1 Introduction

This chapter develops our analysis of the implementation of change by looking at the way issues raised by TXE4 exchange modernisation were dealt with by management and the telecom trade unions at particular critical junctures in the process of change. We will again be concerned with the question of attenuation of corporate strategy, in this case the extent to which corporate industrial relations strategy left area managements room for manoeuvre in their dealings with local trade union representatives. We will also examine two other questions which, according to recent studies, technological change poses for industrial relations. First, how far were existing collective bargaining arrangements adequate for dealing with the issues raised by new technology? Moore and Levie (1985), for example, have presented evidence from a variety of settings which suggests that existing bargaining arrangements are insufficient, at least from a trade union point of view. Another recent study has gone as far as to suggest that 'traditional methods of bargaining are wholly inadequate for technological change' (Wilkinson, 1983: 99; see also Thompson and Bannon, 1985: chapter 7). Second, to what extent and in which ways were the telecom trade unions seeking to influence the introduction of TXE4? In particular, how far were national policies (and national agreements between unions and management) followed in practice by trade union representatives in the workplace?

The core of the chapter will therefore be concerned with industrial relations issues: the national framework of industrial relations within BT; national telecom union policies towards technological change; the negotiation of national and local agreements on TXE4 modernisation; and the implementation of joint agreements at exchange level. We will begin the chapter, however, by exploring the 'strategic position' of the two occupational groups who were directly affected by and therefore had a direct stake in seeking to influence the negotiation of change. These were exchange maintenance technicians and their supervisors.

56

Existing research provides contrasting pictures of the capacity of these two occupational groups to influence the negotiation and outcomes of technological change. A recurrent theme in discussions of advanced automation has been that, whilst the skill-content of direct operative jobs may be reduced, the skill-content and the significance of indirect labour – in particular, of maintenance technicians – tend to increase. The strategic position of maintenance technicians is also underlined by the complex and unpredictable nature of their work. This poses new problems for management in seeking to control their activities (see Bright, 1958; Gallie, 1978: 82–4; Senker *et al.*, 1981; Scarborough, 1984; Willman and Winch, 1985; Cross, 1985). By way of contrast, a recurrent theme in discussions of supervision is that advanced automation and trends in management control strategies in general are leading to an erosion of their previous role as direct controllers of labour (see Edwards, 1979; Child and Partridge, 1982; Buchanan and Boddy, 1983). Our immediate concern in this chapter will be to establish the nature of the strategic position of maintenance technicians and supervisors prior to TXE4 modernisation. Subsequent chapters will examine how far the position of these two groups was transformed as a result of technological change and how far they themselves were able to influence its outcomes.

3.2 The exchange maintenance workforce

Maintenance technicians

The basic grading structure for engineering technician grades (ETGs) in British Telecom at the time of our research had remained broadly unchanged since it was established in 1949 (see table 3.1). For exchange maintenance work, the two most important grades were Technical Officer (TO), the senior technician grade responsible for all major aspects of maintenance work within exchanges, and Technician 2A (T2A), a junior technician grade responsible for more routine tasks. When the grading structure was established, all grades had had 'low status' and 'relatively low pay' (Bealey, 1976: 297). By the mid-1970s, installation and maintenance technicians had achieved an 'elite' (Batstone *et al.*, 1984: 136) occupational position in terms of pay, grading and career structure. In this section we will look at the main features of their labour-market position at the time of the implementation of TXE4.

First, if we look at the development of real wages in the post-war period, we find engineering technician grades in general achieved increases significantly above those of clerical and executive grades within the telecommunications business and substantially greater than increases

Table 3.1 *Grading structure for exchange maintenance technicians (1983)*

Grade	Job
Technical Officer with Allowance (TOA)	Senior technician with chargeship duties[1]
Technical Officer (TO)	Senior technician
Technical Officer in Training (TOIT)	Senior technician in training
Technician (IIA and IIB)	Junior technician
Trainee Technician Apprentice (TTA)	Apprentice

in general (average) wages. In 1960, for example, the real wages of ETG grades were twenty-five per cent higher than average wages, but by 1970 they were seventy per cent higher (see Bealey, 1976: 361, 405). A comparison with wage movements of clerical and executive grades in the civil service during the 1960s (until 1969 telecommunications grades were part of the civil service) also shows what Bealey called a 'more favourable intra-service differential' (*ibid.*: 406).

Second, if we look at the relation between the three main occupational groups within the ETG workforce, 'internal' staff engaged on exchange maintenance and installations, 'external' staff engaged on maintaining, updating and installing cables and ducts, and 'minority' grades composed of motor transport, factories, supplies, and drawing office staff, we find two significant features distinguishing the internal maintenance and installation technicians. By the mid-1970s they had become the numerically dominant of the three groups (over fifty-five per cent, with under twenty-five per cent involved in external work), whereas before 1939 external grades had predominated. In addition, the ratio of senior to junior internal staff was also much higher than in the other two groups, such that by 1983, during the main year of our research, seventy-five per cent of all technical officers in BT were to be found in internal installation and maintenance work. This increasingly elite position of 'internal staff' in the engineering technician workforce was not unrelated to a third feature of their labour market position – their career structure.

Many of the main features of the career structure of engineering technician grades were developed in the early 1960s in the middle of a period of great expansion in the telecommunications network. In 1963 a three-year youth-in-training scheme was instituted which envisaged a fairly quick progression, particularly for those entering the maintenance field, from apprentice via T2A to Technical Officer. Recruitment was largely straight from school, although in years of shortage, there was some direct adult entry at T2A level. From the early 1960s, therefore, formal educational qualifications and training courses began to assume more significance for promotion to TO within the maintenance hierarchy. This emergent credentialism meant that access to the TO-in-Training panel came to depend on the successful completion of a City and Guilds Certificate or Ordinary National Certificate (ONC). Given the stress on formal qualifications and the massive expansion of the telecommunications network from the late 1950s, TOs in exchange maintenance tended by the early 1970s to be both younger and more formally qualified than other engineering technician grades in the business. By 1970, as Bealey has pointed out, 'junior grades were quite likely to find themselves in the "elite" before they were 30' (Bealey, 1976: 402).

Maintenance supervisors

For maintenance technicians with ambitions to go into management, the route into the maintenance supervisor grade to become an Assistant Executive Engineer (AEE) was typically from within the ranks of Technical Officers. In the early 1980s it was estimated by BTHQ that around ninety-seven per cent of maintenance AEE vacancies were filled by promotions from the TO grade. Typically, too, maintenance supervisors had had a long experience as Strowger technicians. Between the late 1960s and mid-1980s the basic pay of supervisors was consistently around twenty per cent above that of senior technicians. As we will see, this was not so much a reflection of the strategic position of supervisors in the workplace, as the outcome of management policy and the success of their trade union in achieving the maintenance of traditional differentials over technician grades. The position of supervisors is examined in more detail in chapter 5.

Study sample of technicians and supervisors

The sample of maintenance technicians and supervisors in our study, involving thirty-four TOs (including TOITs and 'temporary' TOs), ten T2As and seven AEEs, illustrates many of the key features of this structured and stable internal labour market. The mean age of TOs was thirty-four, of T2As twenty-seven, and of AEEs forty-four. Three-quarters of the ETGs had been born in the same county as the exchange in which they now worked. On average the ETGs lived about four and a half miles from their exchange, and fifty-five per cent lived within three miles. All but three of our sample of fifty-one had further education qualifications to City and Guilds or ONC level (the three were all adult entrants), and for over three-quarters (seventy-eight per cent) BT had been their only employer during their working life. On average the TOs had worked for BT for seventeen years, the T2As for seven, and the AEEs for twenty-seven years. The TOs had worked on average for seven years in their present exchange and had been TOs for ten years. The AEEs had all had extensive experience as Strowger technicians.

The technicians' perceptions of exchange maintenance as a career underlined key features of their work within BT. Nearly forty per cent had joined BT initially because of the influence of friends and relations who worked or had worked for the Post Office (in all cases prior to the split of the postal and telecommunications businesses in 1981). When asked to give the main reason why they had joined the Post Office, two main groups of motives emerged, one employer-related and the other job- or career-related. Over twenty-seven per cent of all those interviewed mentioned job security as a reason why they chose BT rather than another employer, while eleven per cent mentioned good pay, nine per cent job prospects and seven per cent training. In terms of career or job, twenty-five per cent said they were seeking some kind of engineering work, twenty per cent that they were looking for an apprenticeship or trade, and fourteen per cent that they were interested in electrical engineering and electronics.

To underline the stability of the maintenance workforce, two other factors may be mentioned. First, nearly half the ETG respondents said that they had never considered leaving BT (eighteen per cent had seriously considered leaving, twenty-seven per cent only vaguely). The reasons given were a roughly equal balance between four factors – a general satisfaction with BT as an employer, job security, pay, and the uncertainties of the job market. Second, when asked about their job expectations ten years hence, just over half the TOs expected to be doing the same job as at present (the others said they did not know). Over half said they would also positively like to be doing the same job. When asked directly if they intended to apply for promotion to first-line supervisor at any time in the future, just under a third of the TOs said they would and nearly two-thirds said they would not. It should be stressed that the responses to this last question were often accompanied by comments that promotion prospects in the future were likely to be severely limited.

In summary, the position of exchange maintenance staff by the mid-1970s, the time of negotiations over TXE4 modernisation, was characterised by a remarkably stable internal labour market offering a high degree of job security and a relatively assured career progression through the ETG grades for those who wanted it. The expansion of the telecommunications infrastructure business in the decades after the Second World War, and particularly the rapid growth and modernisation of the telephone exchange network, had contributed to the creation of a highly profitable business and an expanding workforce with increasingly high levels of formal qualifications. As we have indicated above and will show in more detail in chapter 4, corporate decisions since the 1950s to introduce automatic testing equipment and more reliable exchange systems had reduced the need for large amounts of routine maintenance and increased the need for higher grade staff to carry out the more complex maintenance tasks. In fact, this last point about the relation between work tasks, skills and grades of staff can only be adequately understood in the context of two further factors, the traditional pattern of industrial relations in the Post Office and the strength and policies of the trade unions representing engineering grades. These are the subject of our next two sections.

3.3 Industrial relations and trade unions: patterns and developments

In this section the aim is to characterise the broad pattern of industrial relations in the telecommunications business at the time of the national and local negotiations over TXE4 modernisation and to discuss the structure and character of the two trade unions which had a direct interest and, in one case, involvement in its outcome. The broad policies of the two unions towards technological change will be discussed in the following section.

Industrial relations

As we saw in chapter 2, at the very time TXE4 modernisation was getting underway in the mid-1970s, corporate Post Office management was in the process of modifying its traditional public-service dominated ethos towards a more market-led commercially dominated orientation. The implications of this paradigm shift for industrial relations within the business have been analysed in detail by Batstone and his colleagues (1984: chapter 5) and can be briefly summarised. The traditional pattern of labour relations in the Post Office, which had taken shape after the First World War and achieved its heyday in the 1950s, was based on the positive support of the trade unions for the goals of management and its public-service ethic. In return the unions were given formal recognition and their members enjoyed a number of nationally protected conditions of service. First, they were largely protected from the vagaries of the external labour market by the operation of a 'fair wages' policy and by recruitment and promotion practices which rewarded loyal service and seniority. Second, collective agreements on wages, hours and holidays were nationally applicable throughout the organisation and encouraged 'strong bargaining relationships between top management and national union officials' (*ibid.*: 111). Third, the highly centralised system of bargaining left little scope for local industrial relations initiatives by either management or trade unions. Finally, although there was no formal agreement to that effect, job security was an unwritten but central feature of the traditional industrial relations system.

From the late 1950s, however, there was increasing concern within the ranks of corporate management that the traditional pattern of industrial relations needed to be modified and made more consistent with market and commercial criteria. This had a number of implications for traditional agreements and practices. The first implication of this more 'commercial approach to labour' (*ibid.*: 116) was to break down career structures largely based on seniority and internal recruitment and to encourage more promotion on merit and recruitment from outside the organisation. For Batstone and his colleagues, 'such changes involved an increase in managerial discretion and a reduction in union influence over selection' (*ibid.*: 117). We will examine in detail below how far this new approach was adopted in determining the criteria by which the staff were selected to re-train for TXE4 maintenance.

Second, staffing levels were to be related more closely to the volume of work to be done. Local management were to use the more accurate information on work loads provided by new equipment to change the organisation of work and to utilise labour more efficiently. Third, there was a move away from the 'fair wage' principle towards a new emphasis on productivity and performance in pay determination. In the longer term this suggested the need to reduce the importance of nationally negotiated pay rates. Fourth, the traditional stress on consensus and joint agreement was still formally re-affirmed but at the same time there was a greater emphasis on managerial discretion and autonomy in the workplace. In particular there was a stress on the need for managers and supervisors to increase direct communication with their staff, including the use of local attitude surveys, rather than working at arms' length and relying on the trade unions as a main channel of information (*ibid.*: 122).

As Batstone, Ferner and Terry have pointed out, senior management in the postal and telecommunications businesses was still constrained throughout the 1970s and early 1980s by changing government policies and practices. In addition, many managers at all levels within each business had been brought up on the traditional industrial relations paradigm and remained committed to it. As we will see later in this chapter, the alternative approaches to industrial relations issues suggested by the traditional and commercial paradigms were present in both the national and local negotiations over TXE4 modernisation. However, we must first look at the organisation and character of the two main telecommunications unions.

The Post Office Engineering Union

Trade unionism in the telecommunications infrastructure industry can trace its origins back to 1870, when private telegraph companies were taken into public ownership and the engineering department of the Post Office was established (see Bealey, 1976: 12). However, the POEU itself was not founded until 1919 and it had barely reached a membership of 35,000 by 1939. In fact, as table 3.2 shows, it was really only after the Second World War that union membership really took off in parallel with the massive expansion in the telephone network. In this sense, the POEU was very much a product of the telecommunications boom of the post-war period. This goes some way to explain its positive approach towards technological change and its distinctive character within the trade union movement in Britain: 'British trades unionism is usually depicted as a nineteenth-century phenomenon. It is significant, therefore, that the Post Office Engineering Union is virtually a product of the twentieth century' (Bealey, 1976: 410). By 1983 it was the twentieth largest union in Britain with a membership of around 130,000.

The development of the POEU in the period leading up to the launch of the TXE4 modernisation programme was shaped by two additional features of the telecommunications infrastructure industry, the fact that it was a public-service organisation and that, until 1969, it was also part of the civil service (see Batstone *et al.*, 1984: chapters 8 and 9). As part of the public-service sector, POEU members were relatively isolated from external market pressures. On top of this, the POEU was also party to a system of industrial relations in the civil-service tradition. This meant a relatively stable membership (around ninety-seven per cent from the mid-1960s onwards with the introduction of the 'check-off' system), sole bargaining rights for engineering technicians and 'minority grades', rights to speak to and recruit new staff on their engagement and good local facilities for trade union representatives (normally including an office and, of course, a telephone). In true civil-service tradition the union structure tended to develop in parallel to the structure of the employers' organisation. Thus the POEU developed a highly centralised structure with only limited scope for regional and area bargaining and a

Table 3.2 *Post Office Engineering Union: membership trends (1920–83)*

Year	Membership
1920	19,270
1929	13,315
1939	34,360
1945	45,663
1951	47,844
1957	69,852
1963	82,664
1966	98,532
1969	108,898
1972	125,271
1975	124,682
1978	121,406
1981	132,828
1983	129,950

Source: POEU.

Table 3.3 *POEU structure and joint regulation in BT (1983)*

Union structure	Level	Management negotiators
National Executive Council General Secretary National Full-time Officers	National	BT Board and BTHQ Departments
Union Regional Council	Regional	Regional Director and Departments
Area Co-ordinating Committee/Branch	Area	General Manager, Divisions (e.g. Head of Maintenance)

relatively underdeveloped workplace presence (see Batstone *et al.*, 1984: 221ff). Local organisation was based mainly on geographically based branches and (from the late 1960s) area co-ordinating committees, whose main tasks were to ensure the application of national agreements and to deal with individual and collective grievances specific to the staff in their branch or area. As of 1983, the structure and organisation were as shown in table 3.3.

In summary, the main objectives of the POEU were circumscribed by its structure and history as a union of increasingly well qualified engineering technicians in an expanding public-service organisation with a whole range of civil service traditions. Fair wages, a share in the benefits of increased productivity, improved status, job security, good promotion prospects and a management committed to joint regulation and consensus were the central planks of its policy in the post-war period; not forgetting, of course, a strong commitment to technological change and modernisation.

The Society of Telecom Executives

The other main union representing engineering staff in telephone exchanges was the Society of Telecom Executives (STE). The union joined the TUC in 1966 as the Society of Telecommunications Engineers and in 1969 changed its name to the Society of Post Office Executives. In 1983, after all its members working in the Post and Giro businesses transferred membership to the Communication Managers Association, it was renamed the STE. (To avoid confusion we will refer to the union throughout as the STE, even though for part of the period under discussion it was called SPOE.) At the time of our research, the STE organised supervisors and middle management grades mainly in the engineering field of telecommunications, including exchange maintenance and installation, transmission, planning and research staff. By the late 1970s it also claimed a substantial membership among very senior grades, including General Managers and even some Board members. In 1983 it organised around eighty-five per cent of potential staff, a very high union density for a predominantly management union (see table 3.4). In the same year, its membership amongst first-line supervisors, the management focus of our study, was over ninety-four per cent.

The STE's traditional strategy and organisation were broadly similar to that outlined for the POEU. However, there were a number of differences too. First, as a management union it was extremely sensitive to the need to distinguish between issues which concerned its members in their management capacity and issues which concerned its members as trade unionists. Indeed, as we will see, this distinction was crucial in shaping its approach towards modernisation. Second, its traditional approach towards bargaining issues such as pay and grading was to wait and see what the POEU achieved for its grades and then to claim at least what the POEU had achieved in order to maintain its differentials. Third, the STE started from the assumption that the occupational interests of its members, particularly concerning pay, job security and promotion, would be broadly safeguarded by national telecommuni-

Table 3.4 *Society of Telecom Executives: membership trends (1966–83)*

Year	Membership
1966	7,154
1969	12,944
1972	18,806
1975	22,601
1978	22,567
1981	24,465
1983	22,962

Source: STE.

cations management and that it could trust management to maintain this situation in future national negotiations, if not always in individual cases. All these facets of STE policy were embodied at the time of our research in the person of their general secretary, Kenneth Glynn, who provided continuity and strong 'charismatic' leadership from 1966 until his retirement in 1983.

3.4 The trade union response to technological change

The POEU

In characterising the attitude of the POEU to the question of modernisation in the 1950s and early 1960s, Bealey felt able to conclude: 'it is unlikely that there was any union which accepted change more readily than the POEU . . . [it was] a technologically oriented union with a technocratic leadership' (1976: 331, 367). From the early 1960s it produced a series of policy statements underlining its commitment to technological change and an expansion of the business. This culminated in 1979 in the publication of a 104-page policy document called *The Modernisation of Telecommunications*. The general view of the union towards technological change in the post-war period is clearly captured in the following excerpt:

> POEU members have to make a basic choice. Either we have an electro-mechanical telephone system with limited reliability and service, where the rate of growth in system size and traffic diminishes, resulting in virtually static employment prospects. Or we have a fully electronic telecommunications system with

digital switching and transmission providing the opportunities for new services and markets and more jobs for our members.

It is argued that the best long-term employment prospects for our members rest in the speedy modernisation of the network, so that system size and traffic continue to grow and so that the Telecommunications Business can enter and win a share of the new markets for terminal equipment which will be stimulated by a modernised telecommunications network. (POEU, 1979: 5)

By the time the POEU had produced this report, the 'social impact' of micro-electronics had become a subject of widespread public debate polarised between those who took a pessimistic view of its employment implications and those who took a more optimistic view. British trade unions were to be found in both camps, but the POEU's public position was clear and unambiguous. As one survey of trade union responses to technological change concluded, the POEU adopted 'an optimistic and even enthusiastic approach to micro-electronics' (Robbins and Webster, 1982: 13–15).

So far, developments within POEU policy and organisation have been portrayed as part of a homogeneous consensual internal development. However, we should not overlook ideological and occupational conflicts inside the union in the post-war period. From the 1940s to the 1960s, ideological opposition to the union leadership was consistent though largely ineffective (Bealey, 1977). In the 1970s, however, it regrouped as the 'broad left' and became an increasingly powerful force at the union's annual conference. As we shall see, the broad left was particularly critical of the leadership's modernisation policy and in 1983 it won control of the union's National Executive Council. Since 1945 and even before, there had also been intermittent expressions of dissatisfaction within the POEU ranks from some Technical Officers who felt themselves to be under-represented in a union largely composed of junior technician grades. At various times they threatened to form, and in some cases did form, a breakaway union to represent their special interests (see Lerner, 1961: chapter 3; also Bealey, 1976: especially chapter 10; Batstone *et al.*, 1984: 219ff). Among their number were always a substantial group of TOs working in exchange maintenance.

Some of the most important external challenges to the traditional structure and policies of the POEU came in the wake of the changing commercial and industrial relations climate in the telecommunications industry. Already in the late 1960s, the POEU began to strengthen local union organisation in response to managerial devolution, encouraging the creation of local branch representatives (the equivalent of shop stewards) at workplace level and area co-ordinating committees to represent staff in relations with area management. But the challenge to traditional policy increasingly concentrated on the national leadership's handling of modernisation. By the early 1970s, at the very time national management began to embark on their major programme of telephone exchange modernisation, membership growth appeared to have reached saturation point. Fears of job losses associated with these developments began to surface regularly at POEU annual conferences, and criticisms were made of the Executive's commitment to technological change without apparent safeguards on job security or the rate of its introduction (see Batstone *et al.*, 1984: 236–40).

In 1976, the year in which the first TXE4 exchange was brought into service, the annual conference passed a motion demanding that TXE4 exchanges should have the same staffing levels as the Strowger exchanges they were due to replace. Although this was not achieved, it was one of the pressures which resulted in 1978 in a national agreement between BT and POEU on TXE4 Manpower Requirements. 1978 also saw a major industrial dispute about the 35-hour week involving POEU grades, a campaign again not unconnected with fears about job losses. The dispute led eventually to the reduction in the working week from 40 to $37\frac{1}{2}$ hours. Interestingly, the implementation of this agreement was left to local management and union co-ordinating committees in the telephone areas.

By the late 1970s, then, the policy of the POEU leadership towards exchange modernisation was increasingly under attack. As Batstone and his colleagues have pointed out, 'these discontents and pressures came to be focused in demands for a special conference on modernisation' (*ibid.*, 1984: 237). The leadership eventually responded to this pressure with a number of internal organisational innovations. These included the commissioning from the union's research department of *The Modernisation of Telecommunications*, the holding of a special conference on modernisation in June 1979 and the establishment of a national union modernisation committee, cutting completely across the existing national committee structure, to look at all aspects of modernisation. In 1979, too, as we shall see below, the union engaged in negotiations which led eventually to the conclusion of a national Job Security Agreement.

Most of these innovations were instituted, it should be emphasized, in response to conference resolutions and pressure from union branches, much of which was co-ordinated by the recently formed broad left faction within the union. By the early 1980s, however, System X had become the main focus of attention in internal POEU debates about exchange modernisation. Nevertheless the whole question of modernisation had acted, and continued to act in the mid-1980s, as a catalyst for policy differences within the national union.

One final point should perhaps be noted about these developments within the POEU. One of the side-effects of its centralised structure was the tendency, common to most unions, but particularly strong in this case, to concentrate policy debates at the national level. At the annual union conference, it is true, debates about major policy issues were regular and open. They were also carried over into campaigns concerning the election and composition of the National Executive Council. But although the broad-left organisation had its basis of power in certain metropolitan branches of the union (London, Liverpool, Glasgow), much of the policy debate about modernisation did not filter back to the telephone areas and the technicians in the often isolated telephone exchanges. This, and the fact that TXE4 modernisation was in full swing by the end of the 1970s, meant that changes in the policies and composition of the national union were not readily reflected in local union responses to the implementation of TXE4 modernisation in the areas and individual exchanges. In other words, as we shall see below, there was considerable scope for an attenuation between national union policy and local union practice.

The STE

During the 1970s and early 1980s, the official policy of the STE towards exchange modernisation was that it was a 'management issue', with relevance for the union only in its potential implications for job security. In the mid-1970s, the STE was in fact party to discussions with THQ management on the manpower implications of local exchange modernisation, and in September 1977 it published a document in its monthly journal on the outcome of these discussions. The outcome was a set of agreed guidelines, whose findings were based largely on corporate management's own manpower projections into the late 1980s. The document suggested that there would be no significant reductions in staffing for management grades as a result of local exchange modernisation and promised extensive consultation at area level on the modernisation of individual exchanges. Against this background the executive report to the 1978 STE conference suggested that it had done what was necessary on the issue.

In the event, discontent with the modernisation policy of the national leadership came to the surface at this conference. One motion, though eventually defeated, expressed unease about the apparent inaction of the union at national level. The motion rejected the section of the Executive Council (EC) report on modernisation on the grounds that the EC had failed 'to give a statement of the [STE] policy regarding the modernisation programme and . . . to provide local branches with guidance concerning supervisory staffing levels and training requirements for supervising officers who will be in charge of TXE4 telephone exchanges'. The motion stressed that maintenance supervisors were being faced with completely new exchange systems, and while the technicians were attending twenty-week training courses, supervisors were receiving only two-week 'appreciation' courses which gave them only a superficial understanding. The reply from the EC was that the staffing implications of TXE4 for supervisors would be minimal and that telecommunications management had given assurances that modernisation would have 'no significant impact on [STE] grades'. The main thread running through all the criticisms from the floor of the conference was that the STE was under-estimating the implications of TXE4 modernisation for supervisory grades and was relying too heavily on management forecasts rather than developing its own independent strategy. In his summary of the debate the General Secretary argued that the responsibility for planning and implementing modernisation in a way that would not prejudice the careers of STE members lay in the hands of management and that the union had achieved assurances to this effect. In a classic statement of traditional union policy he said: 'The [STE] was not seeking to manage the Post Office, but to safeguard the interests of its members.'

Many of the criticisms voiced at the 1978 conference were taken up in meetings of the EC during the following year. Concern was expressed by some executive members that the job of the maintenance supervisor would change under the new exchange systems and that the EC was being too complacent. However, the predominant view, as expressed by the General Secretary, was that the maintenance supervisor would become more rather than less important, the span of control (ratio between supervisor and technician grades) would be reduced and there would be increasingly close supervision. The discussion of this issue at the 1979 conference again showed some disquiet from the floor but the executive position was that nothing could be done until the POEU had completed negotiations about the implications of modernisation for maintenance technicians. By this time, however, the concern of the STE, like that of the POEU, was increasingly focused on System X. After 1979 TXE4 did not feature again in discussions of modernisation at its annual conference.

3.5 The negotiation of TXE4 modernisation at national level

We are now in a position to examine the national framework agreed between BT management and the POEU on three particular issues which arose in connection with TXE4 modernisation: staffing levels; job security; and pay and grading. In so doing we will aim to assess the main factors shaping these negotiations and to draw some preliminary conclusions about the effectiveness of collective bargaining procedures and the extent of trade union influence. In the subsequent two sections we will look at negotiations over the introduction of TXE4 in our three telephone areas and the implementation of national and area agreements in individual exchanges.

Staffing levels

In previous sections we have noted a number of conflicting pressures and tendencies concerning question of staffing levels for TXE4 exchanges. First, the reduction in maintenance costs, particularly the cost of labour, was a primary reason behind the corporate management decision to launch the TXE4 modernisation programme in 1973. Second, the gradual adoption by corporate management of a more commercial approach to labour included a strong emphasis on the need to relate staffing levels more closely to the volume of work to be done and to utilise labour more efficiently. Third, there was a parallel stress within corporate management on the need for increased local managerial discretion and autonomy in the telephone areas with fewer constraints to be imposed by inflexible national standards. Finally, the 1976 POEU conference had committed its national leaders to demand that TXE4 exchanges should have the same staffing levels as the Strowger exchanges they were due to replace. For all these reasons, national negotiations over staffing levels were a significant critical juncture for all parties.

In analysing the outcome of the negotiations, the first point to note is that there had been no nationally agreed staffing levels for Strowger exchanges, simply national guidelines (some mandatory, some recommended) on the particular maintenance routines to be carried out. This had resulted in wide variations in staffing levels in individual exchanges (see Batstone *et al.*, 1984: 154). To this extent, the publication in February 1978 of a national interim agreement on TXE4 manpower requirements was a substantial industrial relations innovation.

The main part of the joint agreement, which was issued by corporate management as a national Telecommunications Instruction (TI), laid down a quantitative measure in the form of a 'nomogram' for determining the man-hours needed to maintain TXE4 exchange equipment. Exchange man-hours per annum were to be obtained by a direct reading of the nomogram, which contained two separate scales, one measuring the number of customer connections and the other measuring the level of traffic or calling rate. The aim of this quantitative measure was to establish explicit standardised links between staffing levels and volume of work.

However, this apparently precise national measure was modified by a number of other clauses in the agreement which, as we shall see below, effectively transferred responsibility for determining actual staffing levels to local level. First, the nomogram related only to maintenance of the exchange system proper, whereas the agreement recognised that there were a number of 'other activities' which needed to be considered in arriving at overall staffing levels for an individual exchange. These other activities included other maintenance work in the exchange (non-TXE4 equipment maintenance), other classes of work (line-testing, records, meter-reading, all installation work, cleaning), plus personnel matters such as annual leave, sick leave and training courses. As a broad guideline it suggested that the relation between TXE4 maintenance and these other activities would normally be 60:40.

On top of this, the agreement recognised the need to allow for a number of other local variations, ranging from the operational condition of the equipment and quality of customer service to factors such as area management structure and organisation. In certain telephone areas, for example, it was recognised that some routine exchange work was undertaken by junior technicians who were not counted as part of the staffing complement of individual exchanges. In addition, it was accepted that, in the 'settling down' period of a new exchange, higher staffing levels might well be required to meet transitional problems such as the unfamiliarity of staff with the equipment and higher than normal fault rates. For this reason a 'minimum of three ETG staff should initially be allocated per exchange', the figure to be adjusted to two where appropriate after the exchange had settled down. Finally, local management were required to consult 'at an early stage' with staff and the local POEU branch when determining the staffing requirements in individual exchanges. The interim agreement was to be reviewed 'after approximately two years'. In the event it was withdrawn by BT management in 1982 in favour of new 'work scheduling' procedures utilising 'standard times for jobs undertaken in exchange maintenance' (BT, 1983b: 51). However, by the end of our research period (summer 1984), this new procedure had not yet been used to determine the staffing levels in our case study exchanges.

In a discussion of the negotiations over the interim agreement, Batstone, Ferner and Terry have argued that it represented a concession, both procedurally and substantively, to the POEU:

> THQ [was] forced to concede uniform national standards to the POEU in the face of strong opposition from Regional management, who argued that there was a need for local management discretion to staff exchanges at levels most appropriate for local conditions. (*Ibid.*, 153)

However, these apparently uniform national standards still left a large amount of room for manoeuvre for local managements (and for local union representatives too), particularly in the interpretation of the importance of 'other activities' and local variations. As we will see below, the agreement also exerted an important influence on the selection of staff for re-training and on other issues arising during the implementation process.

Job security

Job security had been one of the outstanding features of industrial relations in the Post Office since the 1920s. The fact that it became the subject of formal national negotiations at the time of the implementation of the TXE4 modernisation programme was in part an indication of a change in the traditional pattern of industrial relations, and in part a response of the POEU leadership to criticisms voiced at successive annual conferences about the longer term implications of technological change for the jobs of engineering staff. Under the agreement, which was signed in 1980, management undertook, without any time limit, that there would no compulsory redundancies for POEU-represented grades. There was a proviso, however, that this undertaking could be withdrawn in the event of circumstances beyond management control. In return, the POEU agreed to co-operate in the planned introduction of new technology and the provision of a high quality service to the customer and that re-training, redeployment and even natural wastage might be necessary in order to avoid compulsory redundancies.

The question of job security has been identified as 'probably the basic motive for organised labour' (Bamber and Willman, 1983: 110) in responding to management proposals to introduce new technology. It has even been suggested that the fear of redundancy and unemployment is 'the major factor influencing unions' views on technical change' (Bamber, 1980: 9). In this context the POEU leadership regarded the agreement as 'unique in that no other British industry faced with comparable technological change has yet negotiated a similar agreement' (Webb, 1979). Without doubt the agreement was a significant industrial relations innovation. However, since job security and union co-operation with technological change had been traditional cornerstones of industrial relations in the business since the 1920s, it is probably best seen as a re-affirmation or formalisation of traditional practice in the changed technological and commercial conditions of the late 1970s. Its relevance to the implementation of change at exchange level will be examined further below.

Pay and grading

One possibly surprising omission in national discussions about TXE4 modernisation was the area of pay and grading. In fact a consensus had emerged between senior management and the POEU, albeit for different reasons, that there were to be no special changes in the terms and conditions of internal maintenance staff selected to work in the new TXE4 exchanges. Instead, increases for the acceptance of technological change were to be paid to all telecommunications staff represented by the POEU in the form of across-the-board productivity payments (see Batstone *et al.*, 1984: 131f). These had been a regular feature of collective bargaining in the Post Office since the 1950s.

For senior management, opposition to regrading and increased pay for TXE4 maintenance staff was based on a concern to reduce labour costs and the argument that TXE4 maintenance involved different but not higher skills than Strowger maintenance. For the POEU, opposition to special increases for TXE4 technicians was based on the concern to retain all senior exchange maintenance staff in a unified national Technical Officer (TO) grade. The union had expressed a strong fear in its policy document of 1979 that the introduction of new technology might separate a new engineering technician elite (often called 'super TO') from the majority of other technicians, thereby fragmenting union organisation as well as creating divisions within the workforce. The union thus opted for a 'broad front' approach to negotiations over the introduction of new technology, rather than using it as a 'bridgehead' to achieve higher pay and grading for specific groups of staff (see Bamber, 1980: 14). In the area of pay and grading, therefore, national management and the POEU did set a framework for the implementation of TXE4 exchange modernisation, not by negotiating changes, but by refusing to put these questions on the agenda for bargaining except as part of a more general discussion about across-the-board productivity increases (of which acceptance of telephone exchange modernisation was but one element). They thus re-affirmed traditional practice in the area of pay and grading rather than attempting to introduce procedural or substantive innovations.

So far this discussion of the national industrial relations framework for the implementation of TXE4 modernisation has concentrated exclusively on the POEU and engineering technician grades. In fact, the STE did not engage in any formal negotiations or agreements with management concerning maintenance supervisors or other management grades directly involved in the conversion and management of TXE4 exchanges. This absence of STE involvement was the direct result of its policy that technological change was essentially a management rather than a trade union issue. It will be argued below that this absence of union involvement was one of the reasons contributing to a relative neglect of supervision in the implementation of TXE4 modernisation in the telephone areas and exchanges studied.

How far was the transition within national management from a traditional towards a more commercial approach to labour reflected in the industrial relations' framework agreed for the introduction of TXE4? The evidence discussed above on job security, staffing levels, and pay and grading suggests, in line with the analysis of Batstone and his colleagues, that a 'balance was struck' between the demands of the new corporate strategy and the traditional approaches which it sought to replace. This balance was the basis for a 'new consensus' (*ibid.*: 143–4) which enabled the implementation of the TXE4 programme without any major national industrial relations difficulties.

If we turn to the question of the adequacy of existing bargaining arrangements in dealing with issues of technological change, some interesting points emerge. The framework agreed was piecemeal and in no way represented a 'new technology agreement' of the type advocated by the TUC and negotiated with limited success by several mainly white-collar unions (see Williams and Steward, 1985). However, existing channels of negotiation did allow management and the POEU to extend the scope of traditional national bargaining to cover issues such as staffing levels and job security. The agreements were also clearly consistent with long-standing and recently re-affirmed commitments by both management and unions to a consensual approach to the introduction of new technology. However, the range of issues covered by national negotiations were relatively limited and the scope left for local variations within them relatively wide. As a result there still remained considerable scope for local management and unions to engage in consultation and bargaining at area and workplace level. This was most evidently the case on the issues of selection for re-training and staffing levels.

3.6 The negotiation of change in Metro, Coast and Town Areas

The issue of staff selection for re-training provided the first critical juncture at which an opportunity arose for local managements and unions to attempt to exert some influence on the outcomes of change. In fact, this turned out to be the only issue over which we found any evidence of formal local negotiations and agreements, although issues such as the phasing of training courses with the installation and debugging of the new exchanges were subject to informal discussions with local trade union representatives.[2]

We have already noted that the traditional career structure of engineering technician grades was based largely on the principles of seniority and internal recruitment, and that the new 'commercial approach to labour' was trying to shift the emphasis towards promotion on individual merit and outside recruitment. For Batstone, Ferner and Terry, the application of these latter principles signalled 'an increase in managerial discretion and a reduction in union influence over selection' (*ibid.*: 117). In the absence of national agreements or guidelines on selection for re-training, our aim in this section is to examine the relative influence of local managements and union organisations in determining the criteria and procedures by which staff would have access to particular jobs within the internal labour market. As we will see, the resolution of this issue had particularly important implications for the occupational distribution of skill within the exchange maintenance workforce.

In Metro and Coast Areas, the general criteria and procedures by which technicians were to be selected to work in the new exchanges were subject to joint negotiation and agreement by local engineering management (at Head of Maintenance level) and trade union branch representatives. In both cases sitting tenants – the existing holders of maintenance jobs in the relevant exchanges – were to be given first choice on the basis of length of service in the exchange as a Technical Officer. In Town Area, in contrast, criteria for selection were established by management alone, albeit with the subsequent acquiescence of local POEU representatives, and the sitting-tenant principle was rejected in favour of the criterion of suitability. This was defined by management, and accepted *de facto* by the local POEU, in terms of experience and maturity as a maintenance TO and aptitude for electronics. Seniority was only to apply where two candidates of equal merit were being considered. In summary, where local union representatives were able to subject the question of selection for training to joint regulation, resulting in both cases in a written agreement with local management, the principle of seniority predominated.[3] Where management established criteria unilaterally, the principles of individual suitability and merit predominated. The reasons for this outcome and its implications will be discussed further below.

One further matter relating to criteria for selection deserves mention here, namely that in all three telephone areas studied only senior technicians (Technical Officers) were considered for re-training. We have already noted above that the 1978 national agreement on TXE4 staffing levels had spoken generally of 'ETG staff' in connection with the new exchanges but in none of our areas were junior engineering technician grades selected or even considered for selection. In Metro and Coast Areas, junior technicians were ruled out *de facto* by the adoption of the sitting-tenant principle – in Town Area, indeed, local management and union representatives came to a formal agreement restricting TXE4 re-training to TOs only. In both these areas, all middle-managers interviewed (Heads of Division and Executive Engineers) explained this restriction largely as a concession to pressure from the local union and none indicated any awareness of a national corporate policy on this issue. When interviewed, union representatives justified their commitment to the seniority principle on two main grounds. First, they argued that TXE4 maintenance should be recognised as highly skilled work requiring highly skilled staff and that the existing TO grade was composed of such staff who had been promoted by management in the past because of their skills and abilities. Second, it was argued that only TOs should be selected for re-training in order to prevent the dilution of skills, that is, the use of lower paid and less skilled junior staff to do highly skilled work. As far as the union representatives were concerned, therefore, influence over the criteria for selection for training was seen as crucial to protecting the position of senior staff within the internal labour market.

In Town Area, the middle manager responsible for selection of staff in his sub-area explained his decision to consider only senior technicians in terms of the refusal of the BT Technical Training College to accept junior technicians for training courses. This was in fact true in the early 1980s, when the demand for training courses was high and the number of places limited.[4] Interestingly, he also explained his decision on the ground of his area management's commitment to adhere to national guidelines on the matter. In fact, as we have seen in the previous section, there were no national guidelines restricting selection to senior staff. However, this particular middle manager was not alone in believing that there were. When interviewed, many TOs and T2As also said that national guidelines expressly excluded junior staff from selection. This was clearly a case where a particular belief, even if it had no basis in fact, managed to exert a powerful influence on the behaviour and choices of the individual managers, union officials and technicians.

As we will see in chapter 6, the exclusion of junior grades from re-training for TXE4 maintenance had important implications for their position within the exchange maintenance workforce and for the division of labour within the new exchanges. It should simply be noted here that the application of the seniority principle, largely as a result of union pressure, led in all three telephone areas studied to the effective exclusion of junior technicians from a present or future career in TXE4 maintenance. Put another way, the principle operated as a form of occupational closure restricting entry to the new jobs to senior technicians only. Not surprisingly, this was a cause of considerable dissatisfaction amongst the small number of junior technicians we interviewed (five in all) who were working in TXE4 exchanges or in Strowger exchanges about to be converted to TXE4. This issue clearly presented the POEU with a potential clash of objectives in the face of new technology, namely to safeguard the jobs and skills of senior staff but also to maintain a clear career structure and good promotion prospects for junior staff.

Procedures for consulting staff whose exchanges were to be modernised were also subject to joint regulation in two of our three telephone areas. In Coast Area, local management prepared a questionnaire in co-operation with local union branch representatives. This was circulated to all senior maintenance staff in the telephone area, irrespective of whether their exchange was to be modernised or not. It asked them to express their views about their future employment within the business, and in particular whether they wished to be considered for re-training for TXE4 or System X. As well as attempting to involve staff in decisions about their future, management used the opportunity afforded by the introduction of new technology (with the co-operation of the union) to gather data about the career expectations of staff. This was in conformity with corporate management's new emphasis, noted above, on the need for increased direct communication between operating managers and staff in the workplace.

In Metro Area, management prepared a letter, again drawn up in co-operation with local union representatives, which asked a more limited range of questions and was sent only to senior technicians in exchanges due for conversion. Again the stress was on involving the staff directly and in meeting their wishes where possible. Following the receipt of answers to the letters, local management in Coast and Metro Areas conducted counselling sessions with individual technicians (but not with maintenance supervisors) about their future employment. This was between two and four years prior to the conversion of their exchanges.

In Town Area, the middle manager with overall responsibility for

TXE4 modernisation adopted a very different approach. He developed a medium-term (five-year) manpower plan long in advance of the modernisation of the three Strowger–TXE4 conversion exchanges under his control. After informal discussions with staff and without the involvement of the local union, he re-deployed what he believed to be the most suitable staff into the three exchanges at least three years prior to their due date for conversion, This conformed very much to his overall sub-strategy for the implementation of change discussed in chapter 2, which placed a high premium on regular personal contact with staff and favoured taking decisions largely on the basis of managerially defined goals rather than rules agreed jointly with the local trade union.

Before we go on to look at the detailed application of these criteria and procedures in our sample of conversion exchanges, it will be useful to give a preliminary indication of some of the reasons for the differences between the industrial relations frameworks established in our three telephone areas. In comparing Coast and Metro Areas with Town Area, what emerges clearly is that different policies and approaches were followed by both management and trade unions in relation to the same problem and that this resulted not surprisingly in quite different outcomes. In Coast Area, where the rules on the procedure and criteria for selection for training were established by joint agreement, local union representatives had pressed for joint regulation right at the beginning of the implementation process. This resulted in a detailed set of jointly agreed rules which were largely in accordance with union objectives. The main reasons for the high degree of initiative and influence of the union in this case were the strong organisation of local branch officials (who had regular area co-ordinating committee meetings to discuss issues arising in the area) and the fact that one of the leading local branch officials was simultaneously employed as a Technical Officer in one of the exchanges due for conversion. His strong personal involvement in this question, his knowledge of the issues and the staff concerned and his union involvement over many years, coupled with his good informal and formal relations with local management, all contributed to the success of the local union strategy.

In Metro Area the union was also well-organised locally, but none of the leading officials were employed in internal maintenance. Union pressure to establish criteria and procedures for selection for training was in fact developed in response to problems which arose when the first Strowger exchange in the area was converted to TXE4, one of the first TXE4 exchanges to be introduced nationally. As a result of this negative experience, the union persuaded area management to set up a local joint modernisation committee in 1978, an innovation which suggested that existing structures for negotiation and consultation were not felt to be adequate. The committee was established initially to agree joint guidelines on selection for re-training but was soon extended to monitor the overall effects of exchange modernisation. In fact, during the period of our research study (1982–4) no meetings of this joint committee were held, since both union and management representatives regarded the progress of modernisation in the area as satisfactory.

In summary, in Coast and Metro Areas strong local union organisation, and in Coast Area the personality of one particularly active union member, appeared to be the major factors in explaining the nature of the criteria and procedures established for selection for TXE4 training. In both cases area managements reacted positively to the union initiative, agreeing to joint negotiations on the issue. It should also perhaps be noted that local union representatives in Metro Area were among the first in the POEU to establish a joint agreement with their area management on TXE4 selection and training, and their agreement was communicated by the national union as a model agreement to all branches, including the branch in Coast Area.

When we examine the experience in Town Area, however, it soon becomes clear that there was another, more negative factor which explains the outcome in Metro and Coast Areas – namely the absence in these latter two cases of a coherent area management policy on selection for training. In Town Area, in contrast, area management had a clear policy developed well in advance of any possible union initiative. The local union, which was comparatively weakly organised, was on the defensive from the beginning, always reacting to management initiative and without any particular policy or objectives of its own. An additional factor explaining the different outcome in Town Area, where the criteria and procedure for selection for training conformed almost exclusively to management objectives, was the role of the middle manager who (as we have seen in chapter 2) both conceived and realised the overall management sub-strategy throughout the implementation process. His strong personality and style, involving clearly formulated objectives and regular direct contact with staff, enabled management to be the most crucial promoter of change in shaping the outcome of this critical juncture in the process.

As with our discussion of the national level we have so far made no mention of supervisors and their union, the STE. Again this is because we found no evidence of any commitment by area STE representatives to establish joint criteria or procedures with local management on selection of supervisors for TXE4. One STE area representative declared explicitly that this question was a management and not a union question, a view which was in broad conformity with the national stance of the STE.

To summarise: where there were negotiations at area level over the introduction of TXE4 exchanges, these were confined to the issue of criteria and procedures for the selection of staff for re-training. However, in both cases where there was joint management–union agreement, the union was able to exert a considerable influence at this critical juncture. For reasons just explained, the STE took no part in formal negotiations and discussions at local level. We will turn now to an examination of the actual outcomes in individual exchanges on those issues which had been subject to national or area agreement between management and unions. We will begin with the issues of selection for re-training and job security.

3.7 The implementation of joint agreements in the case-study exchanges

Selection for re-training and job security

Selection for re-training in our three main conversion exchanges, two of which were in Coast Area and the third in Metro Area, followed the criteria and procedures established by local management and unions. In fact, six of the seven senior technicians selected were sitting tenants. In one exchange (Conversion A), however, one sitting tenant was rejected on two of the additional criteria agreed between local management and union in his area, namely that he was over fifty-two (he was in fact fifty-six) and that he had already been fully trained in two maintenance skills (see note three for details). This particular technician, who had worked for the Post Office and then BT for thirty-one years and in Conversion A for twelve years, felt particularly aggrieved at the reasons for his exclusion and that neither management nor union were prepared to reconsider his case. In the event, though, in conformity with good industrial relations practice and the national Job Security Agreement, he was re-deployed in the same telephone area to a Strowger exchange not due for conversion. In his place a senior technician from another Strowger exchange in the area was selected for re-training on the seniority criterion. In Conversion B there were two sitting tenants and two places for TXE4 technicians, and in Conversion C there were three sitting tenants and three places, so these technicians were selected automatically. In fact, at the time of selection in Conversion C, there had been four sitting tenants, but one had decided to retire after the decision to modernise was announced and before the decision to select was taken. In all these cases, therefore, the incumbent senior technicians were

81

selected. The problems arising from the two exceptions to this rule were resolved by re-deployment and early retirement.

On the issues of selection for re-training and job security, therefore, the terms of the joint agreements negotiated between management and union were fully implemented in the exchanges studied. In this respect, there was no attenuation or loss of control between national agreements (the Job Security Agreement), local agreements (on criteria for selection for re-training) and their implementation in the workplace. The question of staffing levels will be discussed in the next section.

Nevertheless, decisions on selection for re-training made by management and unions at this critical juncture in the implementation process did have a particular outcome in one of our conversion exchanges (Conversion C) with important subsequent repercussions. Although it anticipates our examination of skill acquisition in chapter 4, the case will be discussed here since it shows clearly how outcomes at one critical juncture in the implementation process can influence events and outcomes at subsequent critical junctures.

In this particular case, local management (the Executive Engineer and maintenance supervisor concerned) decided on the advice of the national Technical Training College to withdraw one of the maintenance technicians from the training programme on the grounds that he had not shown the required abilities to carry out TXE4 maintenance. He was subsequently re-deployed to work in a smaller Strowger unit not due for conversion. This was an exceptional case but it did raise questions about the practical adequacy of the various criteria used to select staff for re-training and also about the management of the implementation process.

The technician who was withdrawn from the re-training programme had just completed his fourth course and it was by then over two years since he had first been selected for TXE4 training. The course instructors at the Training College had been concerned from the outset about his suitability for electronic maintenance and this had led to a formal meeting between him and his own supervising officer around one year into the re-training programme. One year later, around four weeks prior to changeover, he was again called to see his supervisor and this time he was recommended to withdraw. The decision was explained by the supervisor in a subsequent interview with us:

> [He] is not capable of absorbing new technology, that's basically what it amounts to . . . he was the weak link in the chain and we could never really rely on him to come up [with the goods] when the situation demands. If we'd had an [exchange] isolation while he was here it would have been hopeless.

The implication of this statement was that the application of the seniority principle had led in this particular case to the selection of someone who was not suitable for TXE4 maintenance work. The technician concerned was forty-two years old, a classic 'Strowger man'[5] who had worked for BT since he had left school at the age of fifteen. Most of his working life had been spent maintaining Strowger equipment. At the time of our first interview around six months prior to changeover, he had expressed some concern over his ability to absorb information on the formal training courses:

> I don't get a lot from a course. It doesn't seem to sink in to my thick skull you know! You come back and you think, 'Oh yeah, well that's what they were talking about, now I understand, I can see it'. Because you've still got this old idea, you know, [on] Strowger you can see everything working, electronic you can't, and you still want sometimes to see something to get it into your brain . . .

At this time, he regarded this as a minor problem, since he was sure it would take him and his colleagues around five years of live experience to become a good TXE4 technician, as he felt it had done with Strowger.

However, when interviewed some five months later, immediately after the decision to take him off the training programme, his perception had changed. His first comment was that he was in full agreement with the management decision to withdraw him from TXE4 maintenance – in fact it had taken a load off his mind. Nevertheless, he was resentful that he had been allowed to re-train over a period of more than two years if it was now so obvious that he was not going to be competent. He felt that the lack of regular counselling by management during his training period and the lack of hands-on experience between courses were among the main reasons for his difficulties in adapting to new technology. These two issues will be explored in more detail in chapter 4 in our discussion of skill acquisition during the process of re-training.

In order to complete our discussion of this issue, it is interesting to examine the reasons given by the technicians as to why they wished to be selected for re-training. The reason given by sixteen out of the twenty-three technicians who had opted for re-training was that training for and keeping up with new technology was all part of the maintenance technicians' job in BT. However, around one-quarter also stressed more negative reasons, such as feelings of boredom and lack of job satisfaction on Strowger maintenance. Significantly, only one of the technicians interviewed identified job security as a positive reason for re-training, although around one-quarter did express fears that they would be left behind if they did not retrain. When they were asked directly whether they anticipated that it would increase their job security, the majority said yes. Not one respondent mentioned the national Job Security Agreement between BT and POEU in this connection, although job security was mentioned by over half our respondents as one of the main positive features of BT as an employer. In other words, it was the traditional time-served pattern of industrial relations in the business which was interpreted by the technicians as the most important guarantee of job security, rather than the new job security agreement.[6] One reason why the technicians failed to mention this agreement may well have lain in their actual experience of staffing levels in the new exchanges. We will consider this issue in the next sub-section.

Staffing levels and wider manpower implications

As we saw above, the national agreement on TXE4 staffing levels, despite containing a clear quantitative measure of staffing requirements for the maintenance of the exchange system proper, still left area management with considerable design space for the development of staffing policies for particular exchanges. In fact, the data from our case-study exchanges shows a significant degree of flexibility and variation in management's approach to individual units. Table 3.5 shows staffing levels in our three main conversion exchanges before and after modernisation.

The most immediate point to note is that only Conversion C showed an overall reduction in staffing between Strowger and TXE4, whereas Conversion A remained the same and Conversion B actually appeared to increase! However, it should not therefore be concluded that local management failed to achieve the objective set by corporate management to reduce maintenance manpower and costs. The figures not only hide significant fluctuations during various sub-stages of the implementation process (for details, see chapters 4 and 6), but require the consideration of a number of additional factors if their full meaning is to be understood.

Among these additional factors we need to take into account the relation betwen staffing levels in individual exchanges and wider area-management training and staffing policies. In Coast Area, for example, area management decided it wished to use the modernisation of Conversions A and B to train additional TXE4 senior technicians, who would then be available as a pool of qualified manpower to meet any future staff shortages. This factor, plus the fact that it was still in a period of initial operation ('settling down') and thus required the nationally agreed

Table 3.5 *Maintenance staffing levels in three case-study exchanges before and after TXE4 modernisation*

Exchange	Before	After
Conversion A (Coast Area)	2 senior technicians 1 'pool' junior technician Off-site supervisor	2 senior technicians 1 'pool' junior technician Off-site supervisor
Conversion B (Coast Area)	2 senior technicians 1 'pool' junior technician Off-site supervisor	2 senior technicians 1 'pool' senior technician 1 'pool' junior technician Off-site supervisor
Conversion C (Metro Area)	4 senior technicians 2 junior technicians On-site supervisor	3 senior technicians 1 junior technician 1 'pool' junior technician On-site supervisor

Note: 'Before' conversion means in each case around eighteen months prior to changeover, and 'after' means eight to nine months after changeover in the case of Conversions A and C and two months after changeover in the case of Conversion B.

minimum staffing level, is why Conversion B is shown as having a staffing complement of three senior technicians. In fact, only two of these three were part of the formal staffing complement of the unit. At the same point in time, that is two months after changeover, Conversion A had also had a staffing complement of three senior technicians, but after nine months it had been reduced to two, as allowed for in the national agreement. In the context of area staffing policy we must also consider that Conversions A and B were among the first exchanges to be converted to TXE4 in Coast Area, and that area management had decided consciously to over-staff them initially in order to build up area expertise. In contrast, Conversion C was the last of ten TXE4 conversions in Metro Area and its staffing levels were determined purely in terms of the requirements of that particular unit.

All these factors – wider management manpower and training policies, the stage in the area modernisation programme, and the stage in the live operation of the particular unit – served to make the implementation of the national agreement by area managements in particular exchanges particularly complex.[7] On one issue, however, there was an unambiguous finding. In none of our three main conversion exchanges did we find any evidence of consultation about staffing levels between management, the staff and the local POEU branch as envisaged in the national agreement. This was a question about which in practice local managements made unilateral decisions. The decisions were in all cases in broad conformity with national guidelines.

In order to understand the wider implications of the figures in table 3.5 we also need to appreciate that the existence of a particular staffing complement did not necessarily mean that all the staff were working on the exchange floor at any one time. We analysed staff attendance records in two of our larger TXE4 exchanges, Conversion D and TXE4 B, over a period of six months between spring and autumn 1983, in other words including the summer holiday period. We found that, for each half-day during a six-month period, the full staffing complement in TXE4 B (which had four senior technicians) was present on the exchange floor for only fifty per cent of the time, whereas the equivalent figure for the other unit was just under seventy-five per cent. Absences were accounted for in each case by a mixture of annual leave, scheduled days off (for senior technicians in these units this amounted to one day every fifteen), sick leave, training courses and, for certain individuals, temporary promotion to replace an absent supervisor. Such workplace realities appeared to justify the discretion allowed to local managements to deviate from national guidelines and to confirm that the implementation of the national agreement showed significant and necessary variations in different areas and exchanges.

This brings us to one of the most important factors affecting the whole question of staffing levels in our TXE4 units, namely the decision by managements in all our telephone areas to retain the individual exchange as the basic reference point for the allocation of staff to particular jobs. As this was the basic principle on which staff were selected for retraining, then by definition staffing levels needed to be a minimum of two, if not three in large units, to cover for regular absences. We saw some signs towards the end of our research, however, that area managements were beginning to adopt a different, more flexible approach to this question. In Coast Area, as we have noted, management had trained two additional senior technicians to be deployed as and when required to cover for staffing shortages in particular units. In Conversion A, for example, one of the two resident senior technicians was absent for all but three weeks over a three-month period in early 1984. During this period he was temporarily seconded to Conversion B to help out during the changeover period, attended a residential training course away from the area and spent nearly two months on temporary promotion to cover for his own supervisor. During his absence from Conversion A he was covered by one of the partly TXE4-trained 'pool' technicians, thus giving the exchange during this period a staffing complement of one fully-trained and one partly-trained technician. In Metro Area, too, area management began to deploy staff more flexibly, taking staff from their 'own' units and allocating them temporarily to other exchanges to assist with particular technical or staffing problems.

These tentative developments in Metro and Coast Areas, where some senior technicians were treated as a part of an area 'pool' to be allocated to particular exchanges as and when required, indicated the beginnings of a more flexible definition of the concept of workplace within exchange maintenance. In digital exchange systems such as System X, the redefinition of the 'workplace' away from the individual exchange building towards an area-based maintenance centre (see Strickland and Hewitt, 1985: 296) will almost certainly take place, bringing with it major implications for maintenance staffing levels, job content, work organisation and the experience of maintenance work itself (see chapter 7).

3.8 Conclusion

Our discussion of the strategic position of exchange maintenance technicians as it had emerged by the mid-1970s revealed a remarkably stable internal labour market. This offered a high degree of job security, relatively high pay and status, and relatively assured career progression. These internal labour-market conditions provided the basis for the traditional pattern of labour relations, which included a highly centralised pattern of collective bargaining at national level, a stress on the principle of seniority in promotion and career structures, and an underlying management commitment to job security. Our examination of national negotiations over the introduction of TXE4 revealed that the outcomes on the issues of job security, staffing levels, and pay and grading, reflected a balance between traditional patterns and a new commercial approach to labour relations. Within this framework it was observed that the POEU was able to exert a significant influence. We also noted that the STE did not see exchange modernisation as a matter of trade union concern and therefore did not seek to negotiate agreements with management. While the national framework agreed with the POEU was piecemeal and did not constitute a new technology agreement, it did allow management and the POEU to bargain over issues directly related to technical change. However, the range of issues covered by the national negotiations was limited and the scope left for local variations within the agreements reached was relatively wide. As a result there still remained considerable discretion for local management and union to engage in bargaining at telephone area level.

In two of our three telephone areas, Metro and Coast, we found relatively successful attempts by local POEU representatives to influence through negotiation the criteria and procedures for the access of maintenance technicians to re-training. In contrast, management in Town Area established the criteria and procedures for access to re-training unilaterally. In the first two cases the local POEU representatives were able to establish seniority as the principle behind selection for re-training. In the latter case management decided that suitability was more appropriate. In all three areas, access to re-training courses was restricted to Technical Officers. This effectively achieved a form of occupational closure for the senior grade at the expense of junior technicians. Finally, we found that nationally agreed guidelines on staffing levels for the new TXE4 exchanges left considerable room for local interpretation and negotiation.

On the issues of selection of staff for re-training and staffing levels, therefore, we found completely different outcomes in our three telephone areas. The explanation for this appears comparatively straightforward. Given the wide discretion which was delegated to area level, the outcome came to depend on the negotiation of change by the local organisational actors, in this case management and unions. In Town Area we found a relatively weak union organisation and a strong middle-manager with a coherent sub-strategy towards all aspects of the process of TXE4 implementation. At the other extreme, in Coast Area we found a relatively well organised union body with clear views on particular aspects of TXE4 modernisation (selection for training, phasing of training courses and post-course experience) and a largely reactive middle-management in the throes of major internal re-organisation.

We have already noted the absence of any policy or influence at either national or local level from the STE. The reasons for this were touched upon above and the implications for supervision will be discussed more fully in chapter 5. However, neither the STE nor the POEU had any significant influence, either nationally or locally, on such issues as skills or the organisation and control of work in the new exchanges. This confirms the findings of many other studies about the limits of formal bargaining procedures and the weak influence of trade unions when dealing with 'control' issues (see Wilkinson, 1983; Williams and Steward, 1985). This does not mean, as we will see, that these are therefore determined unilaterally by management. As Wilkinson has suggested, the 'subterranean' influence of individual employees, and particularly of workgroups, can be quite strong. Moreover, it should also be clear from the evidence presented in this chapter that the POEU nationally and locally, within the confines of traditional collective bargaining issues, was able to exert more than just a token influence on the introduction of TXE4 in the workplace.

4

Maintenance technicians: work tasks, skills and re-training

4.1 Introduction

In the previous two chapters we have examined corporate management strategy towards exchange modernisation and the negotiation of change by management and unions at national level. We have also seen how the varying sub-strategies and responses of management and trade union representatives in our three telephone areas were important factors shaping the different outcomes we found on the issues of selection of staff for re-training and exchange staffing levels. Later in this chapter we will examine a number of important critical junctures in the process of re-training and skill acquisition by maintenance technicians. However, we will begin by exploring in detail the links between the Strowger and TXE4 exchange systems and maintenance work tasks and skills in our case-study exchanges.

Before we begin this analysis, we wish to reiterate some of the points made in chapter 1 about the treatment given to technology in recent research. First, even those writers who are highly critical of treating technology as an independent variable concede that it can play an important part in shaping work *tasks* (see, for example, Buchanan and Boddy, 1983: 244). Second, it has also been suggested that when social and political choices are frozen into particular designs these can have independent impacts on skills and the organisation of work (see Wilkinson, 1983: 21). In connection with this last point, we noted in chapter 1 that the design of the TXE4 exchange system had a number of features which were intended to reduce maintenance requirements and improve system performance and reliability compared with Strowger. We have also seen in chapter 2 that the corporate decision to launch the TXE4 modernisation programme in 1973 was made with the objective of reducing operating costs and improving quality of service. All this suggests that the architecture and technology of the TXE4 exchange system were the result of design choices based on specific managerial objectives. In this and the following two chapters, however, it is our intention to examine empirically the extent to which the TXE4 (and Strowger) engineering systems, *once chosen*, constrained and extended the range of choices open to organisational actors involved in shaping the implementation and outcomes of change in our case study exchanges.

Before we proceed some preliminary comments need to be made concerning the vexed question of skill. A variety of attempts have been made in recent research on technological change to operationalise the concept using a 'task-centred' approach. These have followed in the wake of Braverman's thesis that skill changes need to be analysed in terms of changes in the content of the labour process rather than by such indicators as levels of formal qualification and the duration of training courses (see Rolfe, 1986). A good example of a recent attempt to accomplish this is provided by Crompton and Jones (1984) in their study of white-collar clerical work. Interestingly, though, despite claiming their study to be task-centred, there is very little analysis of the connection between changing clerical skills and changing clerical work tasks. An additional problem inherent in their approach is that skill, defined as the degree of control exercised by workers over their own labour and over other organisational resources, is taken to be more or less synonymous with control. This can lead to considerable confusion, since empirically there is evidence that workers can retain control over their labour despite the de-skilling of the tasks which constitute their jobs (see on this Thompson, 1983: 107).

In this chapter we will adopt a slightly different approach, a modified version of that suggested by Cockburn (1983). Our initial aim will be to present a task-centred analysis, based on the view that skill is rooted in the content of work tasks. We will refer to this dimension of skill as *skill in the task*. We will then distinguish two further dimensions of skill. These are *skill in the person*, that is the skills possessed by individuals accumulated from a variety of sources (training, experience and so on), and the political or *occupational* definition of skill by workgroups, trade unions and managements, who ascribe skilled status to jobs and seek to influence the way they are distributed. By breaking down the concept of skill and operationalising it in this way we will be able to provide a more differentiated analysis of the skill changes that accompanied the introduction of TXE4. One consequence will be that our conclusions will point to the complex and multi-dimensional relationship between technological change, work tasks and skills, rather than any mechanistic link between new technology and 'de-skilling' or 'up-skilling'.

4.2 Strowger maintenance tasks and skills

Our primary data in this section is based on interviews, observation and self-report diaries from two Strowger exchanges, supplemented by interviews with technicians and supervisors in the six other exchanges participating in our study. The two Strowger exchanges were Strowger A in Town Area and Strowger B in Coast Area (see table A, p. 7).

Maintenance tasks

Work tasks of technicians in telephone exchanges can be divided broadly into two main types: those which are concerned with the maintenance of the exchange system proper (e.g. Strowger and TXE4), and those concerned with peripheral equipment and various other activities (e.g. line-testing, meter-reading, information handling) common to all exchange types. The former we shall refer to as 'exchange system maintenance' tasks and the latter as 'other exchange work'. As we are concentrating in this chapter on the relation between different exchange systems, maintenance work tasks and associated skills, we shall be restricting our analysis to exchange system maintenance.

According to data taken from self-report diaries (see Appendix B), technicians in Strowger A and Strowger B spent around two-thirds of their time on exchange system maintenance, which consisted of three main sets of tasks: block routines, night routining and patrol/reported faults. These will be examined in turn.

Block routines, as the term suggests, involved the routine servicing of 'blocks' of exchange equipment. Strowger technology is composed of several thousand moving mechanical parts connected by electrical contacts, all of which are affected by dirt, wear, breakage and misalignment. Block routines consisted of a series of servicing tasks, including testing, cleaning, oiling, realigning and in some cases replacing these mechanical parts and their connections. They were required in order to prevent the progressive deterioration of the equipment and were therefore a form of preventive maintenance.

The second main set of exchange system maintenance tasks derived from the programme of tests carried out by the automatic night routiners. As we saw in chapter 1, the routiner automatically prints out fault dockets for every item of equipment which fails a particular test or which is busy when tested. The initial work task of the maintenance staff arising from the night routiner tests was to retest the items of equipment

4. Re-testing Strowger equipment identified by a night routiner as faulty or busy

identified (see photograph 4) and to use the information provided on the dockets (which included the sequence number of the failed test) to verify whether the fault or busy condition actually represented a fault. The result of this verification process, called 'night routining' by the maintenance staff, was either to find that the equipment was right when tested or to prove the existence, or at least the possibility, of a fault condition. In the latter case the item was temporarily taken out of service ('busied out') before it could affect customer service. For this reason it was established practice in our Strowger exchanges that the checking and testing of the fault dockets was the first task undertaken in the exchange each day.

The initial work task associated with night routining was largely determined by the automatic routiner and was both repetitive and routinised. If there was any doubt in the technician's mind, the item of equipment was busied out. The diagnosis and repair of fault conditions identified by night routiners, which were often carried out later in the day after all the dockets had been checked and tested, involved similar tasks to those associated with patrol/reported faults, the third type of Strowger maintenance task. Unlike block routines, night routining, with its emphasis on testing and correcting automatically identified fault conditions, was a form of corrective maintenance.

The third main type of exchange system maintenance work tasks involved dealing with 'patrol' and reported faults. Patrol fault is a term which refers back to the days when technicians discovered faults *ad hoc* as they patrolled the exchange floor. Such means of fault identification were still employed sometimes during our research, for example, in cases where blatant fault conditions were revealed by pieces of broken equipment ejecting from their location in the racks of switches! However, such faults were now normally identified (or 'reported') automatically by the alarms incorporated into the exchange equipment. As with night routiner faults, the initial maintenance task of the technician was to check and if necessary test the piece of equipment so identified. The other main group of Strowger reported faults were those communicated to the staff from outside the exchange. These came either from BT staff in distant exchanges or from customers whose faults (reported by dialling 151) were received by Repair Service Control (RSC) centres. Where appropriate, customer-reported faults were passed on to the exchange concerned by the RSC. They could be difficult to locate, since the information received from the RSC was often incomplete or imprecise.

This brings us to the process of 'faulting', a set of work tasks which lay at the heart of much exchange system maintenance. The complete process of faulting had four main elements: the identification, location, diagnosis and repair of faults, each of which could be found to varying degrees in all three types of maintenance task. A full understanding of the faulting process will only be possible when we look at the skills required to carry out these tasks. At this point we wish to give a preliminary analysis of those aspects of the process which were shaped by the nature of the Strowger engineering system.

The location and diagnosis of faults depended very much on the quality and quantity of information available. For example, while night-routiner and alarm faults were normally located automatically, many reported faults required much more detective work by the technicians. However, even in these cases the step-by-step switching principle and overall configuration of the Strowger exchange system (with the switches for each stage arranged in successive racks) enabled the technicians to follow through the path of a failed call from one step to the next until the faulty switch was located. Picking out a faulty switch from a group of switches and diagnosing why it was faulty was also facilitated by the appearance of the system, the visible nature of the Strowger technology and the noise often made by a misaligned, worn or jammed mechanical part. In addition the testing of faulty electrical circuits could be helped by the use of a range of maintenance aids.

Most Strowger repair tasks were directly shaped by its electro-mechanical technology. The equipment had a tendency to accumulate dirt and become misaligned, thereby affecting the quality of the connection made by the electrical circuits (the 'crackle on the line'), and sometimes it jammed and even broke. But Strowger repair tasks were shaped by system architecture too. The step-by-step switching principle and the Strowger system configuration, particularly the fact that each switch had the control function incorporated into it (see above, section 1.4), meant that individual fault conditions could be isolated without normally affecting other customers or other parts of the exchange equipment. This was less possible in TXE4 where the control function was separate from the switching function and was shared across a large number of calls or potential calls.

The fact that faults on the Strowger exchange system could be isolated in this way had two important implications for maintenance tasks. First, this meant that faults were seldom sufficiently critical to cause major interruptions or breakdowns in the service provided by the exchange. As a result the technicians were rarely under stress to locate, diagnose and repair faults quickly – they could busy out a switch and come back to it at their leisure. Second, a faulty switch, once busied, could normally be jacked out of a rack and taken away to a repair desk without any critical

Table 4.1 *Proportion of time spent on different types of Strowger system maintenance (%) (total=100)*

Exchange	Preventive maintenance	Corrective maintenance	
	Block routines	Night routines	Patrol/reported faults
Strowger A	40	31	29
Strowger B	49	29	22

effect on the rest of the exchange. Of course there was a threshold at which the removal of large numbers of Strowger switches would begin to affect the grade of service to the customer. In such cases, too many customers would be chasing too few switches. However, the overall threshold in Strowger was far higher than in TXE4. All these factors contributed to the routinised and standardised approach to faulting of Strowger technicians. In this respect Strowger exchange system architecture not only had direct implications for maintenance work tasks, it shaped the whole approach of technicians to exchange maintenance, influencing the pace of work and satisfaction they experienced in it.

Before we go on to look at the nature of the skills required to carry out the work tasks described above it will be useful to provide some quantitative evidence from our two Strowger exchanges on the proportion of time spent on the three types of exchange system maintenance task.[1] At this stage we are interested in aggregate figures for the exchanges as a whole rather than disaggregated figures for individual technicians. These will be examined in chapter 6 when we look at the organisation and control of work and the distribution of work tasks and skill between different grades and individuals. The data presented in table 4.1 presents a clear picture. In both exchanges, despite their different size, number of staff and geographical location, block routines took up the largest proportion of time, followed by night routining and then patrol/reported faults. Just under half the exchange system maintenance effort was spent on preventive work tasks and just over half spent on corrective tasks. We would suggest that the design space available to determine the balance between preventive and corrective maintenance in our two Strowger exchanges was influenced to a significant extent by the nature of Strowger technology, which required a substantial amount of regular block routine maintenance in order to prevent the progressive deterioration of the equipment. We believe this argument about the influence of the Strowger exchange system on the balance between different types of maintenance task carried out by the technicians will be further strengthened when we compare this evidence with that from our TXE4 exchanges (see below).

Strowger maintenance skills

In order to identify the skills required to carry out corrective and preventive maintenance tasks – the skills in the task – we conducted many hours of observation of Strowger maintenance technicians at work (see Appendix B). We also carried out semi-structured interviews which elicited from them descriptions of the procedures adopted in the location, diagnosis and rectification of faults and also their own evaluations of the skills they employed. From this data we were able to construct a qualitative picture of Strowger maintenance skills in the task.

Block routine maintenance tasks in our two Strowger exchanges, and also the repair of night routiner and patrol/reported faults, required mainly manual skills for cleaning, lubricating and adjusting equipment. Some of the adjustments required a high level of manual dexterity – for example, achieving correct tolerances and tensions on parts of the switches (see photograph 5). However, the majority of time spent on block routines involved simple repetitive and routinised tasks of cleaning and lubricating racks of equipment on a modified 'Forth Bridge' principle. Each switch in each block of equipment was serviced according to a detailed programme and once the cycle was completed it was reviewed and, after necessary modifications, begun again. Such tasks allowed little scope for independent judgement or for refined 'manual' or 'mental' abilities (see note nine for an elaboration of these terms).

The scope for independent judgement was also limited in night routining maintenance tasks. As we have seen, the initial task for the technician was to re-test the piece of equipment identified as faulty or busy by the night routiner (see photograph 4) and, if found to be faulty, to remove it temporarily from service. Location and diagnosis of the causes of such faults involved similar skills to those which will now be analysed for patrol/reported faults.

The location of patrol/reported faults was often difficult because of the incompleteness of the information about fault conditions, particularly those reported to the exchange from outside. However, observation and interviews revealed a number of intimate connections between the Strowger exchange system, fault location tasks and fault location skills in the task. The influence of exchange architecture (with its step-by-step

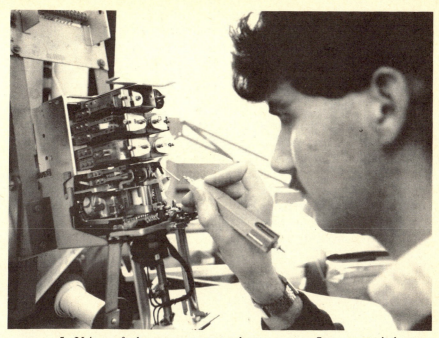

5. Using a feeler gauge to test tolerances on a Strowger switch at a repair bench

switching principle plus a system configuration where the switches for each stage of a call were arranged in successive racks) was particularly apparent as technicians followed through logically and systematically the path of a failed call from one step to the next until the faulty switch was located. This part of the faulting process also required a theoretical knowledge of the exchange lay-out. Picking out a faulty switch from a rack of equipment was also assisted by system appearance and technology, particularly the fact that the moving parts of a Strowger switch were both visible and audible. We witnessed a number of occasions where, despite the persistent chattering of noise generated by the racks of switches in operation, technicians could hear the one switch which was faulty. They demonstrated a high level of perceptual ability, not just in listening but in looking for faulty equipment such as jammed or broken mechanical parts.

Diagnosis of the causes of faults involved similar abilities to those required for locating them. It also demonstrated a number of connections between the exchange system and the work tasks and skills involved. In fact, locating a fault, such as a jammed mechanical part, sometimes meant at the same time diagnosing its cause. Again, this

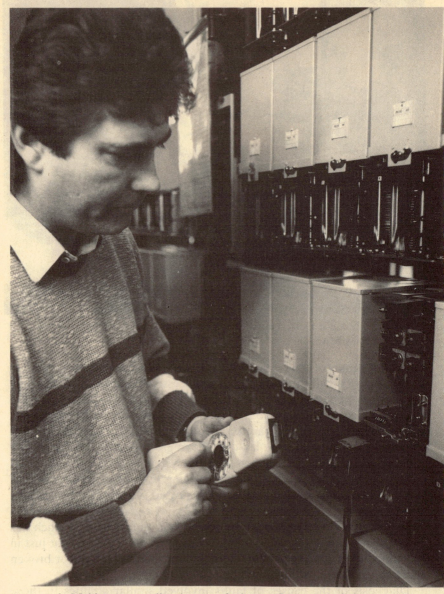

6. Making a test call to locate a fault on a Strowger switch

involved a mixture of refined aural and visual abilities and an understanding of basic mechanical and electrical principles such as Ohm's Law. It could also involve the use of special maintenance aids, for example making a test call via a particular switch (see photograph 6). Repair of faulty equipment called into play manual skills identical to those described above in connection with block routines (see photograph 5).

So far we have shown the range of influences and connections which exist between the Strowger exchange system, particular work tasks and 'mental' and 'manual' skills in the task. However, underlying the execution of many maintenance tasks in our Strowger exchanges were a range of skills which cannot be defined simply as either mental or manual. In fact they can probably best be described as 'experiential' and 'intuitive' skills, based on accumulated experience and knowledge of the fault conditions which could occur and the maintenance practices and techniques which could be used to identify, locate, diagnose and repair them. Such experiential and intuitive skills were also rooted in local knowledge, not only of the layout of the exchange equipment but of the condition and past performance of specific sections of the equipment. For example, we observed on many occasions how technicians were able to locate and diagnose particular night routiner or reported faults with an accuracy and speed which could only be explained in terms of a mixture of accumulated local knowledge and inspired guesswork, backed up by manual dexterity and theoretical knowledge of the principles of the exchange system. This combination of mainly 'tacit' skills was described to us by one senior technician:

> you get what's often known as the 'TO touch'. You don't need to get gauges out, feeler gauges out, that kind of thing. You do it by touch, just by knowing that the tension's about right . . . using experience rather than keep looking at the book.

The prevalence of tacit skills based on accumulated experience, the 'TO touch', also underlined the manner in which Strowger skills had been typically acquired. Not only had a significant proportion of our sample of senior technicians been employed on Strowger maintenance for a number of years, they had normally progressed through a standard career development from apprentice (TTA) through junior technician (T2A) to senior technician (TO). During this career progression 'skills in the person' had been acquired incrementally through a combination of on-the-job experience and practice, including months and sometimes years working alongside senior technicians, plus formal training courses and more theoretical book knowledge. The nature of the Strowger exchange architecture, particularly the fact that individual fault conditions could be isolated and switches taken out of a rack to be examined and repaired without normally affecting customer service or other parts of the exchange equipment, enabled technicians to acquire these skills by trial and error on a live exchange as well as by watching their senior colleagues and asking their advice. As we shall see below, TXE4 common-control exchange architecture did not enable technicians to acquire maintenance skills 'in the person' in the same way, partly because 'diving in' to the equipment could lead to a significant impairment of service and in a few extreme cases take the whole exchange off the air.

These questions will be illustrated further below when we discuss the technicians' experience of Strowger and TXE4 work and their acquisition of new skills during the implementation process. In concluding this section we would simply note the combination of mental, manual and experiential and intuitive skills employed in Strowger maintenance; the strong influence of Strowger exchange architecture, technology and appearance on different work tasks; the generally less strong but no less evident connection with different aspects of skills in the task; and the importance of exchange architecture in enabling the acquisition of Strowger maintenance skills in the person by on-the-job experience and trial and error.

4.3 TXE4 maintenance tasks and skills

Our primary data in this section is based on interviews, observation and self-report diaries from two TXE4 exchanges, supplemented by interviews with technicians and supervisors in four other TXE4 exchanges. The two main TXE4 exchanges studied were TXE4 A in Town Area and Conversion A in Coast Area (see table A, p. 7). Before we begin our detailed discussion of TXE4 work tasks and skills, it is worth underlining that both TXE4 A and Conversion A had settled down into some kind of routine operation[2] at the time of our study. Both were consistently meeting their performance targets and the technicians were experiencing a relatively stable pattern of working. However, we should also note that both exchanges had been operational for only a comparatively short period of time (twelve months and nine months respectively). To this extent, although we shall be treating the data collected from them as evidence on the outcomes of technological change, what we studied was in some respects simply another stage in a continuing process rather than an immutable end-point.

Maintenance tasks

According to data taken from self-report diaries (see Appendix B), exchange system maintenance work in TXE4 A and Conversion A accounted for fifty per cent and sixty per cent respectively of the worktime of the senior technicians, slightly less than their Strowger counterparts.[3] Like Strowger, this work consisted of three main sets of tasks: dormant fault checks (sometimes called system security checks), night routining and patrol/reported faults. These were functionally equivalent to the three main sets of tasks in our Strowger exchanges but their meaning, content and relative importance differed in certain important respects. We shall examine each set of tasks in turn, paying particular attention to the question of how far they were shaped by the nature of the TXE4 exchange system. As in our examination of Strowger, we will then go on to look at the skills required of the technicians to carry out these various tasks.

Although TXE4 exchanges had some Strowger-type mechanical parts which required routine testing, cleaning, lubrication and (sometimes) adjustment, the massive reduction in the number of moving parts in the exchange system and the use of (on the whole) much more reliable electronic components reduced the requirement for this type of routine maintenance. The very term dormant fault checks, broadly equivalent to Strowger block routines, denotes the difference between them. In TXE4 these checks involved the routine testing of the exchange equipment to uncover faults which remained hidden (or dormant) because of the inherent fault-tolerance of the overall exchange system. Depending on the particular piece of equipment, the checks could involve running test programmes or removing cards one at a time to check them on an automatic tester for faulty components or circuits. This was on the whole a highly routinised activity and, as we shall see, constituted only a small proportion of the maintenance effort. Both the proportion of effort and the tasks involved in dormant fault checks were thus strongly influenced by the nature of the exchange technology and the availability and use of automatic testers to check the faulty equipment.

The initial work tasks associated with TXE4 night routining involved the technicians in checking the night routiner fault print-out and, where appropriate, re-testing the piece of equipment identified to check whether it was actually faulty (see photograph 7). If the item was not right when tested, then it could be busied out[4] pending further diagnostic work (and possibly repair) similar to that required for TXE4 reported faults.

Patrol/reported faults were the third main set of TXE4 exchange

7. Re-testing TXE4 equipment identified by the routiner teleprinter as faulty or busy

maintenance work tasks. Within this broad category of faults lay the main difference with Strowger exchange maintenance. As with Strowger, some of these faults were identified via automatic alarms or via reports from customers and other exchanges. However, reported faults from customers were less frequent because of the automatic repeat attempt facility designed into the TXE4 exchange system. Whilst the fault tolerance of the system therefore tended to reduce the number of customer-reported faults, almost all failed attempts were recorded automatically in the exchange on the Fault Print-Out (FPO) teleprinter, a facility not available in Strowger.

Patrol faults, in the original sense of faults discovered *ad hoc* by technicians as they patrolled the exchange floor, had virtually disappeared from TXE4 exchanges. As with Strowger, fault conditions identified by alarms brought up an audible ringing sound and caused a lamp to light up on the rack of equipment in which the fault had appeared.[5] Unlike Strowger, though, information on such faults was directly outputted on a teleprinter. In all of our six TXE4 exchanges this was located on the exchange floor next to or near the night routiner teleprinter. The FPO provided a starting point from which the technicians could seek to clear fault conditions. This brings us directly to a discussion of faulting in TXE4 maintenance.

It is clear from our analysis thus far that automatic equipment in TXE4 exchanges provided technicians with a range of information about fault conditions that had already occurred or were registered as having occurred.[6] However, as explained in chapter 1, since any TXE4 call has a multiplicity of paths available to it through the switching matrix and since the control equipment is shared with other calls made at around the same time on what amounts to a rota basis, a simple line of print identifying the pieces of equipment used in the failed attempt and the broad type of fault condition might not in itself provide enough data to locate and diagnose a fault. In fact the cause of some faults in TXE4 exchanges could be remote from the symptom. It should also be remembered that the TXE4 exchange had no visible moving parts and made no noise which could usefully assist the technicians in identifying the cause of a fault.

One further feature of TXE4 exchange systems with important implications for faulting tasks should also be considered here. Whereas in Strowger the conditions which gave rise to alarms and other service-affecting faults could normally be isolated from the exchange as a whole without a deterioration in exchange performance, TXE4 design only allowed a certain amount of common control equipment to be out of action (either faulty, busied out or removed) before the service to particular individuals or groups of customers would begin to be seriously affected.

As a result of these features of the TXE4 exchange architecture and its implementation in semi-electronic technology, the location and diagnosis of faults could involve a complex set of procedures to trace the path taken by a particular call prior to its interruption and automatic identification as a fault. We shall examine in the next section the nature of the skills associated with carrying out such tasks. At this point we would simply note that, on the evidence analysed above (based on observation of faulting in our two established TXE4 exchanges and on technicians' own descriptions of the faulting process), the location and diagnosis of certain faults could be extremely complex and certainly more complex than in our two Strowger units. This conclusion is supported by the diary data, which revealed that the mean time taken to clear effective (that is proven) faults in our two TXE4 exchanges was two to three times longer than in our two Strowger exchanges (see table 4.2). Perhaps more importantly, an examination of the point of maximum frequency of fault times (the mode or modal value) showed that there was only one peak in the clustering of fault times in the two main Strowger exchanges but two peaks in both TXE4 exchanges (see tables 4.2 and 4.3). This latter finding indicated that while there was a significant cluster of faults in our TXE4 exchanges which took only slightly longer than the main cluster of faults in our two Strowger exchanges, there was also a second cluster of TXE4 faults which took substantially longer (around two and a half times as long as the first TXE4 modal value).[7]

Of course, it can be argued legitimately that the longer mean faulting times in our TXE4 exchanges reflected the relative inexperience of the technicians in comparison to their Strowger counterparts. We also found some complex faults which arose because of exchange extensions or because detailed system modifications were being carried out while the TXE4 units were in operation. However, we would argue that the existence of two main clusters of TXE4 fault times also indicated an inherent feature of the TXE4 exchange system as it operated at the time of our study. This hypothesis was supported by evidence from two other TXE4 exchanges in our study, Conversions C and D, which both showed a similar bimodal distribution of fault times (67/290 and 55/236 respectively) when we collected diary data about two to three months after changeover. Clearly, mean fault times are likely to be reduced as technicians gain in experience. For example, we will see below that the high figure for the second peak in Conversion C clearly reflected the lack of confidence, inexperience and formal training of the technicians two months after changeover.

Table 4.2 *Time per effective fault (minutes): a comparison of Strowger and TXE4 (senior technicians only)*

Exchange	Mean	Mean deviation	Mode
Strowger A	48	22	38
Strowger B	32	11	32
TXE4 A	85	37	40/99
Conversion A	143	66	72/199

Table 4.3 *Time per effective fault (% within particular time periods): Strowger and TXE4 (senior technicians only)*

Time period	Strowger A	Strowger B	TXE4 A	Conversion A
Less than half an hour	19	48	8	—
Between half an hour and one hour	42	45	24	14
Between one hour and one and a half hours	25	3	16	23
Between one and a half and two hours	5	3	32	9
Between two and three hours	5	—	20	14
Between three and four hours	4	—	—	36
Over four hours	—	—	—	5

However, the evidence suggests that a significant number of faults would probably continue to take longer to clear because of their complexity, which in turn derived, to a large extent, from the common control architecture of the exchange system. It would be true to say that this particular implication of the TXE4 system for exchange maintenance was not anticipated at the time of its design which, together with a full range of maintenance aids, was intended to ensure that 'any failure can be quickly detected and diagnosed' (Huggins, Mills and Patel, 1977: 20). In other words we have identified an impact of the exchange system which was not intended at the time of its design.

8. Testing for a faulty component on a TXE4 plug-in unit in a repair room

In contrast to the above, the repair of TXE4 faults, once located and diagnosed down to a particular plug-in-unit, was comparatively straight-forward. The remedy for common control equipment faults normally involved changing the faulty PIU with a spare and taking it to a repair bench for examination in order to identify the faulty component (transistors, resistors and diodes etc.). This was typically accomplished by visual inspection or the use of special test equipment (see photograph 8). The replacement of the faulty component was then effected by the use of a soldering iron. If the fault was too difficult or time-consuming to diagnose and repair, it was sent away to an area repair centre where there was much more sophisticated automatic test equipment. As with Strowger maintenance, the repair stage in the TXE4 faulting process was strongly shaped by the nature of the exchange technology. The common control function was implemented by PIUs composed of a large number of components linked to each other via discrete and integrated electronic circuits mounted on printed circuit boards (PCBs). The implementation of the switching function by means of electro-mechanical reed-relays encapsulated individually in sealed glass 'envelopes' was also highly

106

9. Testing for faulty reed-relays on TXE4 matrix switches in a repair room

sophisticated compared to Strowger switches, and while the reed contacts could fuse or break and thus require testing and replacing (see photograph 9), they did not need routine maintenance comparable to the cleaning and oiling required by Strowger switches. They were, however, subject to routine testing via normal fault checking procedures.

Before we go on to examine the nature of the skills required to carry out these tasks, we will provide some quantitative evidence on the proportion of time spent on the three types of exchange system maintenance task in our two established TXE4 exchanges. The data was

107

Table 4.4 *Proportion of time spent on different types of Strowger and TXE 4 system maintenance (%) (total=100)*

	Preventive maintenance		Corrective maintenance	
	Block routines/ Dormant fault checks	Night routining	Patrol/reported faults
Strowger A	43	30	27
Strowger B	49	29	22
TXE4 A	11	15	74
Conversion A	20	12	68

collected and aggregated in the same way as in our two Strowger exchanges and gives a similarly clear if contrasting picture of the balance between the different types of task. Despite their different numbers of staff and geographical location (they were of similar size measured in terms of exchange connections), patrol/reported faults took up by far the largest proportion of exchange system maintenance time in both exchanges (see table 4.4). In contrast, maintenance tasks associated with the night routiner print-out took up a comparatively small proportion of time, reflecting both the existence of the Fault Print-Out and the smaller amount of exchange equipment which was subject to night routiner testing. The only point of some divergence between the two exchanges related to dormant fault checks, although in both cases the proportion of time spent on these tasks was substantially smaller than that spent on block routines in the two Strowger units. Interestingly, the higher figure for Conversion A was the result of a conscious decision by the technicians to give a thorough servicing to a piece of equipment which had been consistently producing a large number of faults. In this respect, preventive maintenance was carried out in response to particular problems with a particular part of the exchange system rather than, as in our Strowger exchanges, according to a pre-arranged programme of block routines.

However, this particular example of an *ad hoc* dormant fault check does not alter our main finding, namely that corrective maintenance tasks were the absolutely predominant form of exchange system maintenance in our two TXE4 exchanges, in strong contrast to our two Strowger exchanges. Just as in our Strowger exchanges the significant amount of preventive maintenance activities was influenced by the nature of the Strowger exchange system, so we would suggest that the absolute predominance of corrective maintenance activities in our two

TXE4 exchanges was influenced by the nature of the TXE4 exchange system. Its technology was much less subject to wear and tear and comparatively simple to replace but its common control architecture made it an operationally more complex system in which certain kinds of fault location and diagnosis were correspondingly more complex.

Our evidence and analysis have suggested that both the Strowger and TXE4 exchange systems exerted, in their different ways, a number of direct and indirect influences on the balance of exchange maintenance work tasks in our four exchanges. However, this should not be taken to mean that the engineering systems alone determined the proportion of time spent on the different tasks. As we have already noted in chapter 2, BT as a commercial organisation had developed its own corporate maintenance strategy in the face of the conflicting requirements of cost and quality of service to the customer. To offer a fault-free service in either system would have required 'unlimited resources' (BT, 1983b: 8), or at the very least a massive increase in preventive maintenance work way beyond the existing staffing levels of either Strowger or TXE4 exchanges. On the other hand, to offer a very low-cost service would probably have led to a deterioration of the exchange network and a major and probably unacceptable decline in the quality of service to the customer. In this sense BT's exchange modernisation and maintenance strategies influenced the actual balance of preventive and corrective maintenance activities in the two different exchange types. In fact, the TXE4 exchange system was designed and chosen in part precisely because it promised a reduction in the amount of time-consuming routine preventive maintenance work required by Strowger exchanges. However, what we have attempted is to show how, *once chosen*, the Strowger and TXE4 exchange systems influenced the design space available to organisational actors to determine the balance between corrective and preventive maintenance, and also how different aspects of the exchange architecture and technology influenced different elements of the exchange maintenance work tasks in our two Strowger and two TXE4 exchanges. We now intend to take this analysis a stage further by examining the nature of TXE4 maintenance skills and the extent to which they also were shaped by the nature of the exchange system.

TXE4 maintenance skills

As we have seen in the previous section, the massive reduction in the number of moving parts and the use of more reliable electronic components relative to Strowger tended to reduce the requirement for routine checking of blocks of TXE4 equipment. The tasks associated with such checks were highly automated, involving the technicians in running test programmes or removing cards one at a time to check them for faulty components or circuits (usually by subjecting them to some kind of automatic tester). The skills in the task of checking dormant faults were thus mainly incorporated into special test equipment rather than in the person of the technician. The skills exercised by the technicians were confined largely to interpreting information provided by this equipment and did not involve the use of refined perceptual abilities as observed in Strowger maintenance. This was because the technicians were confronted not with racks of visible and audible moving mechanical parts subject to wear and tear but with rows and rows of 'cream coloured covers' containing plug-in units making very little noise and with no visible moving parts. Thus dormant fault checks were largely repetitive tasks requiring nothing like the amount of maintenance effort employed in block routines in our two Strowger exchanges.

Tasks associated with night routiner faults operated on similar principles to those in our Strowger exchanges. However, the provision of fault information on the night routiner teleprinter rather than individual dockets meant that additional interpretive abilities in fault location and diagnosis were sometimes called into play, abilities similar to those required to analyse information from the main fault teleprinter (see below, pp. 113–14). Once located and diagnosed, the repair of faults arising from the automatic night routiners involved similar skills to those employed on patrol/reported faults.

The skills required of technicians to carry out corrective maintenance tasks in our two TXE4 exchanges were in strong contrast to those utilised in our Strowger exchanges. First, the location and diagnosis of patrol/reported faults (and to a certain extent night routiner faults too) was an almost entirely mental activity since there were no audible or visual clues offered by the exchange technology itself. TXE4 faulting tasks thus involved a strong emphasis on mental diagnostic skills, indicating a qualitatively new kind of interpretive ability to that required in Strowger faulting. Not only was an overall knowledge of the exchange system and its common-control principles required but also an ability to interpret fault print-out information (or information from fault reports) and data provided by oscilloscopes and other test equipment (see photographs 10 and 11). Moreover, as we have seen above, certain faults in TXE4 exchanges were far more complex than in our two Strowger exchanges.

Many of the skills required in locating and diagnosing faults in our TXE4 exchanges can be traced directly to features of the exchange system itself. First, the greater susceptibility of common control systems to major service failures required the technicians to think through

10. Using a scopple to locate a TXE4 fault

11. Collaborative faulting in a TXE4 exchange using a storage oscilloscope and charts

alternative explanations and courses of action before 'diving in' to the exchange equipment. As we shall see in chapter 6, this sometimes involved discussions and collaborative working with other technicians (see photograph 11). Second, the intermittent character of many fault conditions in electronics-based systems, the possibility that the cause of some faults could be remote from the symptom and the multiplicity of paths available to calls through the exchange, meant that attempts to locate and diagnose certain fault conditions required both a logical mind and considerable patience to try out a whole series of different possible solutions to the same problem. One technician described how he would often spend hours 'chasing rainbows', and another, recalling many hours spent going down 'blind alleys' before finally locating a particular fault, described the operating principle behind TXE4 as 'Sod's Law' (in contrast to the principle of Ohm's Law behind Strowger!). Third, the very fault-tolerant character and greater reliability of the TXE4 system meant that, unlike Strowger, with its regular and predictable pattern of standard faults, certain fault conditions in our TXE4 exchanges occurred only infrequently. This meant that skill retention, that is the ability to recall how to deal with unusual faults, could add to the difficulty of certain fault-location and -diagnosis tasks.

The extent to which TXE4 faulting tasks involved a strong and new emphasis on mental diagnostic skills, requiring a 'system' appreciation of the relation of individual faults to the exchange system as a whole, was emphasised in all our TXE4 exchanges by the centrality of the fault print-out information to patrol/reported faults. In each exchange the FPO teleprinter (and from 8.00 a.m. until around 9.00 a.m., the night routiner teleprinter too) was the focal point of exchange maintenance tasks, interrupted occasionally by an alarm bell identifying a fault on a particular area of equipment. Periods of time were frequently spent in the interpretation, analysis and discussion of this data, backed-up occasionally by computer analysis. The need for mental diagnostic skills was strongly influenced by the common control principles of the TXE4 exchange system and its concealed and largely inaudible technology mounted on plug-in units.

However, compared to Strowger the repair of faulty TXE4 equipment was fairly straightforward. As we have seen above, for the common control equipment this typically involved taking the faulty PIU to a repair room and using special test equipment in order to locate the faulty component (see photograph 8). The manual soldering skills involved in replacing the faulty component did not really compare in terms of dexterity or 'touch' with those used in the repair of many Strowger faults. The testing and replacement of faulty reed-relays in the switching networks was similarly straightforward (see photograph 9), requiring nothing like the refined manual or intuitive skills necessary for many fault rectification tasks in our Strowger exchanges.

So far in this section we have stressed the strong emphasis on mental diagnostic skills in TXE4 and the weaker emphasis on the refined manual skills so typical of many aspects of maintenance in our Strowger exchanges. However, other skills in the person, based on the accumulated experience of certain fault conditions, were also important components of the technicians' work. These experiential and intuitive skills (an intuition, for example, about which particular path to follow in locating a TXE4 fault) were also enriched, as in our Strowger exchanges, by local knowledge not only of the layout of the exchange but also of the conditions and past performance of various parts of the system. As we have already noted above, in one of our TXE4 exchanges the technicians decided to carry out a thorough overhaul of one section of the exchange equipment which had been consistently producing a number of recurrent faults.

However, the significance of experiential and intuitive 'skills in the person' in our TXE4 exchanges differed from our Strowger findings in certain important ways. First, neither of our established TXE4 units had been in operation for more than a year and so the technicians' accumulated experience of TXE4 maintenance was small compared to that of our Strowger technicians, who had been engaged in Strowger maintenance for an average of about ten years. Second, at the time of our research TXE4 exchanges had only been in operation in British Telecom for a relatively short period of time and the nationally accumulated knowledge of TXE4 maintenance tasks and skills was therefore in its comparative infancy. Third, we have already noted that refined manual skills were less important in TXE4 maintenance tasks than in Strowger maintenance and that the feel or touch associated with Strowger faulting was much less pronounced in our TXE4 exchanges. Fourth, the accumulation of TXE4 maintenance skills was not something which could be acquired by trial and error on the live exchange equipment, that is, by constant practice at continually recurring familiar tasks, since some complex faults occurred only rarely and many were not predictable in their pattern. In our Strowger exchanges skills in the person could be and were acquired incrementally over a long period of time by a mixture of trial and error and 'learning from Nellie' – in other words, working alongside senior technicians. In TXE4 exchanges, by contrast, the trial and error method of learning was not only less appropriate, it could seriously affect customer service. Thus, the common control principles of TXE4 exchanges raised fundamental questions about the acquisition of skills as well as the nature and implementation of these skills in practice. The whole question of skill acquisition for TXE4 maintenance will be discussed in more detail below. Before we do this we will discuss the technicians' subjective experience of changes in maintenance work tasks and skills.

4.4 The experience of maintenance tasks and skills

In previous sections of this chapter we have attempted to demonstrate that there were a variety of complex but clear relationships between technology (two different types of telephone exchange system) and particular aspects of work (work tasks and skills) in the workplaces we have investigated. We now wish to examine attitudinal data on work tasks and skills from our eight exchanges. In our view the data suggests a strong association between different types of engineering system and the technicians' experience of work tasks and skills. However, we feel that to attempt a systematic analysis of this link would require a far more rigorous analysis than our research design allowed. We will therefore confine ourselves to presenting the subjective perception and attitudes of the technicians as evidence which underpins and enriches our analysis of more objective changes in work tasks and skills. In short, this data will be used illustratively rather than analytically.

The contrast already identified between the balance and type of skills used in Strowger and TXE4 exchange maintenance work tasks was clearly reflected in the perceptions of the technicians we interviewed.[8] In order to make this data available in quantified form, we carried out a content analysis of the answers of individual technicians and then grouped their multiple responses into three main categories: mental skills; manual skills; and experiential and intuitive skills.[9] The results are presented in table 4.5 below. This shows an almost equal balance in our Strowger exchanges between the three categories of skills, whereas TXE4 system maintenance was defined by our TXE4 technicians predominantly in terms of mental skills. This quantified data is a rather crude measure of what was clearly perceived by the technicians as a major change in the balance and significance of different types of skills in the task and skills in the person. A fuller picture of the meaning of these responses can be gained by citing in evidence quotations from the interviews.

First, there was a widely expressed view that TXE4, with its strong emphasis on deductive reasoning and a systems approach, was a 'hands off' system, whereas Strowger, with its audible and visible moving parts and emphasis on manual adjustments, was very much a 'hands on'

Table 4.5 *Perceptions of exchange maintenance skills in Strowger and TXE4 (senior technicians only)*

Type of skills	Strowger (n=19)	TXE4 (n=11)
Mental skills	26	28
Manual skills	21	2
Experiential and intuitive skills	20	9

system.[10] One senior technician expressed this difference in terms of what he called the 'dive-in' technique of Strowger maintenance (see photograph 12), in contrast to the more considered mental calculations involved in TXE4 maintenance:

> With Strowger, it's more a dive-in technique, it's a mechanical system. You can actually get to grips with the thing, you could jack things straight out and know it didn't matter, that was it, you'd got it in your hand. You have be sure you're taking the right thing out when you do it on TXE4.

Being sure that 'you're taking the right thing out' partly depended on an overall understanding of the TXE4 system, as another senior technician commented:

> you've got to know a lot more. You've got to take the whole exchange in context rather than just one little piece of equipment . . . In . . . [Strowger] . . . you could isolate and work away on one piece [of equipment]. On [TXE4] you've really got to think of what's happening all through the [system]. A different kind of thinking what the problems are.

Allied to this conception of the difference in skills between TXE4 and Strowger was a perception that the consequences of mistaken action in TXE4 could have major implications for the performance of the exchange as a whole. Additionally, a fault could arise at any time which would require speedy diagnosis and rectification if the security of the exchange system was not to be significantly prejudiced. These perceptions were expressed in the following quotations:

> I think your powers of reasoning need to be a lot greater . . . you've got to think an awful lot more. Strowger you could get by with just walking around keeping your eyes open really,

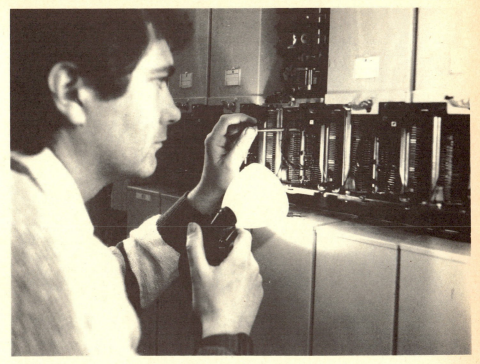

12. Using the 'dive-in' technique in Strowger faulting

and there's not a lot of things that you could do wrong that could cause an absolute disaster in the exchange, whereas with this, you've got to be on your toes all the time, because what you do could knock the exchange off the air, being common control. I think that's in the back of all our minds all the time.

Well, Strowger seemed to be a constant flow of similar problems. It's exactly the same as running a car, we all know how to do plugs, points, condenser, that kind of thing, but when an automatic gearbox goes up the creek, you're suddenly stuck, even though it's part of the same system. It's so different and so irregular that it happens, that's what electronics is like. You suddenly get a fault come out of the blue that's never come up before.

Strowger was more of a mundane day-to-day 'do this do that', but with electronics [i.e. TXE4] it's more exciting because you

117

don't know what's going to happen. You might come in one day and find the exchange is falling off the air. It keeps you on your toes a lot more.

There was also a perception on the part of many of the technicians that some of the skills used in maintenance work on Strowger had been lost on TXE4:

Well you've lost the basic skills of adjustment. Now it's a completely different context really. From Strowger to electronic it's so different. It's literally clockwork to electronics.

Similarly:

[TXE4 work is] very much de-skilled . . . So far as Strowger is concerned, you've got to be good at two things. You've got to be able to do mechanical adjustments and you've got to know how the thing works. TXE4, you've only got to be able to know how the thing works because there's no mechanical adjustments . . .There's not a hell of a lot of skill in unsoldering a transistor. I mean I could teach either of you two to do a good job of that in ten minutes.

However, whilst there was a perception that the manual skills associated with Strowger maintenance had been lost, there was an equally strong sense in which the mental skills required for TXE4 compensated for this. As the latter respondent went on to say:

faults [on TXE4] are a lot more complicated, there's a hell of a lot more to remember. I believe myself that it's going to take me five years to become sort of reasonable at TXE4, whereas I reckon that after I'd been a TO for two years on Strowger there was very little that I couldn't cope with.

A more systematic, if crude expression of this kind of perception was provided by asking the technicians to rank their jobs on a scale of highly skilled, skilled and semi-skilled. As table 4.6 shows, while the majority of Strowger technicians described Strowger maintenance as skilled work, the majority of TXE4 technicians saw their work as skilled to highly skilled.

Attempts to measure job satisfaction are notoriously difficult (see Gruneberg, 1979). We confined ourselves in this study to asking questions concerning 'likes' and 'dislikes' about maintenance work in the two exchange types. While the answers contained references to some wider

Table 4.6 *Attitudes towards Strowger and TXE4 maintenance (senior technicians only)*

Job ranking	Strowger (n=18)[11]	TXE4 (n=14)
Highly skilled	0	5
Skilled/highly skilled	2	3
Skilled	10	5
Skilled/semi-skilled	3	0
Semi-skilled	1	1
Unspecified	2	1

Note: One respondent said part of TXE4 work was highly skilled and part was semi-skilled. This is treated as a multiple answer and counted twice.

aspects of job satisfaction such as staffing levels and supervision, we are including them in this section because the majority of responses, unsurprisingly in view of the focus of our questioning, were directly related to the issues of work tasks and skills.

In relation to Strowger maintenance, likes were particularly associated with faulting activities (see table 4.7 over). Dislikes, however, were strongly linked to routine preventive maintenance work because of its repetitive and boring nature. In contrast, likes about TXE4 work normally emphasised its more interesting, challenging and varied nature compared with Strowger and the better working environment (see table 4.8 over). The most frequently cited dislike about TXE4 maintenance was the occurrence of intermittent faults. Paradoxically, this dislike was also seen as leading to greater job satisfaction once the fault was diagnosed and cleared. Finally, the technicians who had worked on both Strowger and TXE4 systems were asked to compare their overall job satisfaction from the two types of work. It should be remembered that the pay, grading and hours in both types of work were identical. Of the sixteen responses received, fifteen claimed they found TXE4 work more satisfying.

4.5 The acquisition of TXE4 maintenance skills

Earlier in this chapter we discussed briefly how senior Strowger technicians acquired maintenance skills through a mixture of formal training courses and on-the-job experience, including sustained periods in operational exchanges working as junior technicians alongside senior colleagues. In this section we want to focus on the question of how the

Table 4.7 *Likes/dislikes about Strowger maintenance work (senior technicians only) (n=34)*

Likes	Responses	Dislikes	Responses
Clearing faults/faulting	7	Routines	12
Mechanical/visible nature of equipment	5	Paperwork/statistics	4
Serving customers	2	Boredom/familiarity with Strowger system	3
Variety of work	2	Management/supervision	3
Other	5	Other	3
No likes	2	No dislikes	4

Table 4.8 *Likes/dislikes about TXE4 maintenance work (senior technicians only) (n=17)*

Likes	Responses	Dislikes	Responses
More interesting/ challenging/varied than Strowger work	13	Frustrating/ intermittent faults	5
Better working environment than Strowger	8	Lack of experience/ confidence	2
Clearing difficult faults	4	Other	5
Other	1		
No likes	0	No dislikes	5

new skills required for TXE4 maintenance work were acquired by the senior technicians in the exchanges we studied. Our concern will therefore be with the way that 'skill in the person' came about during the implementation of TXE4 modernisation.

The data presented will be drawn mainly from our studies of the conversion of three exchanges: Conversion A and Conversion B in Coast

Area and Conversion C in Metro Area (see table A, p. 7). As a result of our intensive monitoring of these three exchanges before, during and after conversion, we are in a position to describe and explain the differing experiences of individuals and teams of technicians in different workplaces, and also to point to the common and more general features in their acquisition of new maintenance skills. We will also use this evidence in chapter 6 to examine how far choices made at critical junctures during the process of skill acquisition influenced the various forms of work organisation that emerged during the implementation process. In order to appreciate fully the various critical junctures in the process of skill acquisition, we have broken down the conversion of individual TXE4 exchanges into two main sub-stages: installation and de-bugging; and changeover and initial operation.[12] As we will see, these sub-stages raised quite distinctive problems and are therefore treated separately.

Installation and de-bugging

The first main issue that arose during this sub-stage was the timing and relevance of formal training courses. The sheer length and breadth of the course programme, which lasted seventeen weeks in all, gives an initial indication of the potential problems of skill acquisition faced by the technicians. The programme was broken up into five separate courses of between two and four weeks each, all held in BT's Technical Training College (BTTC) in Staffordshire. The first course provided an introductory appreciation of the new system, the three middle courses focused on particular pieces of exchange equipment, and the final course on the maintenance of peripheral equipment and on overall system service.

In our three main conversion exchanges, the phasing of the formal training courses with the installation and de-bugging of the equipment raised a number of problems which required management decision. Area management's aim in all three cases was to programme the five training courses in a two-year period prior to the changeover of the new units. However, a number of factors conspired to upset this goal in two out of our three exchanges. In Conversion B, the changeover date was delayed by nearly a year because of technical problems for which the equipment manufacturer (henceforth called 'contractor') was responsible. The consequence was that the two senior technicians involved in re-training had both completed their formal courses over twelve months before their new exchange was brought into service. A similar experience was noted in the modernisation of exchanges TXE4 A and B.

In Conversion C, in contrast, the installation and de-bugging of the exchange equipment actually proceeded faster than the re-training of

121

staff. The requisite TXE4 courses were either not available at the right time or staff had to withdraw from courses offered to them for personal reasons such as sickness, often causing a delay of some months. The upshot was that four weeks before changeover one technician had received four of the five courses, one three, and the other only two courses. At this point, as we have already seen in chapter 3, the technician with four courses was withdrawn from the re-training programme. He was immediately replaced by a senior technician from another Strowger exchange in the area who had attended only one TXE4 course five years previously. The result was that at changeover, the resident exchange staff were only partly re-trained in terms of the formal training courses, none of them having attended either the fourth or fifth course. Given the importance of mental skills in TXE4 maintenance and the need for an appreciation of the system nature of some faults, it is not surprising that the technicians in Conversion C felt inadequate in terms of skill acquisition at the time of changeover.

In Conversion A, the two technicians had both attended their first training course just over two years before changeover and completed their last course between six and ten months prior to changeover. This was regarded by management and technicians alike as a good fit between the phasing of the formal training courses and installation and de-bugging of the new system. However, it should be noted that, even in this case, the first of the five courses had been completed over two years before the technicians could actually begin live maintenance work in their new exchange. Thus, even without delays in system implementation or in the completion of training courses, there remained the question of providing the technicians with the opportunity to apply their course knowledge and develop their new skills through practical experience.

The next issue arising during installation and de-bugging was therefore the relation between formal training courses and what was normally referred to by the technicians as 'hands-on experience'. Although we have stressed the overwhelming importance of mental skills in TXE4 maintenance, it should not be assumed that these new skills could all be learnt theoretically. As one of our senior technicians commented: 'The biggest thing is experience of maintenance, at any rate getting your hands on the equipment and playing with it.'

All the technicians undergoing re-training in our three conversion exchanges were 'Strowger men' (see chapter 3, note 5), trained and practised over many years in the maintenance of an essentially electro-mechanical exchange system. As such, they had assimilated a particular culture of maintenance, a particular way of thinking and approach to their work captured in such phrases as the 'dive-in' technique and the

'TO touch'. Against this background, it is possible to appreciate the 'culture shock' they experienced at their first re-training course when confronted with a new exchange system with very different maintenance requirements. All our technicians took their first TXE4 course, and some their subsequent courses too, straight from working on Strowger maintenance. Following the course they often went straight back to Strowger maintenance. The problem of skill acquisition in this context is well captured in the following quotation from a senior technician in one of our conversion exchanges, whose sentiments were widely shared:

> The worst thing was that the first week of each course was taken up with forgetting about Strowger, then you get into it the next three or four weeks thinking TXE, then coming straight back here forgetting all about TXE so you could think about Strowger. It was a ludicrous situation which no one other than the people who were doing it would appreciate.

Post-course experience was gained by the technicians in two main ways, by secondment to their new exchange unit prior to conversion and by secondment to another live TXE4 exchange in the vicinity. The technicians' experience of these critical junctures in the re-training process showed wide variations, both in the balance between the two types of secondment and in their relative importance in terms of skill acquisition. This can best be illustrated by looking at each of our three conversion exchanges in turn.

In Conversion A both technicians had completed their formal training courses some six months prior to changeover (which was eventually delayed by just one month) and both had been seconded full-time to their new unit nine months prior to changeover. This had a number of advantages in terms of the acquisition of both skill and confidence in TXE4 maintenance. First, they were able to gain local knowledge by familiarising themselves with their own exchange system lay-out (its overall configuration and particular dimensioning) and with the cabling routes into and out of the exchange. Second, they were able to familiarise themselves with the different areas of the exchange equipment by working alongside the contractors' staff and BT's own installation staff during the last phases of the installation and de-bugging of the equipment. The importance of this experience was underlined by a number of technicians we interviewed and can be illustrated by the following typical quotation:

> We got stuck in . . . at a very early time in the contract and I think it did us a great deal of good. All of the chaps here got the confidence more than anything, that's what you basically

123

need, to get stuck in there and look at something . . . OK, you've got a certain amount of faulting at BTTC, but they're all black and white faults . . . you rarely find a fault like that here.

These comments underline the important link between hands-on experience, skill acquisition and confidence and also the limits to the practical faulting experience which can be gained during formal training courses. However, partly because Conversion A was the first exchange in Coast Area to convert to TXE4, the technicians in this exchange spent only one or two days in a live TXE4 unit (roughly thirty miles away) prior to changeover. They thus felt a certain deficit in the skills and confidence required to maintain a live exchange, since the approach and methods of installation staff (whether from the contractors or from BT's own installation division) were not necessarily appropriate to maintaining an operational exchange. For example, in order to isolate a particular fault, the contractors' staff tended simply to take parts of the exchange out of service, a practice which, as we have seen, could lead in a live exchange to a number of customers being taken off the air. In an informal discussion about two months prior to changeover, the technicians in Conversion A suggested to us that much of what they had to do in the following weeks was to unlearn the contractors' method of faulting. They also stressed that they were having difficulty in remembering information acquired during their formal training courses, and how little they felt the formal courses had prepared them for organising the day-to-day maintenance of a live exchange. This latter point was repeated again and again by the technicians we interviewed:

> [The formal training course] was a good grounding, but not a substitute for practical experience.

> They don't teach you how to fault. They teach you how the system works in a way. I think we'd make excellent design engineers by the time we finish the courses, but we know nothing about faulting techniques.

> Working on a live exchange, with 'subs' [subscribers], real people, real telephones . . . there's no substitute for working on a live system.

In Conversion B, which was also in Coast Area, both senior technicians had completed their courses well before changeover, which was delayed by a period of nearly a year. This delay enabled local management to second them full-time to their new unit many months in advance of changeover and also to second one of them for a period of two months to another TXE4 exchange in order to gain practical experience of the changeover and initial operation of a live unit. In this respect the technicians in Conversion B were the best prepared on changeover day of all the exchanges studied. They had received all the formal training courses, one of them had enjoyed a longish period of post-course experience in an operational unit, and both had spent an extended period of time gaining local knowledge of their own exchange system and learning about the different areas of the exchange equipment from the contractors and BT installation staff. All this resulted in a general feeling of confidence as the changeover date approached.

However, the technicians' apparently successful experience of skill acquisition in Conversion B cannot be attributed entirely to the implementation sub-strategy of Coast Area management. Indeed, the outcomes observed in relation to skill acquisition were to some extent the result of unforeseen circumstances and events beyond management control. The delay of nearly a year in the installation and de-bugging programme arose because the contractors had had to suspend work due to delays in the supply of certain components. Moreover, some months prior to the changeover of Conversion B another TXE4 exchange in Coast Area had suffered major technical problems immediately after coming into service. This had resulted in bad publicity in the local press as customers had experienced a significant deterioration in the quality of the service provided. Understandably, area management was keen to avoid a repetition of this experience with Conversion B and adopted a more cautious approach. The delay in installation provided an additional breathing space in the re-training of the technicians, which, when taken together with management's already established policy of early secondment and its ability to provide post-course experience in a neighbouring live unit, meant that the technicians were particularly well prepared for changeover and that the exchange equipment was fully de-bugged before it came into live operation.

Post-course experience in Conversion C provided a clear contrast to Conversions A and B. As we have already noted, none of the three technicians had completed their formal training courses by the time of changeover. In addition, only one of them had had an extended period of secondment to the new unit (about nine months). This lack of early secondment was for two main reasons. First, the contractors were unwilling to allow too many BT staff to work on the new equipment before it had successfully completed its final acceptance test and become the property of BT. Second, in this particular unit and in Metro Area more generally, the maintenance of the existing Strowger unit appeared to be given as much if not greater priority by management as the secondment of staff to the new TXE4 exchange. Of course these two priorities were not necessarily simple alternatives. This is shown by the case of Conversions A and B, where Coast Area management had arranged the temporary secondment of Strowger technicians from other exchanges to maintain the old Strowger units, which allowed the retrained staff to be seconded full-time to their new units at least nine months prior to changeover. In contrast, the Strowger maintenance supervisor in Conversion C held on to two of the three technicians envisaged for the new unit until around three months prior to change-over, and during these three months both were absent from the exchange for between three and four weeks attending a delayed TXE4 training course. One of these two technicians claimed later that lack of post-course experience in his own unit had been one of the main reasons why he had lacked confidence and been unable to participate properly in one of the final training courses:

> I don't feel confidence on the new system. If only I'd been up
> there [in the TXE4 unit] for some period of time and got to
> grips with it . . . I shouldn't have gone on that [recent] course.
> I went there and of course I looked a fool. I didn't even know
> how to operate the keys to bring it back into service. The
> other blokes knew what they were doing. They must have
> looked at me and thought 'keep an eye on him'.

In the event, all three technicians in Conversion C did spend some weeks on secondment to other TXE4 units in the vicinity. Nevertheless, two of the three technicians told us that during this time they had been given predominantly routine checks and tasks to carry out rather than being attached to experienced TXE4 technicians to learn faulting skills, although one did spend a few days looking over the shoulder of an experienced technician who was working on one particular area of equipment. He thus acquired specific skills on this aspect of maintenance and, as we shall see, tended to specialise in this area in the first weeks of live operation in order to gain confidence and play to his strengths. This particular experience of re-training thus had implications for the organisation of work (see chapter 6) as well as the acquisition of specific maintenance skills. It also touches on one particularly important aspect of the management of change, namely the co-ordination of the re-training programme of individual staff.

In Metro Area (in which Conversion C was located) there was no one member of management with specific responsibility for the training of individual technicians and no regular counselling between courses in

126

order to find out the areas in which staff were experiencing a lack of confidence or skill deficiencies. In the case of the technician who was withdrawn from the TXE4 re-training programme, this lack of counselling was a major cause of criticism. As another technician in Conversion C commented:

> I don't think enough managers ask us enough questions, certainly about the training courses. They just accept that you've been on the courses. They didn't ask us how we felt about them, how we got on . . .

This question of management continuity and co-ordination of the implementation process has already been discussed in chapter 2. We can simply note here that it also had direct implications for skill acquisition.

The importance of post-course experience in the acquisition of new skills in our three exchanges can be summarised briefly. First, it enabled the technicians to apply the more theoretical knowledge they had been taught in the formal training courses. As one technician commented: 'It all starts from the theory learnt on the training courses, and as you get practical experience you realise how it fits together.' Second, experience in their own new units allowed them to gain local knowledge of the exchange layout and also the cabling routes. It also allowed them to practice and build up confidence in maintenance techniques by learning from experts (the contractors' and BT installation staff) and by trial and error, since mistakes while the system was not carrying live traffic did not have any detrimental effect on customer service. Third, periods of secondment to other units enabled the technicians to learn from experienced TXE4 colleagues the faulting techniques required to maintain a live exchange, techniques which were quite different from those used in Strowger faulting and in faulting non-operational TXE4 units. Subjectively, too, the experience of live faulting, particularly at the changeover of another TXE4 unit, could be an extraordinarily intense and important juncture in the process of skill acquisition, as one of the technicians pointed out:

> I was there [at another exchange]. I was there for a couple of days into opening. I think I learnt most in that two days . . . Talk about baptism of fire – that was it! I had that here as well. Working on a live exchange, with 'subs', real people, real telephones . . . there's no substitute for working on a live system.

Before we look at skill acquisition during changeover and initial operation, we should note the importance of area management policies in this whole process of skill acquisition, including their different approaches towards the secondment of staff, the run-down of the old Strowger units and the de-bugging of the new exchanges prior to changeover. We should also note the influence of unforeseen circumstances, both in the case of Conversion B (where there were unanticipated delays in the provision of necessary components by the contractor) and Conversion C (where illness of staff led to delays in training courses). A more complete picture of the significance of skill acquisition will emerge when we examine in chapter 6 the organisation and control of work in our three conversion exchanges. As we will see, the technicians' varying experiences of the process of skill acquisition prior to changeover exerted a considerable influence on their capacity to develop new forms of work organisation for TXE4 maintenance.

Changeover and initial operation

The process of skill acquisition during changeover and initial operation showed certain common features in our three main conversion exchanges. However, the importance of these sub-stages was largely dependent on the previous experience of the technicians during installation and de-bugging. In Conversions A and B the technicians had completed all their formal training courses many months prior to changeover and had spent extended periods of time on full-time secondment to their new units. They had worked over the shoulders of the contractors' and BT installation staff and were fully involved immediately prior to changeover in interim maintenance work, standard checks and final preparations of the exchange equipment. Both the changeover and initial operation of these two exchanges ran relatively smoothly, and the external support of staff drafted in to assist with any technical problems were able to withdraw within a week of the changeover date.

In Conversion C, in contrast, external support from experienced technicians was not only important in preparing the exchange technically for changeover, it played a crucially important role in the process of skill acquisition due to the problems and delays which had occurred during the previous stages of the training programme. Part of the strategy for managing exchange conversion in Metro Area involved using a small team of area experts (called the Special Faults Investigation Unit) to help with the changeover. In the event, the main task of this team (two senior technicians and a supervisor) in Conversion C was to solve a range of technical problems arising from faulty components in the plug-in units. They therefore spent little time working with the resident technicians or involving them in the more general programme of tests. On personality grounds, too, the outside experts were not particularly disposed to spending time in patient explanations of faulting techniques – they were single-mindedly intent on getting down to work and clearing bugs as quickly and efficiently as possible. In contrast, an experienced TXE4 technician from another exchange in the area was also seconded to Conversion C to help during the changeover and he proved to be an extremely patient and good teacher. He spent many hours, especially with one particular technician (who happened also to be a personal friend), explaining how to go about various faulting tasks and also how to organise the maintenance of the live exchange. He also stayed on after changeover to help the technicians through the first ten days of live operation, whereas the team of experts left after three days to carry out remedial work on another unit.

We have already noted the importance of 'learning from Nellie' in acquiring TXE4 maintenance skills. Whereas in Conversion A and B this critical juncture came about during extended periods of post-course experience beginning well before changeover, in the case of Conversion C it occurred during the immediate changeover period at a time of great stress for the technicians. They all agreed in subsequent interviews that without the presence of their colleague from a neighbouring unit their own lack of training and experience could have led to serious consequences for the initial performance of their exchange. The experience of the technicians in Conversion C underlines the fact that the acquisition of new skills is a many-sided process in which different types of learning (formal training courses, hands-on experience in non-operational and live units, support from outside experts during changeover and initial operation) can all feed off one another to provide a rounded preparation for a new range of work tasks. Managerially this implies the need for continuity and co-ordination of different phases of a training programme plus regular counselling of staff undergoing re-training to monitor progress and, if necessary, to take remedial action. While managerial action on some of these issues was evident in our three telephone areas, management monitoring of re-training and skill acquisition was not generally given priority attention.

Two final points should perhaps be noted before we conclude this section. First, we have limited but nevertheless strong evidence that the proportion of time spent on patrol/reported faults, the most complex of TXE4 exchange maintenance work tasks, was much higher during the period of initial operation than after units had settled down.[13] This suggests that the first few months of initial operation were a time when the still inexperienced technicians were involved particularly intensively in learning new faulting skills and practising a more theoretical and hands-off approach to the location and diagnosis of faults. As one technician in Conversion A said at the time in an informal interview: 'You have to get used to not solving faults quickly.'[14]

Second, although it is not directly related to the process of skill acquisition, mention should be made of the importance of the technical condition of the new exchange units for the technicians' experiences of changeover and initial operation. In our three main conversion exchanges the new systems had been extremely thoroughly tested and de-bugged prior to live operation. As a result the technicians were able to devote themselves without too much stress to gaining practical experience of faulting on their new exchanges. In contrast to this experience, the period of initial operation in Conversion D was dogged by technical bugs. During the first three months the technicians spent most of their time trying to reduce the levels of fault print-out, which was being measured in feet of paper rather than the number of lines of print,[15] to manageable proportions. Just after changeover, around thirty feet of print-out was being produced every twenty-four hours! One of the technicians in particular spent all his time for the first two months carrying out simple routine testing tasks to locate all the bugs in the switching area. His opportunity to acquire experientially learnt faulting skills was thus significantly delayed.

4.6 Conclusion

In this chapter we have examined evidence to test our contention that technology, conceptualised as engineering system, can act as an independent variable shaping particular outcomes of change. We began our analysis by looking at the variety of ways in which the architecture, technology and appearance of the Strowger and TXE4 exchange systems influenced the content of the three main sets of exchange maintenance work tasks in our case-study exchanges. We then examined the links between the two exchange systems, the skills required to accomplish these work tasks (skills in the task) and the range and types of skills possessed by exchange maintenance technicians (skills in the person). Finally we traced the different ways in which individual technicians acquired the new TXE4 maintenance skills at different sub-stages and critical junctures in the process of introducing TXE4 in the workplace. We were able to demonstrate that the capabilities of the two exchange systems exerted a variety of different influences on work tasks and skills. These ranged from direct links between exchange architecture and technology and particular aspects of fault location and repair tasks, to less direct but still identifiable links between exchange technology and the overall balance between preventive and corrective maintenance and between exchange architecture and the nature and form of skill acquisition.

A more complete view of the influence of exchange systems on maintenance work will be possible when we have examined changes in supervision and work organisation in chapters 5 and 6. At this point, however, we can make some preliminary observations about the nature of the skill changes involved in the move from Strowger to TXE4. The new skills required for TXE4 maintenance emphasised mental diagnostic and interpretive abilities and system awareness, in contrast to the emphasis on refined aural and visual abilities, manual dexterities, and the 'TO touch' in our Strowger exchanges. We were therefore not able to identify a uniform tendency either towards the 'de-skilling' or towards the 'up-skilling' of work tasks. Rather, both processes were in evidence at the same time. Maintenance tasks in our TXE4 exchanges had been de-skilled in the sense that the manual dexterities associated with Strowger maintenance, particularly Strowger repair tasks, were no longer required. On the other hand there had been a clear up-skilling in the sense that TXE4 faulting involved a qualitatively different degree of mental diagnostic ability. In this respect our findings are similar to those of Senker and his colleagues (Senker *et al.*, 1981; Senker, 1984). They found that the maintenance requirements of automated systems were often reduced compared with non-automated systems and that mechanical skills were being replaced by new electronics and software skills, but that the greater technical complexity of automated systems made many faults more difficult to locate and diagnose. They also found that the promise of self-diagnostic maintenance often failed to materialise or covered only a small proportion of fault conditions.

If there is a need for new and in some senses enhanced skills to maintain automated systems, then the re-training of maintenance staff assumes a particular significance. In this connection, our findings demonstrated the critical importance of management re-training policies in shaping the whole process of skill acquisition. Hands-on experience proved essential to the cementing of the theoretical knowledge gained by the technicians on the formal training courses. To this extent managerial decisions on whether and when to provide periods of post-course experience had a significant bearing on the capacity of the technicians to cope confidently with the maintenance of the new system. In addition, management decisions on the provision of support to technicians during changeover and initial operation played an important part in enabling in most cases a relatively smooth transition. However, in certain cases unforeseen circumstances (such as staff illness and delays in equipment installation), and perhaps more foreseeable occurrences (such as the withdrawal of one technician who was evidently not suited for re-training and the bringing into service of equipment which was not adequately de-bugged), arose which required modifications to management policy and in some cases remedial intervention. In most instances, then, the successful acquisition of skills rested on the general quality of management decisions and in particular the extent to which they provided a broad range of re-training experiences to supplement the formal training courses.

In order to examine further the questions of skills and technological change, we will need to examine the way in which skills were distributed between different grades of staff and different individuals within particular exchanges. We will also need to assess the implications of skill changes for job control and the organisation of work. Before we can do this, however, we need to examine the work tasks and experience of change of the other main actors in the implementation process, the exchange maintenance supervisors. They are the subject of our next chapter.

5

The problem of supervision

5.1 Introduction

In the previous chapter we examined changes in the work tasks and skills of maintenance technicians resulting from TXE4 modernisation. In this chapter we wish to turn our attention to the other group of actors directly affected by the introduction of TXE4 at exchange level – the first-line maintenance supervisors or Assistant Executive Engineers. We intend to explore two main propositions: that technological change throws into sharp relief problems with existing supervisory roles and that it opens up significant design choices for management to redefine such roles within a broader redefinition of the function of supervision.

This latter concern arises directly from a recent debate on the implications of new technology for supervision. According to Buchanan, for example:

> The advantages of new technology may be lost if it is applied
> with traditional management values and assumptions. The
> effective use of new information and computing technologies
> may be dependent on new forms of work organisation. This
> may in turn necessitate a reconstruction of the role of
> management, particularly at lower levels of line management.
> (1983: 79)

Child, too, has argued that new technology poses significant design choices in relation to supervision, for example between the degree of centralisation and decentralisation of decision-making responsibilities (1984: 260). On the whole, recent research has identified a general tendency towards centralisation leading to an erosion of supervisory positions. In the view of Buchanan and Boddy this erosion occurs in three ways: by machine pacing of work operations rather than direct supervisory control; by the automatic capture and analysis of information on operational performance rather than by supervisors; and by the loss of skill superiority of existing supervisors over their subordinates (1983: 249).

However, there are also counter-examples where managements have chosen to develop supervisory roles quite differently in the context of technological change. Dawson (1986) and Dawson and McLoughlin (1986) have shown, for example, how management in British Rail exploited the capacity of new engineering systems to delegate increased decision-making responsibility to supervisory level, creating a new computer-based second-line supervisory position to co-ordinate work-place operations. Whatever the different outcomes, all these examples tend to suggest that management choice is a key variable in shaping the outcomes of technological change in relation to supervision. As in previous chapters, though, we will also be examining how far particular technologies influence the design space within which managements seek to define or redefine supervisory roles.

We will begin this chapter by identifying the nature and range of responsibilities of the Strowger supervisors in our case-study exchanges. Second, we will examine the extent to which, in the absence of any detailed corporate guidelines on the operational management of TXE4 maintenance, the policies developed by middle management in Metro, Coast and Town Areas played a part in shaping the role of the TXE4 supervisors. This will involve an examination of the supervisors' role in both the implementation and routine operation of our TXE4 exchanges. Our general contention will be that although the supervisors in our sample did not experience any major change in their range of responsibilities, their perceived authority to carry them out was in nearly all cases severely undermined. As a result they became even more remote from the exchange floor than they had been as Strowger supervisors. Underlying this development were their lack of training in the supervisory management of TXE4 exchange maintenance, the emergent skill superiority of the exchange technicians, and more generally the failure of management sub-strategies in two of our three telephone areas to come to terms with the new opportunities and constraints presented by TXE4.

5.2 The role of the Strowger supervisor

The corporate view

The general framework within which Strowger supervisors operated at the time of our study was set by a whole range of national guidelines (Telecommunications Instructions or TIs), circulars and memos issued over many years. In addition, all supervisors were required to attend at least two general management training courses (covering questions such as staff management, appraisals and so on) on their promotion or appointment to supervisory positions. However by the early 1980s corporate management had clearly become increasingly concerned about the role of the maintenance supervisor, both in Strowger and in other exchange types. An increasing number of nationally and regionally organised job conferences were held for first- and second-line supervising officers responsible for the maintenance of switching equipment, and to accompany them an updated version of *Switching Maintenance: A Handbook for Supervisors* (BT, 1981) was produced. The handbook, which had been first issued in 1971, was intended by national management 'to provide a concise but comprehensive guide' to the job of the maintenance supervisor, including a definition of the supervisory role culled from various national instructions and guidelines.

The handbook began by giving a broad outline of BT's general aims and its specific national and local maintenance objectives. Overall it defined maintenance objectives as the improvement of both quality of service and productivity (*ibid.*: 4). It went on to describe in detail the information sources available to the supervisor in assessing quality of service, with some guidance about how to use the information. As far as exchange maintenance was concerned, it stated that, while there were comprehensive national and regional guidelines on periodic preventive maintenance, there was still considerable scope for local management initiative. For example, although the recommended frequency of block routines (see chapter 4) was nationally prescribed, the actual programme of routines for each exchange was left to the discretion of the first-line supervisor.

The handbook went on to outline a number of broad areas of responsibility of the maintenance supervisor, including staff training, the control of access to buildings and safety matters, and concluded with a general statement:

> The AEE controls the activities of others and is responsible for carrying out, through the group in his charge, the policy and intentions of higher management. His task is to achieve objectives through the people for whom he is responsible. He should know his staff personally and they should know him. He should be sufficiently up to date with new practices and new systems that he can direct and guide his staff, correct faulty methods and, if he is unable to solve their problems, should know where the answers may be obtained. (*Ibid.*: 49)

The model implied in this statement was a pro-active supervisor engaged in implementing higher management policy at exchange level. It suggested a direct involvement with maintenance staff and a sufficient knowledge of the work they were doing to initiate corrective action where the methods employed were incorrect or technical problems occurred. How far did this model approximate to our findings on the role of Strowger supervisors in our case-study exchanges?

Supervisory roles in the case-study exchanges

The examples of Strowger supervisory roles which we will describe are based on interviews, observation and self-report diaries completed over two-week periods by maintenance supervisors in the two main case-study Strowger exchanges supplemented by interviews from the conversion exchanges.[1] We will begin by describing the supervisory role in Strowger A, because it provided a good example of many features of Strowger maintenance supervision. We will then compare this with our other Strowger exchanges.

Strowger A was one of three Strowger exchanges in Town Area for which this particular supervisor was responsible, and it was by far the largest. His office was in the same building as the exchange, although it was situated on a floor above the two main exchange floors. It was a large exchange in terms of traffic and exchange connections served and had sixteen maintenance technicians, including eight senior technicians and one 'working supervisor' or Technical Officer with Allowance (see above, 3.2). The TOA worked full-time on supervisory activities in the exchange and had an office on one of the main exchange floors. The supervisor himself was a temporary replacement in this position and had only been in charge of the exchange for three months at the time of our research. However, a high degree of continuity in the role was provided by the system of work organisation devised many years previously by his predecessor and by his immediate superior, an Executive Engineer (EE).

The range of responsibilities of the maintenance supervisor in Strowger A during our two-week period of detailed study can be sub-divided into four main categories, each of which is followed by examples of particular work activities observed during this period:

> *Management of contingencies:* liaising with superiors, external staff and customers over particular faults and complaints; ensuring important new customer connections or services were dealt with speedily.

Staff management: approving annual leave and scheduled days off; filling out time sheets; arranging training courses; appraising staff performance; completing accident reports.

Estate management: monitoring stores; health and safety checks; general paperwork; organising car parking; arranging fuel deliveries; sanctioning expenditure on parts for stores.

Monitoring operational performance: collating and interpreting statistical measures of exchange performance; making reports on exchange performance to higher levels of management.

There are three points which we wish to note about the range of responsibilities identified from our field data. First, whilst monitoring exchange performance was undoubtedly the primary engineering management activity in which he was engaged, the role was essentially reactive and administrative. No corrective action to improve exchange performance was taken during our period of observation. According to the supervisor this was only necessary on the rare occasions when performance fell below nationally and regionally established targets.[2] In consequence he had little direct day-to-day involvement in maintenance work on the exchange floor. Essentially the technicians were allowed to get on with their work as long as performance targets were being met.

Second, many elements of the supervisor's role were delegated to the working supervisor (TOA). For example, the latter was responsible for checking staff attendance and various estate management duties and was the main source of technical advice on the exchange floor, especially for junior technicians. Third, whilst the supervisor was a regular visitor to the exchange floor, he relied upon routine visits to his office by the TOA to keep him informed of events (the TOA made at least two regular visits each day to his office, one in the morning to inform him of staff attendance and one in the late afternoon to deliver internal post). All this served to emphasise the remoteness and the essentially reactive and administrative nature of the role of the maintenance supervisor in the management of maintenance operations.

When this data is compared with that from our other Strowger exchanges, we found little evidence of any major deviations in the range of responsibilities carried out by other supervisors. In other words, there was a strong tendency towards the 'administrative supervisor' model noted in the case of Strowger A, with little or no direct day-to-day involvement in supervising work on the exchange floor. One of the most striking illustrations of this was the rarity of occasions upon which the supervisor would be called upon to give advice on working methods or technical guidance. This was of some interest, since in all cases the supervisors concerned had been promoted through the technician grades and had had considerable experience of Strowger maintenance. However, it was evident from our interview data (see below) that the significance of this expertise derived not so much from its frequent practical demonstration as from its perceived importance as the symbol of the supervisors' authority, both in their own minds and in the minds of their subordinates.

Nevertheless, we did find certain variations in supervision in our case-study exchanges. These were largely the result of differences in exchange size (expressed in terms of staffing levels[3]) and in the range of the other responsibilities allocated by area managements to the different supervisors. For example, the supervisor for Strowger A spent a large proportion of his time on activities related to that exchange, since sixteen of the twenty-six staff for which he was responsible were employed there. His other responsibilities comprised two small Strowger units. In contrast, the supervisor in Strowger B spent considerably less time on activities related to that exchange, since only three of the thirty-one staff he supervised were located there. Moreover, his other responsibilities covered four additional exchanges (Crossbar, TXE2 and TXE4) as well as specialist groups of staff such as those charged with maintaining private-branch exchanges in large companies in the area. One effect of the small size of certain Strowger units was therefore to reduce even further the direct day-to-day contact the supervisors had with their staff. This was particularly pronounced where exchanges were situated in relatively isolated locations and the supervisor's office was not located on-site. This was the case in Strowger B and in Conversions A and B, where visits to the exchange were rare and regular contact was maintained almost exclusively over the telephone. In contrast, the role of the supervisor in Conversion C was more like that found in Strowger A. His work related to this exchange accounted for the majority of his time, his office was located on-site, and he was a more regular visitor to the exchange floor.

To summarise this discussion of Strowger supervision, our data would suggest that the 'administrative manager' role involved a somewhat remote relationship to the day-to-day work of the exchange, in which the allocation of duties and the organisation of work was left largely to the discretion of the senior technicians. These findings are consistent with Child's assertion that where the skill and commitment of the workforce is high, there is less need for a strong supervisory emphasis and workgroups can be self-regulating (Child, 1984: 157). This is particularly true where performance targets are consistently being met. However, this picture does call into question the degree to which managerial control was being effectively exercised by the maintenance supervisors. In many ways their position was that of 'lost managers' (Child and Partridge, 1982). Their discretion was partly limited by national bureaucratic guidelines, while an increasing amount of the direct supervisory monitoring of exchange performance was being accomplished by technical devices, for example via the Measurement and Analysis Centres (MAC). In short, it would seem that the Strowger supervisors approached TXE4 modernisation from a position in which their existing role was already relatively marginal and remote. To what extent did the move from Strowger to TXE4 change this position?

5.3 From Strowger to TXE4: supervisors and the process of change

We noted in chapter 2 that the sub-strategies developed by management in Metro and Coast Areas to implement TXE4 modernisation did not involve any clear or consistent policy towards the role of the maintenance supervisor, either in the process of change or in the operational management of TXE4 exchanges once live. We also noted in chapter 3 that, in direct contrast to the situation for maintenance technicians, area management and the STE did not jointly establish criteria and procedures for the selection of supervisors to run the new TXE4 units. In Metro and Coast Areas, in fact, there was no formal selection process. In contrast, management in Town Area developed a clear and coherent policy on the selection and training of TXE4 supervisors and their role in the implementation of the new equipment. In this section we will examine the implications of these implementation sub-strategies for the role of the TXE4 supervisors in the conversion process. This will be followed by an analysis of their role in the routine operation of our two established TXE4 exchanges.

Coast Area – Conversions A and B

In Coast Area three Strowger exchanges were earmarked for TXE4 modernisation in the sub-area with which we were concerned. Two of these three were exchanges participating in our study (Conversion A and Conversion B). Just over a year prior to the changeover of Conversion A (the first of the three exchanges to be converted), local management decided that one of the three maintenance supervisors in the sub-area should assume responsibility for all three TXE4 conversion exchanges. The individual chosen was selected largely on ground of age. He was much younger than his two colleagues, who were aged fifty-eight and sixty-four and both nearing retirement.

139

Two months after being selected, he was sent on a two-week TXE4 appreciation course for supervisors but he did not assume responsibility for the staff in Conversion A until three months prior to changeover. Until that time he had had no direct involvement with the exchange, although he had had some previous contact with the staff in his capacity as co-ordinator of technician training in the sub-area. For a further two months after assuming responsibility for Conversion A he continued to retain a large number of other responsibilities, including the other two TXE4 conversion exchanges in the sub-area, two Strowger units plus the run down of the Strowger unit in Conversion A. It was only one month prior to changeover that he was relieved of all his other responsibilities and was able to devote himself full-time to the new exchange. During this time he occupied an office in the exchange building and was able to observe the preparation of transfer arrangements and ensure that on-site stores were sufficiently stocked with spares. As in all our conversion exchanges, however, the transfer arrangements and the final testing of the system by the maintenance technicians was under the direction of the BT installation supervisor, the clerk of works. To all intents and purposes the maintenance supervisor in Conversion A was a passive observer of these operations, occupying himself with trying to apply the knowledge gained from his appreciation course. This was mainly a matter of familiarising himself with the equipment layout and attempting some very elementary fault diagnosis. This experience demonstrated to all concerned the skill superiority of his technician staff.

The maintenance supervisor's position was made, in his own words, 'somewhat peculiar' by the decision to relieve him of his responsibility for Conversion A immediately following changeover. This decision was the direct result of a more general reorganisation of supervisory duties by area management. In this case organisational change clearly took precedence over technological change. After four months had elapsed and following a further re-distribution of supervisory duties under the continuing area reorganisation, he re-assumed supervisory responsibility for Conversion A – only to lose it again permanently seven months later. In the interim his immediate superiors (including a newly appointed Executive Engineer) had changed area policy towards TXE4 supervision, deciding against the idea of a semi-specialist supervisor responsible for all the TXE4s in the sub-area in favour of spreading the load of TXE4 responsibilities amongst a number of supervisors. The appointment of a new first-line supervisor for Conversion A eleven months after changeover meant that there had been four different supervisors for this exchange and four changes of supervisor during a fifteen-month period from four months before to eleven months after exchange conversion.

This was an extreme example, but it does serve to highlight once again the question of management continuity during the implementation of technological change. The implication of this lack of continuity for the organisation and control of work will be examined in chapter 6.

In Conversion B, by contrast, there was much greater continuity at first-line supervisory level, with the same maintenance supervisor retaining responsibility throughout the conversion process. However, despite this formal continuity, he spent little time in the new unit prior to conversion. During the run up to changeover he was based in an office several miles away and devoted most of his time to his numerous other duties, keeping in contact with his staff largely by telephone. Overall he was overshadowed by his immediate superior, who was the most important representative of maintenance management in the exchange in the weeks immediately prior to changeover. In fact the supervisor's lack of direct regular on-site contact with the maintenance staff in Conversion B during the conversion process was apparently not dissimilar in quantity and quality to his contact with them during his previous years as their Strowger supervisor.

Metro Area – Conversion C

Until a few months before the changeover of Conversion C, there had still been uncertainty about who was to become the supervisor for the new unit. In fact there had been some speculation amongst the technicians that a new supervisor would take over and be located off-site. In the event the previous incumbent Strowger supervisor remained in charge. He was aged fifty-eight and had worked for BT for thirty-six years, fourteen of which had been spent as a Strowger senior technician. He was a self-confessed 'Strowger man' (see chapter 3, note 5), who had been a first-line supervisor for seventeen years and in charge of Conversion C for just under four years. In addition to Conversion C he was also responsible for a smaller Strowger unit and a TXE2 exchange. Both were located a few miles from his office and accounted for four additional maintenance staff. He had attended two TXE4 appreciation courses just over a year prior to the conversion of the unit.

In the weeks and months immediately prior to changeover he had little direct involvement in the preparation of the new exchange. This was the result of what he believed to be the relatively high demands of keeping the old Strowger unit running and the fact that the day-to-day management of the conversion (and of his maintenance staff in the new exchange) was in the hands of the BT installation supervisor and an area-based Special Faults Investigation Unit (see above, pages 128–9). In

141

addition, shortly before changeover area management gave him a general responsibility for all exchange cleaning staff in the area. In the event he was a marginal figure in the run-up to conversion despite having his main office on-site. He made only infrequent visits to the floor of the new exchange and had no direct involvement or discussions with his staff about the way the work would be organised once the unit was operational. Symbolically, on the day of the changeover he observed the 'pulling of the wedges' on the ground floor of the exchange building where the old Strowger unit was located, rather than being together with his staff on the second floor where the new TXE4 unit was housed.

The situation did not appear to change after conversion. He was involved only peripherally in the organisation of TXE4 maintenance and clearly felt unable to make any meaningful interventions. Moreover he also seemed unsure about the nature of his role. One illustration of this was provided on a visit to the exchange about two months after changeover. On our arrival he was attempting to interpret exchange performance statistics in order to complete the required monthly report to area management. No one, he claimed, had told him how to fill out the new forms and he could not explain why particular figures were above the locally established targets (except by reference to the fact that the exchange had only just been brought into service). In the end he abandoned his attempt and the month's performance return was never completed. At the end of the following month the return was completed at his request by the maintenance technicians.

As in the cases of Conversions A and B, the maintenance supervisor in Conversion C experienced the modernisation of his exchange only at the periphery. In none of our three main conversion exchanges was the maintenance supervisor – the person with immediate line responsibility for control of the new unit and its performance – involved in the organisation and management of the maintenance effort of the staff in the first months of its initial operation. This experience in our three conversion exchanges was in some contrast to the experience in exchange TXE4 A, which will be discussed in the next section. Before we look at this, we will suggest some of the ways in which events at particular points in the implementation process provided critical junctures at which the shape of future supervisory roles was decided.

In neither Coast nor Metro Areas, where our three conversion exchanges were located, was there a clear management policy towards the role of the maintenance supervisor in the management of exchange conversion. This had two implications. First, no positive decisions were taken to select TXE4 supervisors based on an overall conception of their role or the abilities required to carry out this role. Second, during the installation, de-bugging, and changeover of the new units, the supervisors had no clear idea of the role they were to adopt. In the event they remained marginal to the process of change in the weeks and months leading up to changeover. In fact, since the day-to-day management of the new units and the maintenance staff at this time was under the control of BT installation supervisors, the maintenance supervisors spent most of their time on other duties, including the run down of their old Strowger units. It would of course have been possible for them to have given their new units a higher priority in advance of conversion and to have chosen to reduce the time spent on their other duties, but, in the absence of guidance to the contrary, none of them did this.

Next, the supervisors' courses they had attended had given them a broad technical appreciation of the new equipment, but little guidance on how to manage and organise its maintenance, particularly in the initial period of operation. Having only been involved in the conversion process on the periphery, it is not surprising that, when they assumed full formal responsibility for their new exchanges and their staff at changeover, they felt unable to influence the organisation of maintenance operations in any significant way. Their feeling of remoteness was compounded by a growing awareness of the skill superiority of the senior technical staff for whom they were responsible. As we will see below, this became even more apparent once the exchanges became live.

In summary, the maintenance supervisors in our conversion exchanges were unclear as to their role in exchange conversion, ill-prepared to manage the exchanges once operational and increasingly aware of the growing skill superiority of the maintenance technicians. In one case personnel and organisational changes overshadowed technological changes, with the result that there was a major break in first-line supervisory continuity.

What were the implications of the maintenance supervisors' experience of change for the outcomes of change? First, their relative lack of involvement in the period prior to changeover prevented them from gaining sufficient knowledge of the new system before they assumed responsibility for it and from appreciating or influencing the forms and methods of working which were being developed by senior maintenance staff during this time. Second, and following from this, they lacked the confidence and the experience to become involved in and influence maintenance operations in the initial operating period of the new system, which was a critical juncture during which new patterns of work organisation, methods of working and priorities in work tasks were established (see chapter 6). The implications of this peripheral experience of change is well captured in the following comment made by one of our supervisors a few days after changeover:

> TXE4 has, if anything, distanced me more from the floor. Being an old Strowger man, I've only got the sketchiest outline of the technology. I can't make a useful engineering contribution. If you've got troubles you feel much happier if you know what you're talking about. I am now purely a paper engineer. On Strowger I definitely influenced the actions taken by the TOs. I could look at a problem and say 'take that course of action' and I knew that if it was done properly it would work. Now I can't say that.

Town Area – TXE4 A

In Town Area a conscious decision was taken by area management to select a specialist TXE4 supervisor well in advance of exchange conversion. The individual who was selected had had six years' previous experience as a senior technician in Strowger maintenance and construction and seven years as a supervisor on Strowger and PABX maintenance. Consistent with area management's view that supervision of TXE4 maintenance required a system-trained specialist, the person selected was soon taken off all other supervisory duties and sent on the full programme of TXE4 technician training courses. He completed his formal training about nine months prior to the changeover of TXE4 A. By that time he had been in charge of its maintenance staff for over a year and had been directly involved as maintenance supervisor in the first Strowger–TXE4 conversion in the area. In the nine months leading up to the conversion of TXE4 A he spent much of his time in the new unit, sometimes even working alongside his maintenance staff and carrying out de-bugging and testing.

He was also involved in making the preparations for the changeover of the new unit. In particular he was able to ensure that the maintenance technicians seconded to the new exchange undertook a programme of work which would be of most use to them when they became responsible for the maintenance of the live exchange. In the weeks immediately before and after changeover he was able to encourage and support the senior technicians in making decisions about new forms of work organisation (see chapter 6). To a very limited extent he was also able to provide additional technical support for his staff in the initial operating period of the new exchange.

The experience of change for the first-line supervisor in exchange

TXE4 A was therefore one of intense and direct involvement. He provided management continuity for maintenance staff throughout debugging, changeover and initial operation and also a limited degree of technical support. This was all made possible by the policy of area management to train him as a specialist and, most importantly in the light of the experience in our other exchanges, to free him from all non-TXE4 responsibilities well in advance of changeover. At the time of our study, about one year after changeover, he had responsibility for three exchanges (two converted TXE4s and one Strowger in the process of conversion to TXE4) and sixteen staff (all maintenance staff in the above exchanges). Management in Town Area had developed a coherent and consistent implementation sub-strategy for TXE4 modernisation. At the heart of this sub-strategy lay a crucial role for the maintenance supervisor throughout the conversion process.

Metro Area – Conversion D

Our study also included one other Conversion exchange, Conversion D in Metro Area. The maintenance supervisor there had been fully trained for TXE4 maintenance whilst still a senior technician and then promoted to assume responsibility for Conversion D before he had had an opportunity to work on a live TXE4 exchange. Due to the arrangement of his responsibilities by area management it proved possible for him to have some involvement with the new unit and its maintenance staff in the three months prior to changeover. This was made easier by the location of his office and his other responsibilities (one Strowger and one Crossbar exchange) in the same building as the new TXE4 unit. His training proved to be of value, particularly during initial operation when there were major technical problems with the equipment. He felt he was in a good position to understand the nature of the technical problems, to discuss ways of overcoming them with his staff and even to make occasional contributions to the solving of particular faults. Almost a year later, however, his staff had become on his own admission much more confident and competent than him and the technical gap between them had widened considerably.

This supervisor saw his role largely in terms of a manager motivating a highly skilled technician workforce. His main concern was to monitor the performance of the exchange and to encourage his staff to improve its performance. In some ways he had adopted the role of what might be termed a system manager. It must be borne in mind, however, that this was not the result of area management strategy, neither had he received any specific training for TXE4 maintenance supervision. The role he had constructed was largely his own adaptation of the role of administrative supervisor. He had been helped in this by his temporary skill-parity with his technicians during installation, changeover and initial operation. The importance of both this and the previous case is that they illustrate the alternative design choices that were available in relation to the role of the TXE4 supervisor. We will return to this issue below. First we need to pursue our analysis of the implications of area management implementation sub-strategies by examining the role of TXE4 supervisors during the routine operation of our case-study exchanges.

5.4 From Strowger to TXE4: supervisors and the outcomes of change

In the previous section we examined the implications of area-management policies for the role of the TXE4 supervisor in the implementation of change. We now wish to follow through this analysis and consider the outcomes of change as evidenced by the data from our two established TXE4 exchanges, TXE4 A (twelve months after change-over) and Conversion A (nine months after changeover). We will be particularly concerned to contrast the implications of the implementation sub-strategy pursued by Town Area management (TXE4 A) with that adopted by Coast Area (Conversion A).

As a logical development of their approach to the selection of TXE4 supervisors and their role in implementation, Town Area took the view that the role of the TXE4 maintenance supervisor should be that of a 'system-trained specialist'. According to this view the supervisors required the same formal training as the maintenance technicians in order to carry out their responsibilities. They also needed to specialise in the management of TXE4 units rather than cover a spread of different exchange types. In consequence the supervisor in TXE4 A had attended the full programme of technician training courses, his responsibilities were exclusively concerned with TXE4 exchanges, and his span of control was relatively small, covering sixteen maintenance technicians of whom four were located in TXE4 A. Further, as we saw in the previous section, area management's policy meant that there was a continuity in supervision in all of their TXE4 exchanges throughout the implementation process and into routine operation.

In direct contrast and in keeping with their approach towards the selection of TXE4 supervisors and their role during implementation, there was no attempt by Coast Area management to redesign the role of the maintenance supervisor. There was a clear view that supervisors did not need full system training in order to exercise their responsibilities, and while the idea of a specialist supervisor had been considered, in the

146

event other organisational contingencies took priority. In consequence the supervisor in Conversion A had only been given a two-week TXE4 appreciation course. Further, as well as being in charge of Conversion A, he was also responsible for a wide range of other duties (four other exchanges of three different types) and had a large span of control covering twenty-four maintenance technicians, of whom only two were located in Conversion A. Moreover, as we saw in the previous section, Conversion A experienced considerable discontinuity in first-line supervision during the implementation process.

Aside from these points of contrast there were a number of strong similarities between the two supervisors' jobs. Both their offices were located off-site in buildings three or four miles from their respective exchanges. Both had fully trained, high quality staff and the general level of exchange performance were broadly similar. There were no areas in which either exchange was performing substantially below target or where there were particular staff problems. Both supervisors adopted a broadly participative approach to supervision, although in practice the form this took differed significantly, as we shall see. The size of both exchanges, measured in terms of the number of exchange connections, was similar and both units were situated on one floor of a dedicated exchange building. However, TXE4 A had a slightly larger staffing complement, reflecting not only the slightly greater number of lines and the higher level of traffic but also the fact that one extra senior maintenance technician had been drafted in temporarily to help with a new extension to the unit.

In examining the main work activities of the two TXE4 maintenance supervisors we will use the classification of four categories developed in connection with Strowger supervision, namely the management of contingencies, staff management, estate management, and the management of operational performance. Looking first at the management of contingencies (excluding, as before, staff contingencies), the supervisor of Conversion A left this totally to the senior technicians in the exchange. At first glance this appears to be in strong contrast to his opposite number in TXE4 A, who was regularly to be seen on the exchange floor talking over particular problems and contingencies with his staff, occasionally offering advice and even participating collaboratively in solving certain faults. However, as a result of observation and interviews with both the supervisor and his senior technicians, it became clear that his involvement made only a minor contribution to the management and solution of technical or other contingencies. Its primary function was to enable him to carry out two of his other main activities more effectively, namely staff management and the management of operational performance.

The content of staff management and estate management activities in our two established TXE4 exchanges was virtually identical to that found in our Strowger exchanges. As far as estate management was concerned, responsibility was devolved in both cases from the off-site supervisor to one senior technician. As for staff management, the range of activities (arranging leave, replacement staff, training courses, appraisements etc.) was common across all Strowger and TXE4 exchanges. Also, as we have already noted, both TXE4 supervisors adopted a broadly participative 'high trust' approach to staff management, encouraging their staff to achieve effective performance predominantly by self-discipline rather than discipline imposed by 'low trust' direct supervision (Fox, 1985).

However, the 'high trust' approach of the supervisor in TXE4 A involved him in frequent visits to the exchange, amounting to the equivalent of one and a half days per week. During his visits, he occasionally attached himself to individual technicians, partly to 'keep his hand in' but also to observe the technicians' performance. In this respect his regular attendance on the exchange floor enabled him to gain an extensive understanding of the progress of the staff under his formal control, putting him in a good position to counsel them on career development and to carry out their annual appraisements. He was also able to intervene to ensure that the staff did not over-specialise on particular pieces of equipment, a practice which he believed would prove to be detrimental to exchange performance (see chapter 6).

In contrast, the supervisor in Conversion A was on his own admission a rare visitor to the exchange (less than once a month), maintaining contact largely by telephone. When interviewed, he did express a strong wish to become more involved in the management of the exchange but felt prevented from doing so by his large number of other responsibilities. As a result, although he carried out the same staff management activities as his opposite number in TXE4 A, this was done in a remote fashion and without the accumulated first-hand knowledge which he would have been able to acquire if he had made more regular visits to the exchange. His style of supervision was thus more *laissez-faire* than that of his more actively involved counterpart in TXE4 A.

This contrast in the different styles of supervision is also directly relevant to a comparison of the supervisors' role in the management of operational performance. Although the supervisor in Conversion A regularly received and checked Measurement and Analysis Centre (MAC) and other figures on exchange performance, he did not use them to initiate corrective action or to try to improve performance. Since they were regularly on target, he apportioned only a small amount of his time to the exchange, devoting himself predominantly to 'more pressing' activities ensuing from his other responsibilities. In contrast, the supervisor in TXE4 A was regularly involved in discussions with his staff about improving operational performance and spent much more time on collating and evaluating a whole range of exchange performance data. His regular visits to the unit clearly put him in a good position to assess the operational performance of the exchange. However, in both cases the degree of supervisory involvement in the management of operational performance was perceived to be largely dependent on the extent to which national and area management targets were being met. As we have suggested above, this represented a reactive rather than pro-active approach to first-line supervisory management.

In summary, area management sub-strategies played an important role in shaping the process and outcomes of change for the supervisors in both TXE4 A and Conversion A. In neither of our exchanges, though, were supervisors given any training in how to manage TXE4 exchange operations and maintenance, or issued with guidelines or assistance in establishing which performance criteria were most important in the monitoring of exchange performance. Even in the case of TXE4 A – where the supervisor was system-trained, directly involved in the implementation of change and a regular visitor to the exchange floor – he was able to make only occasional contributions to the day-to-day management of the unit and the improvement of exchange performance. In this sense we would suggest that the role of the TXE4 supervisor in the operational management of exchange performance was in many respects at least as remote as that exercised by their Strowger counterparts. However, there is a sense in which some of our TXE4 supervisors were rendered more remote. This was a result of the new skill superiority of the TXE4 maintenance technicians and the fact that, symbolically at least, in our Strowger exchanges the supervisors' own experience as Strowger technicians continued to serve as an important source of authority *vis-à-vis* their staff. To explore this point further we need to examine the subjective perceptions of both supervisors and maintenance technicians.

5.5 Perceptions of the changing role of the maintenance supervisor

In our interviews with maintenance supervisors and senior technicians we attempted to discover whether there were any perceived differences in authority relationships between Strowger and TXE4. Both groups were asked whether they felt the supervisor had more, less or about the same say over the work of senior staff in TXE4 compared with Strowger. Seven out of the fifteen senior technicians who were asked this question felt that the supervisor had less say over their work and none said they had more. These perceptions were explored further by questions about differences in the way work was supervised under the two different exchange systems. Interestingly, the technicians in the smaller TXE4 units with off-site supervisors tended to say that there were no major differences, suggesting that they had retained the autonomy over the day-to-day control of their work which they had enjoyed as Strowger technicians. At the opposite extreme, those in exchanges with an on-site supervisor, where the Strowger division of labour had been highly sectionalised, said that the supervisor now had less control over the day-to-day running of the exchange.

The supervisors themselves saw the comparison between their activities in Strowger and TXE4 in different terms. Two of them argued strongly that the technicians' skill superiority meant that they had to rely much more on their staff. As one of them put it:

> Now I'm completely in the hands of my staff. All right, I'm lucky, sixty-six per cent of my staff I'm quite happy to be in their hands. You've got to rely on your staff even more so on TXE4 . . . In my situation I think a little learning can be a dangerous thing. If I try and assert my authority on something I know nothing about, we could get into real trouble.

The significance of this point is emphasised when we consider the rather different response of the system-trained first-line supervisor in TXE4 A. He believed that, whilst in Strowger his role had been mainly 'administrative', with TXE4 he was much more involved in a technical capacity:

> The difference is, on the Strowger load there was rarely an opportunity to join in and fault, because the faults generally were relatively simple and they didn't struggle on them. And so you'd go to an exchange and I suppose, if anything, waste the blokes' time. Perhaps in ten years time, when these lads are really familiar with the exchange – and already I'd say they were more familiar than I am – in ten years time they'll probably just clear the faults as a matter of course and my involvement may be a waste of time. Perhaps they already think that! But I think that's the main difference. With Strowger it was more of a paperwork and organisational exercise, whereas in TXE4 that element still exists, but there is more of a technical content as well.

The supervisor in TXE4 A was the only one who believed that the technical content of his work had increased in TXE4 and even he stressed that his staff were already technically more familiar with the system than himself. This point was underlined by the other system-trained supervisor in our sample (Conversion D). He stated unequivocally that, after eleven months of exchange operation, the 'technical gap' between himself and his staff was 'broadening'. Despite attending the full set of TXE4 technician courses, his lack of daily hands-on experience meant that his technical ability and understanding was declining – as he put it, 'after eleven months, technically I'm a wally'.

As a result this supervisor, together with one other who had some experience of supervising other common control systems (TXE2 and PABXs), did not see any major difference between supervising work in Strowger and TXE4, stressing that both systems required the same 'managerial' role of monitoring exchange performance. This is illustrated by the following statements from these two supervisors when asked to compare their role in both exchange types:

> Identical, no difference at all. There's nothing very much new about TXE4 is there? It's just a different sort of switching system, it requires a great deal less effort on routine maintenance than Strowger, but the practice, what you're actually doing, is the same . . . For any exchange the task is to see that the exchange operates as efficiently with the least cost during its normal working life, and seeing that effort is not wasted, and ensuring that the staffing is adequate but not too generous, seeing that sufficient effort is put into the areas that show well or badly on statistics . . .

> There's no difference really. I'm still the unit manager in just the same sense. When all's said and done, my job really is to monitor performance and correct as necessary.

This brings us to the question of the perceived attributes required to supervise TXE4 maintenance. For purposes of comparison a similar question was put to Strowger technicians about Strowger maintenance supervision. According to most Strowger technicians the two main attributes required of a Strowger supervisor were staff management abilities and an up-to-date understanding of the exchange system. The latter was perceived to be necessary to enable the supervisor to deal adequately with technical problems and to give advice (see table 5.1). The TXE4 technicians interviewed similarly emphasised staff management abilities but also stressed that the supervisor needed to place more trust in his staff because of their skill superiority. At the same time they felt that a supervisor should have sufficient understanding of the exchange system to appreciate the problems that the staff faced (see table 5.2).

Table 5.1 *Attributes of a 'good' Strowger supervisor*

Attributes	Citations (n=21)
Staff management abilities (leadership; communication skills; able to earn respect of staff; backs up staff)	14
Up-to-date technical understanding of Strowger in order to be able to deal with technical problems/give advice	10
Trust technical staff to get on with job	5
Other	4

Table 5.2 *Attributes of a 'good' TXE4 supervisor*

Attributes	Citations (n=15)
Staff management abilities (personal interest in staff; backs up staff; sorts out staff problems)	7
Trusts staff to get on with the job	6
Basic understanding of TXE4 and its differences from Strowger	5
Same training as technicians/experience as a TXE4 technician	4
Ability to provide technical back up	3

TXE4 technicians were divided in their perception of the degree of technical understanding required by their supervisor in order to carry out the job. Of the eighteen technicians asked, five indicated that they regarded some degree of technical understanding as essential, six indicated that it was not essential but an advantage, and another six suggested that it was not important. Data from our interviews with Strowger technicians revealed a slightly different emphasis, with seven regarding some degree of technical understanding as essential, three not essential but an advantage, and four not essential at all.

The TXE4 supervisors' own perceptions of the same question were similarly conflicting, but they all gave clear expression to the changes that they felt had taken place in their authority *vis-à-vis* their senior technicians. Their answers are particularly important for our evaluation of supervision and will therefore be cited at some length:

System-trained supervisor

I work on the principle that I never get someone to do something I can't do myself. I expect them to do it better than me, but I wouldn't ask any one to do anything I wouldn't have a go at. Now a lot of people say that's not necessary to be a supervisor, but I think the only way to get a good team spirit going is to at least have the respect of the blokes, or attempt to get it, and to be able to ask them sensible questions . . . I've been a TO . . . and it's quite frustrating when you've got a problem and they [the AEEs] dismiss it all the time because they don't want to understand it really.

Supervisor trained previously as TXE4 technician

It's nice to know what a Supervisory Processing Unit does, what a Marker does,[4] but my technical knowledge is dwindling all the time, obviously, because I haven't got hands-on. I could still tell you how a call goes through the exchange, but anyone who went on a one-week course would catch up to me in a week . . . When I first took this job it frightened the life out of me if blokes knew more than me, it took two management courses to knock that out of me . . . I think the biggest hang-up AEEs have got is trying to keep one step ahead of the blokes all the time, so they don't know more than you. That syndrome is fatal on this job, because they always will . . . I have to accept that I am not running the show, the TOs are . . . My role is largely to motivate staff. The manager of TXE4 is basically a man manager, my job is ninety-eight per cent man management.

Supervisors having attended TXE4 'appreciation' course

I said that I was willing to be system-trained, but I didn't think it was necessary, and my EE backed me up on that. Since then [BT management nationally] have said exactly the same thing . . . and as far as I'm concerned I agree one hundred per cent. I went on an introductory course for four weeks, with certain elements from other courses and a bit of management thrown in, but basically until I actually got into the exchange with some time to spare, I can't say that I really understood the system. I don't now, well not to any great depth, because it requires time working on it before you understand what you're doing.

I've always felt that the first-line supervisor should have a minimum of good working knowledge of what's on the floor, my views haven't changed. I feel it is necessary, [but] I have to live without it. I've got a very sketchy idea of what goes on . . ., but we will never get to the stage of the AEE really knowing the system. Until you've had about ten or fifteen years at it, you don't know, and by that time this system should be out, so we'll never be in that stage.

Supervisor with neither TXE4 system-training nor TXE4 'appreciation' course

My opinion on the AEE's job is that if you're an AEE you should be able to do the TOs' work, because if you're controlling staff and asking staff to do certain things, if they know you can do those things as well, they will respect you, plus you can also see the problems they come up against. I mean, I don't know what problems they come up against now. They tell me, but I don't know if it's true or not.

When the supervisors were asked directly about their TXE4 'appreciation' courses they felt they did not provide sufficient information about the management of exchange performance, and only gave a superficial view of the technical workings of the exchange system.

What is immediately apparent about the answers cited above is the connection drawn by the supervisors between technical training and knowledge on the one hand and the degree of supervisory authority and legitimacy on the other. Some argued that the ability to do the job oneself was an essential prerequisite for effective supervision and that therefore detailed system-training and hands-on experience were crucial for the exercise of supervisory authority. Others, in contrast, argued that such a view was 'fatal', since the staff would become ever more technically aware and competent than the supervisors. According to this view effective supervision should not be built on a high level of technical expertise but on the development and application of management skills and abilities. However, none of them (with the partial exception of the system-trained specialist supervisor from TXE4 A) argued that full technical training was required so that the supervisor could actively engage in maintenance work and give technical support and back-up to staff. The question which remained, then, was what kind of technical expertise was required by first-line maintenance supervisors in order to do their job effectively and maintain credibility with their staff. Significantly, this was an issue which was the subject of a major review by headquarters management during our research. We will conclude this chapter with a brief examination of developments in corporate views on the role of the TXE4 supervisor.

5.6 Changes in the corporate view of the role of the TXE4 supervisor

By the early 1980s a number of senior managers within BTHQ had come to the conclusion that while general concern had been expressed in many quarters about the problem of the exchange supervisor no one within the organisation had overall responsibility for resolving the issue. It was also felt that, at exchange level, TXE4 supervisors were still geared to the Strowger system of working and were therefore not responding adequately to the challenge of new exchange systems. Indeed, many maintenance supervisors were considered to have become so remote as to be little more than 'estate' managers, looking after accommodation matters and signing time-sheets. In the context of the new commercial paradigm and discussions about the management of digital exchange systems, the problem of supervision came to attract the increasingly close attention of corporate management.

During discussions with BTHQ personnel in 1981 and 1982, our attention was drawn to two conflicting strains of thought amongst senior managers about the supervision of semi- and fully electronic exchange systems. One view was that there was, or should be, a clear division between management functions and technical functions. From this perspective the solution to the problem of supervision lay in the enhancement of the existing working supervisor role and a corresponding redefinition of the role of the first-line supervisor. In each exchange one senior technician would thus become a 'super-technician' with many technical management responsibilities, while the first-line supervisor, now largely divorced from direct involvement in the day-to-day control of maintenance operations, would become a system manager responsible for the monitoring of overall exchange performance and for staff management. The other view was that there should be a merging of management and technical functions at first-line supervisory level, with supervisors fully system-trained and able to carry out a direct and pro-active role in controlling day-to-day maintenance operations and performance. The hiatus over the role of the AEE in TXE4 maintenance management was essentially resolved in 1983 in favour of a modified version of the system manager concept, that is without the up-graded 'super-technician'.

This brings us back to the question with which we concluded our previous section. What degree of technical competence and, more generally, what kind of training was required for the TXE4 supervisors to fulfil their new role? As we have seen, they had previously received a maximum of two relatively short system-appreciation courses. These had concentrated on giving a technical overview of how the exchange system worked without the practical hands-on training undergone by the technicians and with little or no exchange management content. Against this background it was not surprising that the majority of our TXE4 supervisors continued to operate in the same way as they had in their Strowger exchanges, although in most cases without the degree of authority that came from direct knowledge or experience of the work they were supervising. In 1983, however, BTHQ decided to change the training curriculum, replacing one technical system appreciation course with a course dedicated to the management of TXE4 maintenance. This new course was called appropriately 'TXE4 Exchange Management'.

While this represented a corporate decision against the full technical training of TXE4 supervisors, it did give them much more explicit guidance on how to manage TXE4 units and a detailed definition and explanation of their responsibilities and duties, including the use of maintenance aids, interpretation of different exchange performance indicators, staff organisation and working practices, and managing system modifications and extensions. This new course programme clearly recognised the skill superiority of the technician workforce, while at the same time suggesting that the authority of the supervisor rested not in the technical ability to carry out maintenance tasks, but in staff management and the management of operational performance. Whether this solution will lead to different outcomes to those observed in our case-study exchanges remains to be seen.[5]

5.7 Conclusion

In this chapter we have seen how the introduction of TXE4 threw the role of the maintenance supervisor into sharp relief. We concluded from an examination of national policy and our own empirical data that the role of the Strowger maintenance supervisor was essentially that of an administrative manager standing in a remote relationship to the day-to-day work of the exchange. While this was consistent with the view that where the skill, commitment and 'self-control' of the workgroup are high a strong degree of supervisory emphasis is not required, we also pointed

156

out that this role called into question the effectiveness of the management control exercised by the supervisors. In this respect we suggested that the Strowger supervisors were 'lost managers' (Child and Partridge, 1982), with a limited range of discretion and with many aspects of their role replaced by bureaucratic and technical control devices.

Our data on the role of TXE4 maintenance supervisors during the implementation process revealed that the majority were unclear as to their role in exchange conversion, ill-prepared to manage the exchanges once operational and increasingly aware of the skill superiority of the maintenance technicians. On the other hand data from our fourth conversion exchange and from exchange TXE4 A provided counter-examples where system-trained maintenance supervisors had assumed responsibility for their exchanges prior to changeover and had been more directly involved in the implementation process. These two examples showed the possibility of alternative design choices for the role of the TXE4 supervisor.

Our data on the role of supervisors in operational TXE4 exchanges confirmed the possibility of alternative role-models. In Conversion A the non-system-trained, non-specialist supervisor remained a marginal figure in the management of day-to-day maintenance operations. By way of contrast, the system-trained specialist supervisor in TXE4 A had a greater involvement in the day-to-day work of the exchange so that he was in a better position to assess its operational performance. However, his intervention to improve performance was limited in the main to reactive adjustments in instances where national or area management performance targets were not being met. Further, we found that in neither of the cases where the supervisors had had full system-training did this resolve the question of the skill superiority of the technicians.

Nevertheless, our data on perceptions of the changes in the supervisory role suggested that system-training did prove to be important, not so much because it enabled the supervisors to engage in more direct control of the technicians' work or to give them technical advice but because it provided them with an important aura of authority. They understood the work of the technicians in sufficient detail to be able to appreciate the problems they faced, to discuss various solutions to problems as they arose and occasionally to offer advice. This was precisely the function performed in Strowger exchanges by the supervisors' accumulated experience as Strowger maintenance technicians. In the cases where this knowledge was made redundant by the introduction of TXE4 and was not replaced by anything else, the remoteness and largely administrative nature of the supervisor's role became even more pronounced.

What factors, then, explain the different outcomes of change in relation to supervision? Clearly the initial absence of a detailed national management policy on the role of the TXE4 supervisor was crucial, since it meant that there was considerable design space for local managers to devise their own supervisory policies. However, the absence of any corporate guidelines also meant there was no outside impetus for area managements to seek solutions to the problem of supervision. In the event this problem was largely neglected in the implementation sub-strategies of area managements in both Coast and (particularly) Metro Areas. Even where some consideration was given to the supervisory role, as in Coast Area, this was still given a low priority in relation to other organisational considerations. The importance of area management implementation sub-strategies is underlined by the contrast with Town Area. Here, a conscious decision to make a system-trained specialist supervisor the lynch-pin of the implementation sub-strategy meant that area management was able to exert a positive influence on the role of the TXE4 supervisor and the wider implementation process.

The influence of the maintenance supervisors' trade union, the STE, on the implementation of the modernisation programme at both national and area level was minimal. The STE's official view, that decisions on the role and training of TXE4 supervisors were matters of managerial prerogative, meant that there was no official policy and no attempt to negotiate on this issue. We found no evidence to contradict this in our three telephone areas. The STE's influence on the role of the TXE4 supervisor was simply non-existent.

Turning to the supervisors themselves, their capacity to influence the outcomes of technological change rested largely on their existing strategic position within the organisation. We have already seen in chapter 3 how their position in the internal labour market owed more to the acceptance by corporate management of the maintenance of existing differentials over the POEU than on any occupational power that supervisory grades and their union were able to wield in the workplace. Similarly, our data on Strowger maintenance supervisors showed that their role was sufficiently remote and reactive to suggest that their capacity to influence change would be marginal. It was only in the cases of the system-trained supervisors that we found some evidence of supervisory influence on the outcomes of change, both in terms of their own role in the management of change and, as we will see in chapter 6, in terms of the organisation and control of work in their exchanges. This brings us to our final question. How far did the nature of the exchange systems influence the way supervisory roles were defined?

Our broad answer to this question is that the introduction of TXE4 tended to highlight existing problems of supervision rather than change the nature of supervisory activities in the way that the tasks of maintenance technicians were changed. The main factors influencing TXE4 supervision were, as we have seen, corporate management policy, local management implementation sub-strategies, and the relatively weak strategic position of supervisors compared to senior maintenance technicians – a point underlined by the absence of intervention by the STE at either national or telephone-area level.

However, there were two technical factors which acted as constraints or opportunities in the shaping of supervisory roles in our case-study exchanges: First, both Strowger and TXE4 were automated exchange systems and both had bolted-on or incorporated into them fault-monitoring devices which provided supervisors with a growing body of information about exchange performance. In fact, the semi-electronic TXE4 exchange system had a greater inherent capacity than Strowger for allowing automated monitoring and interpretation of fault data, although specific software-controlled systems for the use of TXE4 maintenance supervisors were only introduced towards the end of our project.

Second, the nature of the Strowger exchange system, particularly its electro-mechanical technology, was such that it required substantial amounts of routine preventive maintenance. This feature of the exchange system enabled national, area and supervisory management to lay down in some detail the programme of activities to be carried out by the technicians over the course of a week or even year. The TXE4 exchange system, in contrast, did not need anywhere near as much routine preventive maintenance and the type and nature of TXE4 faults were much less predictable in their maintenance requirements than Strowger. These features of the TXE4 exchange systems constrained the extent to which supervisors could lay down programmes of work for their staff and suggested the need for a more flexible system of work organisation and, by implication, a different type of first-line supervisory role. This question takes us directly to the theme of our next chapter – the organisation and control of work at exchange level. Here we will see more clearly the influence of the two different exchange systems on the nature of supervisory management and the extent to which supervisors themselves were able to influence the new forms of work organisation which emerged during the implementation process.

6

Work organisation and the emergence of team autonomy

6.1 Introduction

In the previous two chapters we have examined changes in the work tasks and skills of maintenance technicians and changes in the role of maintenance supervisors. We argued that whilst some TXE4 work tasks had been de-skilled in the sense that the manual dexterities associated with Strowger maintenance were no longer required, there had been a clear up-skilling in the sense that many TXE4 work tasks required a qualitatively different degree of mental and diagnostic ability. The situation of the exchange supervisors was rather different. In the absence of management policies and trade union or workgroup pressure to redesign their role and re-train them for it, the introduction of TXE4 equipment served to highlight further the already remote relationship of supervisors to maintenance work on the exchange floor. In addition, the emerging skill superiority of the maintenance technicians served to undermine what the supervisors perceived as the traditional basis of their authority – their long personal experience and knowledge of the work they were supervising. Clearly these developments also had major implications for the organisation and control of work. Our concern in this chapter is to compare the forms of work organisation and job content in our case-study Strowger exchanges with the outcomes of change in our TXE4 exchanges and to examine how these outcomes emerged at critical junctures in the implementation process.

We also wish to pursue further our analysis of the influence of engineering systems on the outcomes of technological change. In the previous chapter we saw that the two exchange systems, which exerted a range of influences on the work tasks and skills of the technicians, were a less significant factor in shaping the role of the supervisors. However, job content and work organisation have been identified in previous research as areas in which technology, particularly automated technology, can be an important factor extending and constraining organisational choice. As

Gallie has argued in his comparative study of automation in British and French oil refineries:

> Broadly speaking, the argument that control functions are decentralised onto the work team seemed to us the most persuasive of the various propositions that have been put forward [by 'new working class' theorists such as Blauner and Mallet] about the transformation of the control systems with advanced automation . . . There were clear signs in both countries that automation is conducive to a certain degree of team autonomy. (Gallie, 1978: 220, 221)

Other writers such as Andrew Friedman (1977) have also identified a trend towards 'responsible autonomy' as opposed to more direct systems of management control. However, Friedman has argued that this applies only to highly skilled 'core' (as opposed to 'peripheral') workers and is normally the result of a management strategy to secure their allegiance to organisational objectives rather than a product of the independent influence of technology.

Friedman's distinction between core and peripheral workers is part of a wider debate concerning the possibility of increasing divisions between different occupational groups as a result of technological change. This question has not only been analysed by academics (such as Friedman, 1977; Thompson, 1983: chapters 5 and 7; Child, 1984: chapter 7; Clark *et al.*, 1984), but has generated much interest in trade union circles (see TUC, 1979; POEU, 1979: 82; Moore and Levie, 1985: 519–20) and amongst personnel and industrial relations managers (see Atkinson, 1984; Atkinson and Meager, 1986). In this context it has often been argued that new technologies will lead to and in some cases reinforce a segmented or dual internal labour market within work organisations, forming a split between an elite of highly skilled workers and a pool of semi- and unskilled workers with little opportunity for mobility between them (see on this Thompson, 1983: 134ff). This is contrasted with traditional internal labour markets, which typically have an incremental career structure progressing more or less automatically through a series of clearly defined stages.[1] As we will see, this was an important issue arising from TXE4 modernisation in our case-study exchanges.

We will begin this chapter by examining the division of labour and the control of work in our case-study Strowger exchanges. This will provide a benchmark from which to assess the changes resulting from the introduction of TXE4. Second, we will examine the emergence of new forms of work organisation during the installation and de-bugging of our TXE4 conversion exchanges. Third, we will examine the nature of job content and work organisation during the initial operation of the same exchanges. Finally, we will examine the outcomes of change in our two established TXE4 exchanges, looking at both the organisation and control of work and the occupational distribution of skill between senior and junior technicians. We will conclude by assessing how far the main organisational actors, management, trade unions and workgroups, shaped the outcomes of change, examining the factors which influenced the choices they made.

6.2 The organisation and control of work in Strowger exchanges

In this section we will examine the organisation and control of work in the case-study Strowger exchanges. This will be broken down into a number of distinct issues, including the overall division of labour between individual technicians, the method of work execution (whether individual or collaborative) and the detailed content of individual technicians' jobs. We will also examine the relative influence of the technicians and their supervisors on the day-to-day control of work. We start with a discussion of the organisation and control of work in Strowger A.

Strowger A

As we have seen in chapter 4, just under half the time worked by senior technicians on exchange system maintenance in our two Strowger exchanges was spent on preventive block routine tasks, while just over half was devoted to corrective tasks involving the identification, location, diagnosis and rectification of faults. In Strowger A all exchange system maintenance work was divided into five 'loads'. These covered all maintenance tasks on specific areas of equipment in geographically defined sections of the exchange. In addition there were three specialised maintenance duties (including special faults and private circuits). These five loads and three duties were each allocated to one senior technician. Our observation and interview data revealed that demarcation between these loads and duties was extremely rigid. There was no job rotation, indeed the idea was frowned upon by the technicians. The majority of the technicians had been responsible for the maintenance of the same area of exchange equipment for several years – the record was in fact twenty-three years.

Reflecting this rigid division of labour, none of the time spent by the five senior technicians on exchange system maintenance (and recorded in the daily diaries) was spent working collaboratively with other senior

162

Table 6.1 *Job content of technicians in Strowger A (% of time spent on particular activities)*

Work activities	Senior technicians							Junior technicians			
	1	2	3	4	5	6	7	8	9	10	11
Corrective maintenance											
Patrol/reported faults	8	10	22	38	29	24	0	3	5	10	49
Night routining	26	25	33	33	32	19	0	11	0	9	22
Preventive maintenance											
Block routines	36	42	18	25	34	0	0	53	42	0	24
Other exchange work											
(incl. specialised duties)	30	23	27	4	5	57	100	33	53	81	5

colleagues. However, seven of the nine junior technicians in the exchange were attached to seven of the eight senior technicians, both to help out with their work and to learn maintenance techniques and skills on-the-job. The remaining two junior technicians were responsible full-time for routine 'provision of service' work, essentially connecting and disconnecting customer lines. While these last two technicians were working under a highly formalised division of labour, the full extent and nature of the division of labour between the senior and junior technicians will become more apparent when we look at the content of their individual jobs.

The diary data allows us to present a detailed quantitative picture of the content of the jobs of the individual technicians surveyed over a period of four weeks (in this exchange, seven out of eight senior technicians participated and four out of seven junior technicians, see Appendix B). This data was supplemented by periods of observation of exchange maintenance work and interviews with senior and junior technicians and their supervisor. The job content of the senior technicians with exchange system maintenance loads (numbers 1 to 5) showed a varied mix of preventive and corrective activities. Where the technicians had specialist duties (numbers 6 and 7), the amount of exchange system maintenance was reduced and in one case completely eliminated.

Data on the job content of junior technicians engaged in exchange system maintenance activities showed two distinct patterns. First, in the two cases where junior technicians (numbers 8 and 9) were attached to

163

senior technicians with an exchange system maintenance load (numbers 3 and 5 respectively), their jobs comprised the more routine and mundane tasks, that is, block routines and 'other exchange work'. This arrangement clearly enabled the senior technicians to reduce the amount of less satisfying tasks in their load. In the two cases where the junior technicians were more experienced, their jobs were similar to those of their senior colleagues. In one case (number 10) a junior technician assisted with a specialised duty, while the other (number 11) regularly covered for absent senior technicians with exchange system maintenance loads. Interestingly, in this latter case the junior technician tended to deal with the less routine corrective maintenance activities rather than the more routine preventive tasks. Given a normal rate of absence due to sickness and holidays and the operation of a system of one scheduled day off for each senior technician every three weeks, this junior technician spent most of his days covering the exchange system maintenance loads of his senior colleagues.

How was this system of work organisation and allocation of jobs established and controlled? In fact, as we have already noted in previous chapters, it had been established by a previous maintenance supervisor several years before within the broad guidelines laid down nationally for block routine maintenance of Strowger units. Within this framework the individual technicians had a considerable degree of individual autonomy in the organisation and execution of their work activities on a daily and weekly basis. In the absence of major contingencies, technical problems with particular parts of the equipment or problems with a particular load, the supervisor and working supervisor (see above, pages 136–7) were content not to interfere with the work of their senior technicians and simply to receive daily verbal plus weekly and monthly written reports. These normally confirmed the generally satisfactory performance of the exchange and thus of each exchange load.

In summary, in Strowger A there was a rigid formal division of labour between individual senior technicians and, on the whole, between senior technicians and junior technicians. However, this latter division was not so rigid as to prevent the junior technicians doing a small amount of corrective maintenance and night routining, and in one case it was sufficiently flexible to allow a junior technician to cover the maintenance loads of senior technicians in their absence. Moreover, the remoteness of the exchange supervisor meant that the senior technicians enjoyed considerable individual autonomy in the day-to-day control of their work.

Table 6.2 *Job content of technicians in Strowger B (% of time spent on particular activities)*

Work activities	Senior technicians	
	1	2
Corrective maintenance:		
Patrol/reported faults	18	13
Night routining	35	32
Preventive maintenance:		
Block routines	17	22
Other exchange work	30	33

Strowger B

How did this pattern of work organisation compare with our small Strowger unit, Strowger B? In fact, here there was also a clear division of labour into what amounted to loads but these applied only to block routine maintenance. There was no formally established division of labour in relation to corrective maintenance tasks, and in practice the technicians moved flexibly across each other's loads where necessary. Interestingly, about sixteen per cent of the overall time recorded by the three senior technicians on exchange system maintenance was spent working collaboratively, compared with none in Strowger A. Based on our observation and interview data it appeared that this collaborative working was usually occasioned by the perceived advantage of having two pairs of hands to accomplish certain night routining tasks. In general, though, the technicians in this exchange, as in Strowger A, worked predominantly alone.

Table 6.2 shows the job content of two of the three senior technicians in Strowger B (data from the third technician was insufficient for inclusion). As in Strowger A, there was a varied mix of tasks in both loads, although the amount of block routine work was being run down prior to the planned modernisation of the exchange. There were no specialised duties (such as special faults) and no resident junior technicians in the unit, although one junior technician was employed to carry out routine provision of service work in Strowger B and in two other small local exchanges in the vicinity. In other words, the more mundane exchange maintenance tasks and 'other exchange work' (apart from provision of service work), which were allocated in Strowger A to junior technicians, were carried out in Strowger B by senior technicians.

How was this system of work organisation and allocation of jobs established and controlled? We saw in chapter 5 that the maintenance supervisor was located off-site some miles away and was an infrequent visitor to the exchange, although he was in daily contact by telephone. This being the case he left all aspects of the organisation and control of work completely in the hands of his team of technicians, two of whom he had known and trusted for many years. As he commented:

> I've got a very good team of TOs whom I can trust to get on with their work. They know what I want, we've worked together for years . . . I can let them get on with it . . . I don't run the sort of ship where I want every problem brought to me. I encourage them to try and work it out for themselves.

The technicians thus enjoyed a high degree of autonomy from their supervisor in organising and controlling their work. There was also evidence, however, of a less individual, more collective involvement on the part of the technicians in the organisation and execution of corrective maintenance tasks in the exchange.

Supplementary data on Strowger work organisation

Before we examine our data on the outcomes of change in our established TXE4 exchanges, it is important to relate our findings from Strowger A and B to evidence on the organisation and control of Strowger work in our four conversion exchanges and in our two TXE4 exchanges prior to conversion. This information is particularly important, since it provides the benchmark for the changes that resulted from the introduction of TXE4. Our evidence here is based almost entirely on retrospective interviews. Therefore it has not been subject to the same cross-checking and corroboration as our data on Strowger A and B. Nevertheless we were able to gain a good idea of the forms of work organisation and control in these exchanges to supplement that already presented.

In three out of the five exchanges (Conversions C and D and TXE4 A) the forms of work organisation and control appeared to have been very similar to those observed in Strowger A. That is, a rigid overall division of labour (incorporating junior technicians), combined with a predominantly individual execution of work, involving a high degree of individual autonomy in the day-to-day control of work but with responsibility for the overall distribution of duties resting with a first-line or working supervisor. In contrast, the form of work organisation and control in the smaller Conversions A and B appeared to have been more similar to that of Strowger B. In these exchanges there was a less rigid and largely informal division of labour between the senior technicians (mainly on preventive maintenance tasks), very little collaborative working and no involvement of junior technicians in exchange system maintenance activities. The day-to-day control of work was based on individual technician autonomy from the supervisor, and the senior technicians had a large degree of collective involvement in the overall organisation and control of work. The reasons for these differences will be discussed further below.

6.3 The emergence of team autonomy: installation and de-bugging

In this section we will examine the emergence of team autonomy as the basic principle of work organisation in all our TXE4 exchanges. We will concentrate particularly on the installation and de-bugging sub-stage of the implementation process. In general it is at this sub-stage in the introduction of new technology that workgroups have been found to exert the strongest influence on the outcomes of change (see Wilkinson, 1983).

Conversion C

We will start with Conversion C, as this represents perhaps the clearest example of a major change in the organisation of work from Strowger to TXE4. It will be recalled from chapter 5 that at the start of our period of study in this exchange around nine months prior to changeover there had been some doubt amongst the technicians as to who was to be the maintenance supervisor for the new unit. At this time they believed that it would not be their existing Strowger supervisor and that whoever the new supervisor might be, he would be located off-site. As it turned out, they were to be proved wrong on both counts. Nevertheless these perceptions were at the heart of a collective decision they made about eight months prior to changeover, that they themselves would have to take responsibility for deciding how the work was to be organised. In other words, the breathing space created by the delays in the appointment of the new supervisor coupled with the absence of any explicit area management policy towards the role of the TXE4 supervisor provided the technicians with the opportunity to decide informally on their own new form of work organisation. As one of them said in an interview around six months prior to changeover:

> We've decided [how the work will be organised] between the
> three of us. There's no way the governor here at the moment
> would allow us to do that, but we have heard more than
> strongly that he is going. So we've decided that we have got to
> try and organise this place before a new governor comes and
> tells us what we are going to do . . . We thought why not try
> and organise it between the three of us rather than wait and
> see what happens.

From what they already knew about TXE4, the technicians were
convinced that work could not be organised in the way to which they had
been accustomed in their Strowger unit, where a formal load system had
been in operation for as long as any of them could remember. As one of
them commented:

> I can't see the sections [i.e. load system] working. I spoke to Z
> [one of the other technicians in the unit] about this. We've got
> to completely change our attitude and he agreed . . . We'll be
> working more in pairs.

This view had been shaped by a number of factors, in particular the
experience of faulting during formal training courses (where they had
been encouraged to work in pairs), by observation of TXE4 maintenance
in other exchanges during periods of post-course experience and
informal discussions with other senior technicians in their own telephone
area.

Essentially, the idea they adopted was to have a flexible arrangement
in which two of them would work together faulting the exchange system
(patrol/reported faults and some night routiner faults), while the third
would take responsibility for all other duties including dormant fault
checks, routines on remaining Strowger-type equipment and other
exchange work such as special faults, coin and fee checks, and so on. The
plan was to rotate responsibilities once every three or four weeks so that
everyone would have regular experience of exchange system maintenance.

In the next section we will examine how far this planned form of work
organisation was put into practice during the initial operation of Conversion C. What the foregoing serves to illustrate, however, is a phenomenon also observed in our two other conversion exchanges, namely the
attempt by senior technician workgroups to make decisions autonomously
from the exchange supervisor about how the work in the new exchange
was to be organised.

168

Conversions A, B and D

How far was Conversion C typical of our other TXE4 exchanges? In fact some form of team autonomy emerged prior to changeover in all the other units for which we have data (Conversions A, B and D and exchange TXE4 A). However, two important points should be noted in this connection. First, unlike Conversions A, B and C, the supervisors in Conversion D and TXE4 A were both fully trained technically on TXE4 and much more directly involved in the conversion of their new units prior to changeover. In other words, although team autonomy was still crucial to the basic organisation of work in these two units, it was an outcome of change not only determined informally and autonomously by the workgroup but also with the encouragement of the maintenance supervisors. Nevertheless, the fact that team autonomy still emerged as the basic principle of work organisation in these two units suggests that the reasons for its emergence cannot be simply explained in terms of the role of the supervisor in exchange conversion or the skill superiority of the technicians over their supervisors. The main reasons, as we will argue below, must be located elsewhere.

A second point of divergence between our sample of TXE4 units lies in the extent to which team autonomy was a new development. In Conversions C and D and in TXE4 (units of between 12,000 and 15,000 exchange connections), it contrasted strongly with the previous sectionalisation of Strowger duties into rigid maintenance loads with virtually no collaborative working. However, in Conversions A and B (units of 9,000 and 11,000 connections) team autonomy was largely a continuation of the previous practice under Strowger. The only difference the technicians expected to find in practice (as reported to us in interviews prior to conversion) was a greater degree of collaborative working on TXE4 maintenance. Interestingly, they believed this would be a temporary phenomenon resulting directly from their lack of experience. As we shall see the outcome turned out to be somewhat different.

6.4 The emergence of team autonomy: changeover and initial operation

In this section we will examine the forms of work organisation operating in our case-study exchanges about two to three months after changeover. We will first look at the exchanges (Conversions C and D) in which the emergence of team autonomy marked a significant shift from practice under Strowger. We will then look at the smaller exchanges (Conversions A and B) in which team autonomy was more an extension of the system that had already existed under Strowger.

169

Conversion C

As we saw in the previous section the three technicians in Conversion C had decided collectively prior to conversion that there would be a flexible system of work organisation in their new unit and job rotation once every three or four weeks. Under this system all of them would work regularly on the more challenging and satisfying non-routine exchange system maintenance tasks. This was based on two assumptions – that their supervisor would not try to impose an alternative system of work organisation, and that all three technicians would be fully trained and of roughly equal experience and confidence at changeover. As it turned out, they were correct in the first assumption but wrong in the second.

As we saw in chapter 5, even though the existing Strowger supervisor remained in post to take charge of the new exchange, the perceived skill superiority of the technicians and his own lack of knowledge of TXE4 meant that he had little inclination to attempt to influence what was happening on the exchange floor in the first few months of live operation. Even so, the technicians were convinced that he would attempt to impose some of his own ideas on them. On several occasions in the days and weeks immediately following changeover they told us during informal discussions that a staff meeting to decide on the organisation of work in the new unit was imminent. To their surprise, however, the meeting never took place. As one of the technicians commented of their supervisor: 'He gives the impression he doesn't want to get involved. Everything is down to us, whereas in Strowger he seemed to want to be in charge.'

Given this lack of involvement on the part of the supervisor, it might have been thought that the technicians would have had no difficulty in instituting their previously discussed plans for the organisation of work. However, as we saw in chapters 3 and 4, the acquisition of new skills in this exchange was handicapped by delays in the formal training programme, inadequate post-course experience and (four weeks prior to changeover) the withdrawal of the technician who had undertaken the most courses. The upshot was that on the day when the new exchange opened two of the technicians had only attended three of the five formal training courses and the third had only attended one course and had no direct experience of TXE4 maintenance at all.

As we noted in chapter 4, area management was well aware of these problems and drafted in a more experienced technician to see the resident staff through the first ten days following changeover. It was in this period that the resident technicians, together with their more experienced colleague, changed their long-worked-out plans and devised a new form of work organisation which took account of their relative degrees of inexperience. First, it was agreed by the team that the newly recruited colleague with no experience of TXE4 maintenance could not be allowed to carry out maintenance tasks on the exchange system proper. As we saw in chapter 4, the nature of TXE4 system architecture constrained the extent to which new skills could be acquired incrementally through hands-on experience in a live exchange. This technician was therefore allocated semi-permanent responsibility for all other exchange work, including the special faults duty. The planned principle of job rotation was therefore shelved. Where possible, though, it was decided that the inexperienced technician would look over the shoulder of his other two colleagues pending his attendance at formal TXE4 training courses.

The other two resident technicians took over joint responsibility for all exchange maintenance tasks. However, again reflecting their incomplete formal training and lack of confidence, they decided to specialise where possible on particular sections of the exchange equipment rather than work collaboratively. In some respects this was a return to the kind of division of labour which had operated under Strowger. However, this sectionalisation was different from the Strowger load system in a number of important ways. First, it was evolved informally as a temporary solution to a transitional problem of lack of confidence and expertise. Second, exchange system maintenance on one section of TXE4 equipment still required overall system awareness since the diagnosis and rectification of some faults required both system knowledge and the need to trace fault symptoms in one part of the exchange to causes in different parts of the exchange. Third, despite specialisation, the technicians did adopt a comparatively flexible approach which meant that they spent some time working together to solve particularly complex faults.

We are able to give some quantitative expression to the division of labour in Conversion C from diary data collected during the second month of initial operation. As table 6.3 shows, during this period the two technicians working on exchange system maintenance (numbers 1 and 2) spent the majority of their time on patrol/reported faults and virtually no time at all on routine dormant fault checks. In contrast, the newly recruited technician (number 3) spent the vast majority of his time on other exchange work. Despite their decision to specialise on particular sections of equipment, technicians 1 and 2 did tend to work together much more than was evident in our Strowger exchanges. In fact, twenty per cent of time recorded on exchange system maintenance in Conversion C was spent in collaborative team-working (according to the technicians, there had been virtually no collaborative working in Conversion C when it had been a Strowger unit). More importantly, perhaps, in

Table 6.3 *Job content of senior technicians in four TXE4 exchanges (initial operation) (% of time spent on particular activities)*

Work activities	Conversion A		Conversion B			Conversion C			Conversion D		
	1	2	1	2	3	1	2	3	1	2	3
Corrective maintenance:											
Patrol/reported faults	65	57	88	69	58	68	76	0	62	52	31
Night routining	8	14	0	0	12	13	21	16	4	33	27
Preventive maintenance:											
Dormant faults	6	9	0	2	7	1	0	0	0	0	0
Other exchange work	21	20	12	29	23	18	3	84	34	15	42

contrast to our small Strowger unit (Strowger B) collaborative working in Conversion C was concentrated on patrol/reported faults rather than night-routining tasks.

To summarise thus far: during the initial operation of Conversion C the form of work organisation adopted continued to be decided collectively by the senior technicians autonomously from their supervisor. The form of work organisation they chose involved a significant amount of collaborative or team-working on corrective maintenance tasks. Both of these facts were in contrast to the time when Conversion C had been a Strowger unit. However, the allocation of work tasks within the team of technicians turned out to be more sectionalised and inflexible than planned prior to live operation, with one technician working semi-permanently on other exchange work and the other two specialising on particular pieces of the exchange equipment rather than working across the whole of the exchange system. This can largely be explained by the lack of formal training and post-course experience of the technicians, their lack of confidence and, in one case, lack of basic system-knowledge.

Conversion D

The initial operation of Conversion D was dominated by serious technical problems with the equipment. This was in contrast to Conversion C where the de-bugging of the equipment had been thorough and highly effective. In the period immediately following the changeover of Conversion D work had been particularly hectic, with the three resident senior technicians struggling to keep down the length of the fault print-out. These difficulties were compounded by the same problem as in Conversion C – the relative inexperience of the staff. Only one of the three technicians had attended the full five training courses, although all had spent at least three months in live TXE4 exchanges gaining post-course experience. Against this background area management decided, as in the case of Conversion C, to draft in a more experienced TXE4 technician from another unit whilst the technical difficulties persisted.

Although, as we saw in chapter 5, the supervisor of Conversion D was fully trained on TXE4, it was largely at the instigation of the maintenance technicians that a new pattern of work organisation emerged in the weeks following conversion. Two of the resident technicians and their experienced colleague from a nearby unit took collective responsibility for all exchange system maintenance tasks and adopted a flexible pattern of working, although the two resident technicians tended to specialise on specific parts of the exchange equipment in order to build up their expertise and confidence. The fourth technician, who did not participate in our study, dealt with all other exchange work (including special faults). According to the supervisor and the other technicians, this man, though fully trained for TXE4, felt unsuited to working under pressure and unable to cope with the more flexible and complex demands of TXE4 system maintenance. He was therefore allowed to carry out the more routine and less complex tasks.[2]

Again we are able to supplement these findings with quantitative diary data collected around two months after changeover. As table 6.3 indicates, the job content of the three technicians engaged in exchange system maintenance varied far more than in Conversion C. First, the more experienced TXE4 technician from a nearby unit (number 1) spent the majority of his time on patrol/reported faults, mainly trouble-shooting on the most complex faults. The rest of his time was spent on other exchange work. In contrast, the least experienced technician in terms of formal training courses (number 3) spent under a third of his time on patrol/reported faults, with which he felt far from confident, and over forty per cent of his time on other exchange work. Both technicians 2 and 3 spent a significant amount of time on night routiner faults, where technical problems were producing a high level of print-out. In fact twenty-nine per cent of overall time recorded by the technicians on night-routining was spent working collaboratively, a figure far higher than in any of our other TXE4 exchanges during either initial or routine operation. In contrast only seven per cent of time on patrol/reported faults was recorded working collaboratively, a figure far lower than in our other TXE4 exchanges. This reflected the high level of faults occurring in the exchange and the fact that, despite having a complement of three technicians working on exchange system maintenance, they all had to work individually to keep abreast of problems as they arose.

In summary, the forms of work organisation and control practised in Conversions C and D during initial operation were in strong contrast to the time when they had been Strowger units. The overall form of work organisation was now decided collectively by the technicians autono-mously from their supervisor. The actual system of work organisation chosen by them involved a more flexible and team-oriented approach to the division of labour and work execution. However, technicians in both units did tend to specialise at this time on familiar pieces of equipment in order to gain experience and confidence. Also the least confident senior technician in both exchanges was excluded almost totally from exchange system maintenance and thereby confined to 'other exchange work'. The organisation of work during the period of initial operation was thus shaped significantly by the level of training, experience and confidence of the technicians gained prior to changeover and by the technical and operational condition of the exchange equipment, also influenced largely by events prior to changeover.

Conversions A and B

How far were these forms of work organisation and control in evidence during the period of initial operation in the two slightly smaller conversion exchanges? In fact the organisation of work in Conversions A and B was similar in a number of respects to that in Conversion C. First, in terms of job content patrol/reported faults predominated, with a very low level of night-routining and routine dormant fault checks. Second, decisions about the overall organisation of work and the day-to-day execution of work were taken collectively by the technicians with no involvement from their supervisor. Third, there were no major technical bugs in the equipment which might have required a temporary sectionalisation of duties or a particular set of routine equipment checks to be carried out. Hence they adopted a more team oriented and flexible division of labour and engaged in a higher level of collaborative working than in the case of Conversion D.

However, job content and work organisation in these two exchanges did show some differences to both Conversions C and D. In Conversion A both senior technicians had completed all their courses and were of roughly equal levels of experience and ability. They were therefore able to adopt a more fully fledged pattern of flexible team-working during initial operation. This is confirmed by the diary data collected about two months after changeover (see table 6.3). The division of labour was marked by a roughly equal split between the main sets of work tasks, with both technicians spending the major proportion of their time on patrol/reported faults. There was also a significant amount of collaborative working, with thirty-eight per cent of the time on patrol/reported faults and twenty-six per cent of the time on dormant fault checks spent working together. According to the technicians this reflected their lack of familiarity with many of the problems that were occurring and also the complexity of many of the faults. As one of them commented:

> Every fault is a new one . . . In-service faults are different
> from those before BIS [brought-into-service or changeover
> day] . . . You have to get used to not solving faults quickly.[3]

By way of contrast, in Conversion B there was a more discernible division of labour. In this exchange one of the technicians (designated officer-in-charge by his supervisor) was much more confident and experienced than his two other colleagues. He not only tended to assume responsibility for allocating work tasks and duties on a daily and weekly basis but also spent the overwhelming proportion of his time (eighty-eight per cent) trouble-shooting on the more complex and difficult patrol/reported faults (see table 6.3). Of the other two technicians, one (number 3) was not fully trained but had been seconded to the exchange to gain post-course experience. He was given almost all the night-routiner faults and dormant fault checks to carry out as well as a significant amount of other exchange work. However, he was competent and confident enough to be allocated a number of patrol/reported faults. The other resident senior technician carried out a range of duties, dominated by patrol/reported faults but also including nearly thirty per cent of his time on other exchange work. The amount of collaborative working on exchange system maintenance in Conversion B was twenty-five per cent, very similar to Conversion C (twenty-three per cent). The figure for Conversion A was significantly higher at thirty-eight per cent. The extent of the technicians' collective autonomy from supervision in Conversions A, B and C was summed up by a comment from the technician officer-in-charge in Conversion B, who observed that as long as the exchange was performing roughly to target they were left to run things as they wanted.

What are the general implications of these findings? First, we should note that all the exchanges had some form of team autonomy in the organisation, control and execution of work during initial operation. In no case was there a formal division of tasks into loads based on particular geographical areas of the equipment as in Strowger. In three of our four exchanges the maintenance supervisor was not involved in establishing the system of work organisation and in the fourth (where the supervisor was fully system-trained and had been directly involved in the conversion of the exchange prior to changeover) he participated in discussions on work organisation but in the end ratified the collective proposal of his team of senior technicians. The extent to which team autonomy and the lack of supervisory involvement was a new feature of work compared to Strowger depended to a large extent on the size of the old Strowger unit, measured in terms of number of staff and exchange connections. The smaller the Strowger unit the less likely it was that the general approach to TXE4 work organisation would be new. However, three aspects of job content and work organisation were uniformly new compared to Strowger – namely the predominance of patrol/reported faults over all other exchange system maintenance tasks, the relative absence of a rigid division of responsibilities between the technicians for routine preventive maintenance, and the significant amount of collaborative working. We shall see in the next section how far this was maintained during the routine operation stage.

However, there were also differences between our four conversion exchanges. For example, team autonomy did not always mean that all members of the team participated equally in decisions about job content and work organisation, nor that there was no division of labour between the technicians. While in Conversion A there was virtually no division of labour between the senior technicians, in all the other exchanges there was some degree of sectionalisation of duties. This was mainly for transitional reasons, such as the high level of bugs in the new equipment and the uneven levels of formal training, post-course experience and confidence of individual technicians.

6.5 The emergence of team autonomy: routine operation

The final part of our examination of job content and work organisation relates to the stage of routine operation in Conversion A and TXE4 A. Analysis of data from Conversion A will be particularly important, as it will allow us to assess the nature of changes in job content and work organisation between the period of initial operation (two months after changeover) and a period in which the exchange and the staff had settled down into a more routine pattern of working (around nine months after changeover). The second established exchange, TXE4 A, was not studied as a conversion unit. However, it is also particularly interesting because of its size (it was a slightly larger exchange than Conversion A with 12,000 lines and a staffing complement of three rather than two senior technicians) and because it was the most mature established TXE4 exchange in our sample, having been in operation for twelve months. Since only two exchanges are being considered and since our findings for each were broadly similar, we will discuss them together.

In neither exchange was there a formal division of labour between the senior technicians, who saw their responsibilities in terms of the whole exchange system rather than a particular area or piece of equipment. In other words, the team approach to the overall organisation and control of maintenance tasks, which we found to a greater or lesser extent in the period of initial operation, was also in evidence in the routine operation of both Conversion A and TXE4 A. In exchange TXE4 A, though, there was an informal degree of specialisation in that individual technicians regarded themselves as especially skilled and experienced on particular sections of equipment. To this extent, when a fault arose on a particular section, the specialist tended spontaneously to assume responsibility for it. From interviews with the technicians and their supervisor we gathered that the specialist skills had been developed by the technicians during the training courses and post-course experience, when they had happened

Table 6.4 *Job content of senior technicians in exchanges TXE4 A and Conversion A (routine operation) (% of time spent on particular activities)*

Work activities	TXE4 A senior technicians		Conversion A senior technicians	
	1	2	1	2
Corrective maintenance:				
Patrol/reported faults	40	34	40	42
Night routining	5	10	9	4
Preventive maintenance:				
Dormant faults	5	6	14	10
Other exchange work	50	50	37	44

(almost by chance) to specialise on or get on particularly well with, these pieces of equipment. However, it should be stressed that this was nowhere near as pronounced as in Conversions B, C and D during the period of initial operation, where specialisation had come about either through lack of experience and confidence or because of particularly high levels of faults. In fact the existence of a degree of specialisation in TXE4 A did lead to the only case during our research where a TXE4 supervisor intervened in and altered the organisation of work of his senior technicians, insisting that if it became too rigid it would cause problems when the specialist was absent from the exchange.

If we turn to our quantitative data on job content and work organisation in these two units, then we find considerable similarities between the relative proportions of time spent by the senior technicians on different types of work activity (see table 6.4). For all four technicians studied, patrol/reported faults constituted a large proportion of exchange system maintenance activities, whereas the amount of night routining tasks and dormant fault checks was comparatively small. This was in strong contrast to the situation we found in our two Strowger units. For all four technicians, too, the proportion of 'other exchange work' was higher than for their comparable colleagues in the Strowger units.

If we compare the job content of the senior technicians in Conversion A with that during their initial operation of the same exchange, what is most striking is the reduction in the proportion of overall time devoted to patrol/reported faults (down from sixty-five per cent and fifty-seven per cent to forty per cent and forty-two per cent respectively) and the corresponding increase in the time devoted to other exchange work (up from twenty-one per cent and twenty per cent to thirty-seven per cent and forty-four per cent respectively). As the exchanges settled down, the level of patrol/reported faults dropped and the technicians became more experienced, reducing the amount of time needed to clear faults. This allowed more time to be spent on other tasks, including dormant fault checks and other exchange work. We shall examine the implications of this data in more detail below.

One particular feature of work organisation and job content that we noted during the initial operation of our TXE4 units was the tendency for senior technicians to execute more tasks, particularly patrol/reported faults, collaboratively. In this connection we raised the question of whether this was purely a part of the process of skill acquisition and whether once fully trained, more confident and experienced the technicians would revert to the pattern of Strowger maintenance, with its strong emphasis on individual autonomy and working. Our data from Conversion A is particularly useful in allowing us to test this proposition as we have data on collaborative working from both initial and routine operation. In fact this shows that, while thirty-two per cent of time recorded on exchange system maintenance during initial operation involved collaborative working, the equivalent figure for routine operation was fifty-two per cent. Thus collaborative working increased significantly as the technicians became more experienced and the new equipment settled down. Additional support for this conclusion is provided by exchange TXE4 A, where the equivalent figure was forty per cent, a figure far higher than for the initial operation of any of our four conversion exchanges.

We would suggest two main explanations for the tendency of senior technicians to increase the amount of collaborative working as their exchanges settled down into routine operation. First, since there was an overall reduction in the volume of patrol/reported faults, when such faults did occur more than one of the technicians wanted to become involved. In other words, it was not that the fault necessarily required the effort and skills of more than one technician, rather it was because the technicians had fewer patrol/reported faults to go round that they tended to work more collaboratively. In fact we observed and were also told of occasions when an alarm or sudden burst of fault print-out on the teleprinter caused two or more technicians to leave their more mundane tasks in order to become involved in locating and diagnosing the new system fault.

However, there is also a second possible explanation. It could be

Table 6.5 *Collaborative working preferences (senior technicians only)*

Preferences	Strowger (n=19)	TXE4 (n=13)
Prefer to work alone	10	1
Prefer to work with others	3	7
No preference	5	5
Don't know	1	0

argued that once the main bugs in the equipment had been ironed out the faults that occurred were likely to be of sufficient complexity (and sometimes of sufficient threat to the quality of customer service) that working in pairs was both more advisable and more effective. Some support for this view can be gleaned from the data already presented in chapter 4, which suggested that there was a significant cluster of highly complex faults in all the TXE4 exchanges for which we have data, faults which were certainly much more complex than patrol/reported faults in our Strowger exchanges. We would argue that there is evidence to support both these explanations for increased collaborative working and that in particular cases one of the explanations may be more valid than the other. It is interesting to note, however, that over half the senior Strowger technicians interviewed preferred to work alone, while only one out of thirteen TXE4 technicians interviewed expressed such a preference (see table 6.5).

If we now turn to the question of who determined the overall system of work organisation in our two exchanges and who was responsible for the daily and weekly allocation of work tasks, the conclusion is that both were largely in the hands of the technician team. We have already noted in chapter 5 that the exchange supervisors in TXE4 A and Conversion A exerted relatively little influence over the organisation and execution of work on a day-to-day basis. As far as Conversion A was concerned, this was a continuation of the autonomy developed by the technicians during changeover and initial operation. However, in exchange TXE4 A the supervisor had been system trained on TXE4 maintenance and encouraged by his local management to take an active part in the process of exchange conversion. As a result he had participated in discussions with the technicians during the changeover period about the general system of work organisation which would operate in the new unit. Nevertheless, once the exchange had settled down, our observational data and interviews with both the supervisor and his staff confirmed that he was not involved in the daily or weekly supervision of the work of his senior technicians to any greater extent than his counterpart in Conversion A, who had neither been system-trained nor involved directly in the process of change. In other words, the autonomy of the senior maintenance technicians *vis-à-vis* their supervisors, which we noted during the initial operation of our four conversion exchanges, appeared to be very much a feature of routine operation too, irrespective of the personal involvement or technical expertise of the supervisor.

6.6 Perceptions of changes in the organisation and control of work

Our findings on the contrasts between work organisation in Strowger and TXE4 exchanges were partly based on and certainly strongly supported by the perceptions of supervisors and technicians. First and foremost, they all stressed consistently the need for team autonomy and flexibility in the organisation of work. The contrast between the two exchange types was particularly strong for those who had previously worked in medium and large Strowger units. Technicians and supervisors alike point to the dangers that sectionalisation of work duties and specialisation of expertise might have for the quality of service provided by TXE4 exchanges, particularly for the efficient functioning of the 'central brain' of the exchange, the Main Control Unit (MCU). As one senior technician commented:

> I still think the main difference is you've got to adopt a more flexible attitude on TXE4 as regards day-to-day stuff. You've got to really know where the trouble is on common control, whereas on Strowger you can be rigid, 'that's X's job, it's in his section'. In TXE4 you can't just say . . . 'I'm the MCU man', you've got to be reasonably good at everything, you can't afford specialisms or specialists in a TXE4. If you've got specialists you can lead yourself into trouble as regards staffing, because if your MCU man is [absent] and there's two MCUs out, that's the exchange effectively cut out.

The need for flexibility underlined in the above comment did not necessarily imply the rejection of any kind of specialisation but more the rejection of too great a sectionalisation of work or specialisation of knowledge. This is illustrated by the following response of one of the system-trained TXE4 supervisors:

> *NTRG:* Can you work a load system on TXE4?
> *Supervisor:* I don't think so. Well you could say to somebody perhaps, 'do a load system for dormant fault routines', but you

can't do a load system [for the rest], not in my view, anyway, because you lose expertise. [However] the lads do tend to adopt certain areas which they prefer to fault on. X for example had worked more on cyclic stores, so we regard him as the cyclic store man, Y is the MCU man and Z is the network man.[4] Now that's only really because when they did the commissioning, those were the areas that they commissioned.

Interestingly the origin of this informal specialisation was traced by the supervisor to the experience of the technicians during the de-bugging of the equipment during which time they were allocated to particular sections of equipment. We found such specialisation in a number of units, also during initial operation. The reaction of this particular supervisor was not to stop it altogether since specialist knowledge was clearly a strength within the technician team. However, he stressed the need to ensure that it did not become too rigid:

The manager's stuck with this problem, and if . . . the guy who does MCUs goes on two weeks' holiday, what's going to happen to that? . . . I've got to keep the figures good by playing to my strengths, but also make sure that the blokes don't get so out of touch with another bit of equipment, come the day, they haven't got a clue what anybody else is doing.

These quotations illustrate the influence of TXE4 common control exchange architecture on the division of labour in our TXE4 exchanges. However, the importance of exchange technology for both job content and work organisation was also underlined in our interviews. Whereas Strowger's mechanical technology tended to require a large amount of routine preventive maintenance leading to regular and predictable patterns of working, so the semi-electronic TXE4 technology required less routine preventive maintenance, with patterns of work and work tasks which were also less predictable and routine. This is captured in the following comment from a senior technician:

The mere fact that the work [in Strowger] was divided into routine tasks, that isn't done in TXE4 . . . [Routine work in Strowger] was regarded with considerable importance by management and they expected to see that it was completed . . . There is some set routine work [in TXE4], but one doesn't have the week or the month organised quite the same way. There is a greater flexibility in what one does.

6.7 The division of labour between senior and junior technicians

So far we have neglected one aspect of job content and work organisation which featured prominently in our Strowger exchanges, namely the division of labour between senior and junior technicians. It will be recalled that in all our medium and large Strowger units we found junior technicians attached to the maintenance loads of senior technicians carrying out a mixture of exchange system maintenance tasks, normally the more routine tasks such as block routines plus other exchange work. In the case of Strowger A, one of the more experienced junior technicians covered regularly for absent senior colleagues and in practice the content of his job was very similar to that of a senior technician. At the other extreme we found that in all Strowger exchanges at least one junior technician carried out no exchange system maintenance tasks at all and was confined to provision of service work at the periphery of the exchange system.

In short, the tasks carried out by junior technicians in our Strowger units were extremely variable. However, the expectation and the practice was that as they became more experienced they would prepare themselves for promotion to the senior technician grade by learning practical exchange maintenance skills and techniques on the job working alongside their senior colleagues. There was, therefore, a strong connection between the division of labour, the acquisition of skills and a career structure which envisaged a gradual but clear progression from junior to senior grade. How did this situation in our Strowger exchanges compare with the experience in TXE4?

As we saw in chapter 3, decisions made at area level, often as a result of joint management–union agreements, meant that no junior technician was selected to re-train for TXE4 maintenance in any of our three telephone areas. Given the basic 'systems' knowledge required, this effectively prevented junior technicians from engaging in TXE4 maintenance. The clearest point of contrast between the job content of junior technicians in our Strowger and TXE4 exchanges was therefore that in none of our six TXE4 units was any junior technician engaged in any exchange system maintenance tasks.

For the junior technician whose duties covered both Conversions A and B, this represented no change, as he had always been confined to provision of service work only. However, for those who had previously worked in medium or larger Strowger units, this represented an important change, not just in job content but also in career structure and career expectations. This can best be illustrated by the example of two junior technicians in Conversion C. The contrast for them was heightened by

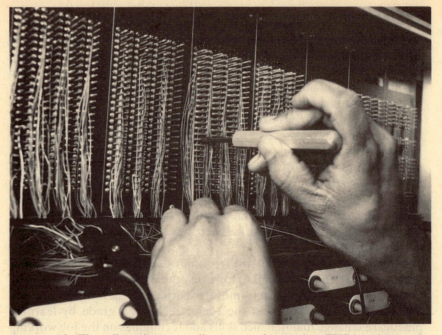

13. Threading wires on cyclic-store equipment in a TXE4 exchange

the fact that in the three months prior to changeover, when their senior colleagues had been either on training courses or seconded to the new unit, they had effectively been working as senior technicians with a full range of Strowger maintenance duties. However, when they moved into the new TXE4 exchange on the day it was brought into service, they found themselves suddenly restricted to provision of service and other routine work such as threading wires on cyclic-store equipment (see photograph 13). In the weeks and months following changeover, they had little or no working contact with their senior colleagues. When we returned to the unit for final interviews about eight months after changeover, neither of them had had any experience of TXE4 exchange system maintenance and neither of them expected to in the near future.

For the more ambitious of the two junior technicians this major change in the pattern of working and in career expectations was exacerbated when all the staff in the unit were informed by area management that the number of exchange maintenance staff in the area would be drastically reduced over the following decade as a result of System X modernisation. Just a few weeks after this he resigned from BT, despite the attempts of his supervisor to keep what he regarded as a very bright and

184

competent technician. The junior technician had intimated to us in an interview just prior to his resignation that he saw no career prospects in exchange maintenance and that exchange modernisation appeared to have down-graded the work of junior technicians. This view was supported by the two other junior technicians we interviewed working in TXE4 exchanges. Not surprisingly, of all the supervisory and technician staff in our study it was the junior technicians who were most dissatisfied with the outcome of technological change. As far as the junior technicians were concerned TXE4 exchange modernisation had resulted in the replacement of an open and progressive internal labour market by a closed and segmented one, with reduced job satisfaction, de-skilling of the content of their jobs and frustrated career expectations.

6.8 Conclusion

This chapter has been concerned with changes in work organisation and control resulting from the introduction of TXE4. We found that the combination of the skill superiority of the maintenance technicians and the remoteness of the maintenance supervisor led to the emergence of a new form of work organisation based on team autonomy. This involved both collective technician control over day-to-day maintenance work in the exchange and a more flexible and collaborative approach to work execution. We also showed how this new team autonomy arose at various critical junctures during the implementation of change and how more flexible and collaborative approaches to work organisation were an emergent feature in each of our conversion exchanges.

The extent to which the forms of work organisation in our TXE4 exchanges differed from the situation when they were Strowger units depended to a significant extent on the size of the exchange unit. In the case of the larger TXE4 exchanges the degree of change was quite marked. In these cases the organisation and control of Strowger work had been based on the load principle, involving a high degree of individual autonomy for the senior technicians in the day-to-day control of their work, combined with a rigid formal division of labour. In the case of the smaller TXE4 exchanges the new forms of work organisation were, rather, a development of the practice under Strowger. However, the degree of flexibility and collaboration in the execution of TXE4 maintenance tasks in these exchanges did mark a significant departure from Strowger practice.

We also noted another major change in work organisation in the TXE4 exchanges concerning the overall division of labour between senior and junior technicians. In Strowger exchanges it was the expectation that junior technicians would prepare themselves for promotion to the Technical Officer grade by learning exchange maintenance techniques on the job alongside their more senior colleagues. However, this strong connection between the acquisition of skills and a career structure which envisaged a gradual but clear progression from junior to senior grades was effectively broken in our TXE4 exchanges. Here we found a rigid division between the job content of senior and junior technicians. This demarcation, which derived from prior decisions by management and union representatives on criteria for selection for retraining, effectively excluded junior technicians from working on TXE4 maintenance. From the point of view of the individual junior technician and of junior technicians as an occupational sub-group within BT, TXE4 exchange modernisation pointed towards an increasingly segmented and closed internal labour market leading to low job satisfaction, de-skilling of job content and frustrated career expectations.

Our final task in this chapter is to review the ways in which various actors were able to shape these outcomes of change and the factors which influenced their choices and actions. Turning first to corporate management, the lack of detailed national guidelines on the operational management of TXE4 maintenance meant that they had little or no influence on how work was organised and controlled at exchange level. Further, the reduced need for large amounts of routine preventive maintenance in TXE4 limited the extent to which job content could be determined by national guidelines. Indeed, the only evidence of corporate management influence on work organisation that we could trace was the encouragement given at the national Technical Training College for technicians to work collaboratively on faulting exercises. This was a practice which the technicians continued to adopt on return to their own exchanges.

Turning directly to the role of the exchange supervisors, the extent to which they were in a position to influence the organisation and control of work depended largely upon area management's implementation sub-strategies, in particular area management policy towards the role of the TXE4 supervisor. In the absence of clear policies in two of our three areas, the supervisors in our conversion exchanges had an even more marginal and remote influence on the day-to-day work of TXE4 exchanges than they had had under Strowger. However, even in the cases where area management did have a clear policy towards the role of the TXE4 supervisor and/or where the supervisors had been system-trained they did not exert a major influence on job content or work organisation.

This brings us to the role of the maintenance technician workgroups. All our evidence suggests that they were the main actors shaping the outcomes of change in terms of work organisation and job content. As we have seen, the emergence of team autonomy was in all cases on the initiative of the exchange technicians. In effect they filled the vacuum created by the introduction of TXE4 and the inappropriateness of traditional forms of Strowger work organisation. Through informal contacts amongst themselves it was the technicians who devised, developed and passed on the new forms of work organisation. In this respect our data confirms that of Wilkinson (1983).

The significance of the technician workgroup was enhanced by the absence of any trade union influence on questions of work organisation. As we saw in chapter 3, such issues were not traditionally part of the collective bargaining agenda; this remained the case in the negotiations over TXE4. However, there was one important issue over which trade union influence was clearly in evidence. This was in relation to the division of labour between senior and junior technicians. Here, local union insistence on the adoption of the seniority principle as the criteria on which technicians were to be selected for re-training was instrumental in the rigid division that emerged in TXE4 exchanges between the work of senior and junior technicians and the blocked career structure for junior maintenance technicians which resulted from this.

This brings us to the question of the design space available to organisational actors in choosing new forms of work organisation, in particular the constraints and opportunities arising from the capabilities of the different exchange systems. In the case of Strowger, although the step-by-step architecture did involve a clear technical inter-relation between the switching stages, each of the stages was nevertheless discrete. Thus the functional configuration of the switching equipment enabled the division of work into discrete areas of maintenance responsibility. As a result it was possible in our Strowger exchanges to adopt a highly formal division of labour with rigid demarcations between the responsibilities of individual technicians. Further, because of its requirement for regular, planned, preventive maintenance, the electro-mechanical technology used to implement the Strowger architecture acted as a strong imperative towards the formal allocation of individual maintenance responsibilities divided according to specific areas of the exchange equipment. However, our data suggested that the size of the exchange installation and hence the number of staff involved was an important mediating factor shaping the division of labour. In small exchanges informal forms of work organisation were more prominent. In larger exchanges the adoption of a formal load system appeared to be the norm.

Turning to the TXE4 exchange system, the common-control architecture involved a far greater functional interdependence of the exchange equipment compared to Strowger. The TXE4 exchange was an integrated system where, unlike Strowger, the cause of faults could be remote from the point at which symptoms occurred. The possibilities for sectionalising the work into loads were therefore more limited. In fact our data suggested that the range of choices of systems of work organisation was strongly constrained by the common-control architecture of the TXE4 system, indeed that there was a strong imperative towards more flexible and collaborative forms of work organisation. This imperative derived from the need for faulting activities to take into account the exchange system as a whole rather than just one element of it. There appeared to be positive disadvantages in over-specialisation by individual technicians on particular parts of the exchange equipment, whereas in Strowger such specialisation had been positively encouraged. Moreover, the intrinsic complexity of some fault conditions contributed to the greater tendency in TXE4 to work collaboratively. Finally, the nature of TXE4 technology, which did not require anything like the amount of regular, planned preventive maintenance as in Strowger, also reduced the need to allocate formally specific areas of maintenance responsibility to individual technicians.

It should be stressed that the choices of particular forms of work organisation in our case-study exchanges cannot be exclusively explained in terms of the nature of the two exchange systems. In particular, the process by which the new forms of TXE4 work organisation emerged showed quite clearly the influence of other factors. For example, differences in the level of skill and competence of the technicians during initial operation often meant a formal division of labour was necessary. Similarly, technical problems with the equipment often required the adoption of alternative forms of work organisation in order to overcome them. This was certainly the case in Conversion D and, indeed, in exchange TXE4 B, which, in spite of being the oldest of the TXE4 exchanges we studied, suffered considerable technical problems during (but not because of!) our fieldwork in the unit.

The evidence presented in this chapter strongly supports the view that automated systems are conducive to a form of work organisation based on team autonomy, where control over day-to-day work operations is exercised by the workgroup independent of direct supervisory control. For some writers, such as Friedman, this kind of 'responsible autonomy' is largely to be explained as the result of a deliberate management strategy to achieve greater control through the increased motivation and commitment that derives from the exercise of worker discretion. However, our data does not reveal evidence of management influence over work organisation to anything like the degree implied by this proposition. Rather, it seems that the technician workgroups made choices and decisions within constraints imposed not just by management but also by the nature of the exchange systems as well. This shows once again that in order to understand the full implications of technological change for the organisation and control of work at workplace level it is necessary to take into account not only the influence of social choices, but also the role of engineering systems in shaping outcomes of change.

7

System X: centralised maintenance and a new industrial relations?

7.1 Introduction

While conducting the research reported in this book we were acutely aware that we were studying an organisation undergoing rapid change. Indeed, when our initial discussions with national telecommunications management began in mid-1980, the business was still part of the Post Office. By the time our research report was completed in January 1985 it had been split off from the Post Office, renamed British Telecom, partially 'liberalised' and transformed into a public limited company. During the course of our fieldwork we encountered many instances of the effects of these changes, but throughout this period the impending introduction of an all-electronic digital exchange system, commonly referred to as System X, was increasingly at the forefront of the minds and actions of managers, trade unions and individual employees, particularly those directly concerned with exchange maintenance. Accordingly, although it was not the focus of our research, we believe our story would be incomplete without relating our findings to some of the future implications of System X. Moreover, it is important that our study of TXE4 is seen in its wider context as an intermediate step towards the development of fully electronic exchange systems.

Two initial points should be made about the following discussion. First, we can only consider the potential implications of digital exchange systems in Britain, since at the time of writing there were still only a small number of System X exchanges in operation. Second, our analysis is not based on primary data collected from interviews about national and local modernisation strategies or from observation and interviews concerning changes in work tasks, skills, supervision and work organisation. What we have done is to use available published sources to address some of the questions we have discussed in connection with the change from Strowger to TXE4. As we will see, these sources indicate that System X modernisation will represent a continuation of some of the developments we have identified in our findings on TXE4 but also a

190

radical change in the way exchange maintenance is organised and managed.

7.2 System X and the integrated digital network

The term 'System X' was coined in the early 1970s by engineers engaged in designing a viable fully electronic exchange system: 'X' represented the problem to be solved. By the mid-1980s, as we shall see in the next section, it had been adopted by BT as the main but not exclusive solution to the problem. In this section we will examine its distinctive features as a new type of exchange system.

Following the failure of the Highgate Wood experiment in 1962 (see above, pages 42–3), the development of a fully electronic exchange system in Britain depended on further advances in digital transmission, switching and control techniques. Initial technical advances were most pronounced in the transmission area. In exchange systems such as TXE4, where switching is implemented in electro-mechanical form, the speech path is made through the electrical contacts of the switch, which remain closed throughout the duration of the call. The electrical signal transmitting the speech itself is continuous and is known as an analog signal. While electronic devices present many problems for switching analog signals they nevertheless provide excellent digital switching characteristics. In order to capitalise on this capability, the analog speech signal must first be converted to digital form as a sequence of electrical pulses or bits (binary digits). By the mid-1960s the British Post Office had successfully developed a technique, first invented in 1939, for transforming analog speech signals into digital form and back again. This process, known as Pulse Code Modulation (PCM), has been used since then at an increasing rate in the transmission of traffic between exchanges.

Turning from transmission to switching techniques, electronic devices are capable of operating at very high speeds; in fact, one device can service many digital speech signals simultaneously. This technique, known as time-division switching, realises the potential of electronic switching devices in an extremely efficient manner. However, the development of digital switching proceeded at a slower pace than digital transmission techniques. Between 1968 and 1975 an experimental digitally switched exchange, the first of its kind in the world, carried public traffic in West London. This was accompanied by the trial of another experimental exchange in 1971 at Moorgate, a trial which combined digital switching with common control implemented in electronic technology. These two experiments were to be significant landmarks in the development of System X.

The final strand was the use of electronics techniques in the common control area of digital switching networks. We have already seen how one form of electronic implementation of common control was used in TXE4, where the program was stored in the form of threaded hard-wire units. However, developments in computer processing techniques and micro-electronics in the 1970s made it feasible to store the program in the form of software, thus making it possible to alter the functions performed by the exchange by use of a computer terminal. Such flexibility contrasts with the more cumbersome methods involved in physically changing hard-wired plug-in-units such as are used in TXE4.

The culmination of developments in these three areas – transmission using PCM, switching using time-division techniques and common control using software-based stored program control – was the System X exchange system. Like TXE4, System X was designed according to a modular systems approach, where each exchange unit is in effect assembled from a selection of hardware and software building blocks (see Brander and Burville, 1985: 223). This has meant that the system can continue to evolve over time and use can be made of new technologies as they become available and cost-effective. For example, with advances in micro-processor technology, the physical size of the processor area within the overall system has already been reduced by a factor of thirteen since the original design in the mid-1970s and its processing power has increased four-fold (*ibid.*). The flexibility provided by the software components of the system also means that new facilities and services (both for customers and for the management of the network) can be built in without major changes in the hardware. We will return below to the crucial importance of software in enhancing the capabilities of System X. We would simply note at this point that digital exchange systems incorporating a modular design are generally much more flexible and capable of modification than previous systems –indeed, it may soon be possible to incorporate optical switching techniques into the system without altering the basic architecture (*ibid.*: 225).

Another distinctive feature of System X is that the range of services offered by individual units can be enhanced enormously when they are interconnected with other digital exchanges in a multi-purpose 'integrated digital network' (IDN). In this respect System X is in fact a family of exchanges, composed of a three-tier hierarchy: digital main switching units, which are broadly equivalent to the present trunk or national exchanges; digital principal local exchanges, which are broadly equivalent to the old Group Switching Centres and provide a number of interconnecting links, for example, between digital and analog exchanges; and digital local exchanges, which will replace existing local exchanges. The IDN will be created gradually as exchanges at these three levels are progressively modernised, interconnected with digital transmission systems and supported by fast inter-processor common-channel signalling (see Price and Boulter, 1985: 311).

From the customer's point of view System X promises a reduction in the number of faults and improvements in the time taken to set up calls and the quality of line provided. It also holds out the possibility of a greatly enhanced range of voice and non-voice (text, data, graphics, etc.) services for the office and the home.[1] It is intended that these will become the basis of an Integrated Services Digital Network (ISDN), through which customers will have direct access to the network facilities and be able to satisfy an ever-increasing range of data and voice telecommunications requirements (see Price and Boulter, 1985: 311–17). In the words of two senior engineering managers in British Telecom: 'System X is the focal point of plans geared to meet the future demand for telecommunications facilities' (Boag and Frame, 1985: 222).

7.3 System X modernisation strategy

In chapter 2 we analysed the development of the TXE4 modernisation strategy and the extent to which it was influenced by the adoption of a more commercial approach within the business. In this section we will examine the influence of the commercial paradigm in shaping the System X modernisation strategy up to the mid-1980s. The modernisation strategy can be traced back to the late 1960s when a team composed of representatives of the British Post Office and the three main equipment suppliers (GEC, Plessey and STC) was set up to identify the criteria on which to base future developments in exchange systems. It was from this team that the concept of System X emerged. The development programme proper began in 1976 and in 1977 the first major contracts for the manufacture of System X exchanges were signed between the BPO and the three equipment suppliers. In anticipation of the export potential of the exchange system a new company was also formed to market the system overseas.

An important landmark in the development of the modernisation programme and strategy was reached in July 1980. In this month the first System X exchange to carry live traffic was brought into service at Baynard House in London and the Post Office Board agreed an accelerated digital modernisation programme to be organised around a Network Master Plan (see BT, 1982: 6–8). This plan envisaged the digitalisation of all large local Strowger exchanges and all trunk exchanges by 1992 and the complete digitalisation of the network (the complete ISDN) by 2014. Within a year, however, this plan was already being criticised at senior levels within the organisation:

Insufficient emphasis had been given to meeting marketing criteria. This had become particularly important in view of the new competitive environment [within] which BT was required to operate . . . as a result of government legislation during 1981 . . . The marketing requirements of modernisation are long-standing, namely to deploy System X so as to make its unique facilities available to those customers most likely to benefit from them. However, the advent of competition sharpens the need for a commercial approach that takes account of costs, potential revenue and the risk of loss to those competing networks when planning the modernisation of the BT network. This is particularly important in the early stages when the supply of System X equipment is limited by the constraints of industry . . . A revised deployment strategy for local exchange equipment has therefore been prepared for application to the 1982 Network Master Plan. The implementation of this strategy will clearly lay heavy emphasis on the deployment objectives of System X. (BT, 1982: 6)

This is a clear expression of the factors shaping BT modernisation strategy from the early 1980s and of the growing predominance of a commercial approach within the organisation. Under pressure from the 'political contingency' in the shape of the 1981 Telecommunications Act and government plans to privatise the business, BT modified its System X modernisation strategy to give increased emphasis to marketing criteria and to concentrating the implementation programme around leading marketing areas. These were identified as those having the highest numbers of potential customers for the new services and as being most vulnerable to competition from competing networks. Against this background it is not surprising that large business customers were increasingly being singled out for special consideration (Boag and Frame, 1985: 220).

Consistent with this approach, too, was the decision taken by the BT Board in 1984 to provide a second source to the home-based System X by purchasing digital exchange equipment from the Swedish company Thorn–Ericsson (*Financial Times*, 9.10.84). Following the re-organisation of the System X equipment manufacturers in 1982, as a result of which STC withdrew and Plessey took over as prime contractor with GEC as the main sub-contractor (see Brander and Burville, 1985: 223), there had been major delays in the full-scale implementation of the new system due (according to informed sources) to 'major software problems' (*Financial Times*, 11.3.85).[2] In this context, the existence of a second

194

source, sometimes known as System Y, can be seen as the creation by BT of a more competitive environment for its traditional equipment suppliers. By the time of the privatisation of BT in 1984, therefore, the commercial paradigm dominated both corporate business strategy and the System X exchange modernisation strategy.

7.4 System X and the centralised control of maintenance

British Telecom's overall objectives for digital exchange maintenance were and are still broadly similar to those applying to systems such as TXE4, namely to combine improved quality of service with more efficient use of manpower and other resources (see Baty and Sandum, 1985: 277). However, from the early 1980s its corporate policy towards the organisation and control of System X maintenance operations has been quite distinct from previous practice. Although the terminology has varied over time, what has remained consistent is the intention to use the new technical capabilities of System X to facilitate the introduction of 'centralised control' of maintenance operations away from the individual exchange (*ibid.*; see also BT, 1982: 35–46). Corporate management envisages the establishment of computer support systems in Operations and Maintenance Units (OMUs) which will be linked into a number of System X exchanges. The aim is that the OMUs will become the focal point for the maintenance of all System X exchanges in particular geographical areas. In addition, the OMU itself will be part of a wider Operations and Maintenance Centre (OMC), whose facilities will be used not only by maintenance staff but also by clerical and administrative grades dealing with sales, billing and fault enquiries (see Strickland and Hewitt, 1985: 287).

There are two particular aspects of the OMU/OMC concept which suggest that the organisation and control of System X maintenance work, although still evolving and subject to modifications during the implementation process, will be radically different from that of previous exchange systems. First, it involves a redefinition of the concept of workplace. Hitherto, as we have seen, the workplace of maintenance technicians has been co-terminous with the boundaries of a particular exchange building. However, the use of software-based stored program control in System X – which provides for the automatic capture, interpretation, transmission and display of data on all aspects of exchange performance – allows the point of control of maintenance operations to be removed from the exchange floor to a remote computer centre. This means that exchange alarms and other fault information can be routed directly to the OMU and that, on the basis of the information provided, initial decisions can be made on the nature of a fault and whether a site visit is necessary. Linked to this, it is envisaged that the OMU will be under the overall control of an 'engineering maintenance manager' (Baty and Sandum, 1985: 277) who will be the communication and co-ordinating point for all aspects of exchange maintenance in a particular area. Second, the proposal that the OMU should be part of a wider Operations and Maintenance Centre (OMC) breaks down the traditional isolation of exchange maintenance activities and incorporates them into a range of wider computer-based support systems, all geared to improve customer service. BT is at present engaged in introducing an integrated Customer Service System (CSS), which is intended to provide a common data base on all aspects of customer service, such as billing, faults, equipment sales, installation and maintenance (see Strickland and Hewitt, 1985: 286). It will eventually be possible for the data base to be accessed by a number of different operating functions within the organisation.

These two aspects of corporate policy towards System X maintenance organisation have wide-reaching implications for the traditional working practices and job territories of maintenance technicians. They are made possible by distinctive features of the exchange system itself, including software-based stored program control and built-in self-diagnostic maintenance capabilities, which reduce preventive maintenance tasks to a minimum and transform the nature of corrective maintenance. Indeed it is anticipated that some faults will be so infrequent that maintenance staff will be faced with a major problem of skill retention. It is likely, therefore, that working on simulated faulting exercises will form a significant part of maintenance activities. Further, because of the likely complexity of some software faults, a special 'fault escalation procedure' is being devised so that particularly difficult problems can be directed 'up the line' to centrally located maintenance specialists. All these developments imply radical changes in the content and organisation of maintenance work and this has been reflected to varying degrees in the responses of the trade unions concerned.

7.5 Union policies towards System X modernisation

In chapter 3 we examined the policies of the POEU and the STE towards technological change and TXE4 modernisation. In this section we want to look briefly at the policy response of the two unions towards System X modernisation. We will then examine the national discussions and negotiations between management and unions on the key workplace issues identified in chapters 3 to 6, namely staffing levels, job security, pay and grading, re-training, skill and work tasks, supervision and the organisation and control of work.

At the time of writing (mid-1986), the development of POEU policy towards System X modernisation had had two main focal points, its 1981 Annual Conference and 1984 Special Policy Conference. These will be discussed in turn. In its report to the 1981 conference, the POEU Executive concentrated on two main issues. First, it stressed the desirability of national interim agreements on the introduction of System X pending the conclusion of full agreements on all matters affecting POEU grades. Second, it pointed to the need for an immediate response to management's intention to introduce a centralised organisation for System X maintenance. On this latter question the executive proposed that the maintenance organisation adopted should 'reflect the traditional arrangements for maintenance of exchanges, especially in terms of facilitating on-site maintenance to the maximum practicable extent' (POEU, 1981: 57). The conference debate, however, focused on the implications of System X for maintenance staffing levels and the more general manpower requirements within the business. Two motions were passed, one proposing that System X exchanges should be staffed according to TXE4 staffing levels (a parallel to the 1976 POEU conference motion proposing that TXE4 should be staffed according to Strowger staffing levels), and the other that the union should not co-operate with the full-scale implementation of System X until a national agreement on staffing levels and wider manpower objectives had been concluded. In fact little headway was made with these demands between 1981 and 1984, by which time BT was in the throes of privatisation and adopting a much tougher approach to industrial relations within the business (see below).

Against this background, the POEU Executive (which in 1983 had been taken over by a broad left majority, see above, pages 67–8) decided to call a special conference to review its policy towards new technology and to place it in the context of other recent developments within the business, particularly the proposed re-organisation (implemented in the spring of 1985) of the ten telephone regions and sixty-one areas into thirty more autonomous and powerful districts. As in the mid-1970s, therefore, technological change and particularly telephone exchange modernisation became the focus for a wider internal union debate about the adequacy of existing union policy and methods.

Although the document presented by the POEU Executive to this conference, entitled *Making the Future Work – The Broad Strategy*, made reference to questions such as skills, inter-union relations and management control of work, the section on new technology was dominated by the issue of manpower and jobs:

197

In virtually *every* area of the telecommunications network – terminals, transmission and switching – the new technology will reduce the manpower requirements of the business . . . [However] over the next three years the most dramatic reduction in manpower will occur in exchange maintenance. Although there is no agreed staffing standard for System X, one informed summary of the *eventual* relative manpower requirements of Strowger, Crossbar and System X exchanges is 10:4:1. (POEU, 1984: 7; original emphasis)

The document also quoted a report from stockbrokers Scrimgeour, Kemp-Gee and Co. about future exchange maintenance requirements. This had suggested that, in terms of man-hours per exchange connection the comparison between Strowger Non-Director (the type we examined in our study), Crossbar, TXE4 and 'settled down' digital exchanges would be as follows:

Strowger	0.45
Crossbar	0.25
TXE4	0.22
Digital	0.1

The response to these projections, proposed in the Executive document and endorsed by the conference, centred on one prime demand: a thirty-two hour, four-day week for all POEU grades plus a major reduction in overtime working. This was an extension of the demand for a thirty-five-hour-week advanced in the late 1970s, which had led after prolonged industrial action to a reduction in the working week to thirty-seven and a half hours. The other main demand was for the negotiation of a 'national framework agreement' between BT and the POEU to cover all relevant aspects of BT's modernisation programme. While this envisaged the introduction of a new national consultative framework through which the union would be informed of all major technological developments proposed by BT, it was intended to leave detailed negotiations to established procedures and committees.

In summary, the new POEU policy was an attempt to link new procedures with traditional bargaining arrangements. Future union co-operation with System X modernisation was seen as conditional on a programme of nationally negotiated benefits and, above all, on a reduction in working hours.

As for the STE, it participated from the late 1970s in a range of national consultative meetings on various aspects of System X modernisation, including the role of the maintenance supervisor in System X maintenance. However, its generally reactive and passive approach persisted. At its 1980 Conference, for example, a motion was proposed from the branch covering the new Baynard House System X exchange suggesting that the union should develop its own policy on the role of first- and second-line supervisors in System X maintenance and the management of Local Administration Centres (subsequently renamed Operations and Maintenance Centres, see above). However, the motion was opposed by the executive, whose spokesman suggested that the union's 'traditional posture' of waiting for the Post Office to make its own proposals, following initial discussions with the POEU, was the best position to adopt. The view of the Executive was accepted by the conference.

One final development in union policy with potential implications for the implementation of System X exchange modernisation involved the rationalisation of union structure. Between 1983 and 1985 clerical and administrative/managerial staff in BT, who had previously belonged to two civil service trade unions (CPSA and SCPS), transferred membership to the POEU and the STE respectively. By 1985, the POEU (now under its new name, the National Communications Union) had become the single BT union representing the vast majority of non-management grades, including engineering technician, clerical and computer, and sales staff.[3] The STE had reached a similar position as regards supervisory and management grades by 1983. Therefore, while conflicts might still arise within the BT workforce over the distribution of work between different occupational groups following the introduction of System X, such conflicts are unlikely to be exacerbated by the kind of inter-union rivalries which have occurred in other organisations (see Moore and Levie, 1985; Clark *et al.*, 1984; Thompson and Bannon, 1985).

7.6 The negotiation of System X modernisation at national level

Since we have no primary data on the industrial relations implications of System X modernisation in particular areas, we will confine this discussion to developments in national negotiations between management and unions. Of course, these are likely to be subject to modification during later stages of the implementation process, particularly at workplace level, but they already indicate a number of interesting parallels and differences to our findings on TXE4 modernisation.

The first point to note concerns changes in the industrial relations climate between the initial negotiations and discussions about System X in the early 1980s and more recent discussions following the liberalisation of certain aspects of BT's activity in 1981 and privatisation in 1984. In 1981 an interim agreement on System X modernisation was negotiated between national management and the POEU. This was to be reviewed following the introduction of the first units. The centrepiece of the agreement was concerned with 'the interim maintenance organisation' (BT, 1982: 35). The agreement confirmed management's strategy to centralise the administration and control of maintenance but also emphasised the need to provide job satisfaction for maintenance staff by allowing them to identify with particular 'workloads' (see *ibid.*). However, a System X maintenance workload was not defined in terms of a particular exchange building or section of equipment within it as with Strowger. Rather, it was to be composed of two sets of responsibilities, maintenance activities in one or more exchange units, plus a range of duties in an Operations and Maintenance Unit. The OMU duties were to be allocated on a rotating basis, so that over time every technician would have responsibility and experience in the three main aspects of OMU work: exchange maintenance control (overall surveillance of System X exchanges and co-ordination of day-to-day maintenance in an OMU area); technical support (assisting field technicians in analysing fault symptoms using available diagnostic aids in the OMU); and operations support (collecting and interpreting bulk fault information from the exchanges). Staff responsible for maintenance duties were classified in the interim agreement as Technical Officer grades, thus ensuring that initially only TOs or TOs-in-Training were to be selected for re-training.

At the beginning of the System X programme the interim agreement also envisaged the selection and re-training of staff additional to requirements in order to meet maintenance needs during the early and middle phases of the programme. There were no agreements on the criteria by which technicians were to be selected for re-training, apart from the fact that they should be TO grades. However, given the likely reductions in the total number of maintenance staff and the redefinition of the workplace away from the individual exchange building, the clear implication was that staff would be selected by management on grounds of individual suitability rather than seniority. There were no guidelines on the roles of junior technicians or maintenance supervisors in System X exchanges. As we saw above, it was not until later that more public statements were made by BT about the role of 'engineering maintenance managers' (Baty and Sandum, 1985: 277) in the co-ordination of all aspects of exchange maintenance work in an OMU area.

This interim agreement on maintenance organisation certainly represented an extension of the scope of national agreements on exchange modernisation compared with TXE4, particularly as regards job content, the organisation of work and certain aspects of selection for re-training. However, it should be remembered that this was an interim rather than final agreement, that the potential implications of System X for job content and work organisation were far more radical than they had been for TXE4 and that the agreement still left open a number of questions such as staffing levels, manpower objectives, pay and grading, supervision and the control of work. This is important, because between 1981 and the end of our project there were no further national agreements between BT management and either the POEU or the STE on System X implementation.

So far we have made no reference to the issue of pay and grading. In fact the wider question of the re-organisation of the engineering technician grading structure had first been discussed at national level in 1978 (see Batstone *et al*. 1984: 149ff). For management, changes in the grading structure were seen as a means of achieving a more flexible utilisation of labour. However, developments in the System X modernisation programme clearly threw a whole range of pay and grading questions into much sharper relief. These included not only the relations between junior and senior technicians, highlighted in our study of TXE4 maintenance and again in the interim agreement on System X, but also those between senior maintenance technicians in System X exchanges and other exchange types; between senior technicians and maintenance supervisors; and between engineering and clerical administrative grades. By the end of 1985 none of these questions had been the subject of national agreements. Nevertheless, proposals made by BT at various times since 1980 would suggest that they are likely to be crucially important in future relations between management and unions.

Of particular interest in this respect was the proposal made by BT in the winter of 1982/83 to create two categories of Technical Officer, one on a higher scale (subsequently dubbed a 'Super-TO') and the other on a main scale. The express intention was to implement a radical change in inter-grade ratios, and in particular to increase the proportion of junior to senior grades in exchange maintenance. The figures quoted in the proposal showed a long-term reduction in the total number of senior technicians on exchange maintenance from around 15,000 to around 9,700, with just over 1,000 on the higher scale and just under 8,700 on the main scale. At the same time the proposals envisaged an increase in the number of junior technicians on exchange maintenance from about 4,500 to just over 9,000, plus the creation of an additional 2,600 'general duties' posts specifically related to System X and its enhanced maintenance requirements.

In the eighteen months following the adoption of the 'Broad Strategy' in November 1984, the POEU/NCU made little headway in the achievement of its objectives on System X modernisation. By the middle of 1986 it had failed to reach a national agreement on staffing levels and appeared unlikely to in the near future given the devolution of significant areas of management responsibility to the newly created district managers. So far, therefore, the NCU has maintained its formal policy of non-co-operation with System X modernisation, while continuing discussions with BT and progressing its wider campaign for a thirty-two-hour week.

7.7 Conclusion

We can draw no final conclusions on System X modernisation. By the middle of 1986 the programme was only just entering its implementation stage and the outcomes remained highly uncertain. All we can do is give one or two indications of the climate in which future developments are likely to take place. First, there are clear indications of a change in corporate industrial relations strategy within BT. In October 1984 Michael Bett, then corporate director of personnel, subsequently Managing Director of Local Communications Services (LCS) (the largest Division within BT), was quoted as seeing a 'perceivable shift in attitude' in industrial relations within the organisation. He referred particularly to management's strong commitment to reduce overmanning, to restructure pay and grading in the light of new technology and to devolve wide areas of bargaining and consultation to local level (*Financial Times*, 17.10.84). The *Financial Times* entitled its report of Bett's statement: 'End of the line for a cosy way of life.' Changes along these lines would undoubtedly mark the end of an era for the traditional system of collective bargaining and industrial relations within the business.

Second, running parallel to this development in industrial relations strategy was the ever increasing predominance of the commercial paradigm in the setting of overall corporate objectives. This achieved a new expression in 1985 in senior management proposals to transform BT into 'Top Telco by 1990' (*Financial Times*, 28.11.85). According to the *Financial Times*, the 'Top Telco' policy set the new district general managers a series of very specific financial and manpower targets. The LCS division, for example, was required under this policy to improve its contribution to profits by three per cent per annum between 1985–6 and 1989–90. To achieve this objective it would have to increase customer use of the network and to reduce costs, including a reduction in staff of 4,000 in the first year. On the industrial relations front district general managers were urged to 'examine existing arrangements with unions, both local and national, and to change practices which are no longer consistent with running the business excellently' (*Financial Times*, 28.11.85).[4]

Fears and anxieties often find an outlet and expression in humour. For exchange maintenance technicians within BT the major fears associated with the introduction of digital technologies are manpower reductions and unemployment. As we have seen, System X exchanges are believed to require much less maintenance effort than digital ones and much of what remains is likely to be carried out remote from the exchange building. In fact there was a widespread anxiety amongst the Technical Officers we interviewed that hands-on maintenance might eventually be all but eliminated in System X exchanges for fear that it might cause more faults than it solved. At the beginning of our research, in 1981, a common joke within BT ran:

> Q. What is the staffing level for a System X exchange?
> A. One man and a dog.
> Q. What is the dog for?
> A. To make sure the man doesn't touch the equipment.
> Q. What is the man for?
> A. To feed the dog.

By the end of the project, the joke had changed slightly:

> Q. What is the staffing level for a System X exchange?
> A. A dog.
> Q. What is the dog for?
> A. To stop anyone from breaking into the exchange.

8
Conclusions

8.1 Introduction

This book has had two main themes: the way managers, trade unionists and workgroups seek to shape the processes and outcomes of technological change; and the extent to which given technologies (conceptualised as engineering systems) can act as an independent variable influencing the way outcomes of change are socially chosen and negotiated. Our principal focus in examining these questions has been on the implementation of new technology in the workplace. Thus, although we have examined corporate management strategies and industrial relations at national level, our main interest has been in the significance of these national frameworks in setting the parameters within which the implementation of change takes place at workplace level. In this concluding discussion we will summarise the main arguments of the book and then discuss the broader implications of our analysis. At each point we will relate our findings to those of other recent investigations of technological change. We begin by reviewing the conceptual framework which has guided our analysis.

8.2 Summary of the argument

In chapter 1 we discussed a number of sociological approaches which have been used to investigate technological change in the workplace. We noted that much recent research has tended to emphasise the importance of choice in the social shaping of technological change, concentrating attention on such questions as the nature and role of management strategy, the influence of trade unions and collective bargaining, and the capacity of workgroups to influence changes in the organisation of work (see for example Buchanan and Boddy, 1983; Wilkinson, 1983; Child, 1984). While accepting many of the insights of such studies we argued that they have tended to neglect the influence of technology on the outcomes of technological change. While agreeing that outcomes cannot be explained exclusively in terms of the capabilities of 'the technology', we suggested that it was equally erroneous to reject the notion that it can have an independent influence.

In order to substantiate this view, we argued the need for a concept of technology which was accurate in engineering terms and concrete enough to allow us to analyse its influence in detail at an empirical level. To this end we introduced and elaborated the concept of 'engineering system'. Our starting point was that technologies used in work organisations are not only pieces of hardware and software but also systems based on certain engineering principles and composed of elements which are functionally arranged (configured) in certain specific ways. All engineering systems, therefore, have three basic elements: system principles, an overall system configuration and a system implementation (or physical realisation) in a given technology. The first two elements we termed the system architecture and the third the system technology. We also alluded to two further aspects of engineering systems. First, in any particular installation an engineering system design is normally dimensioned to suit a specific user or workplace. Second, engineering systems have ergonomic and aesthetic features which play a significant part in their visual and audible appearance, or what we have termed system appearance.

To demonstrate the applicability of this definition, we used it to analyse the technologies which formed the main focus of our empirical investigation, the electro-mechanical Strowger and the semi-electronic TXE4 telephone exchange systems. The Strowger system has an architecture based on a step-by-step switching principle, with control and switching co-located. This architecture is implemented using electro-mechanical technology. The system appearance provides both aural and visual expressions of the switching process, with many hundreds of visible switches mounted on rows of floor to ceiling racks making an audible staccato rattle.

In contrast, the TXE4 system has an architecture which combines common-control and matrix-switching principles. Unlike Strowger, the control of the switching process is accomplished by equipment which is separately located but commonly accessible to all the switching area (hence common control). The common-control equipment is implemented using electronic technology, while the switching equipment is implemented using electro-mechanical technology (though not the same as that employed in Strowger). The switching process is extremely quiet and both switching and control equipment are hidden in racks of plug-in-units. The system appearance of TXE4 is thus in vivid contrast to that of Strowger, with few aural or visual indications of its operation. We also noted the enhanced fault-tolerance and functional interdependence of TXE4 equipment compared to Strowger and its more comprehensive automatic fault monitoring and reporting capabilities.

In chapter 1 we also pointed to some of the weaknesses of previous attempts to treat technology as an independent variable shaping organisational behaviour. As a result we underlined the need to understand technological change as a *process*, as a series of analytically distinct stages with a number of critical junctures at which organisational actors can intervene to shape particular outcomes of change. The main stages identified were initiation, decision to adopt, system selection, implementation and routine operation. Once the stages leading up to system selection have been accomplished, the social choices made become 'frozen' in a given technology, or, as we now prefer it, engineering system. We also argued that, at least from this point onwards, it makes analytical sense to suggest that technology so conceived is one of the factors which defines the design space within which organisational actors may attempt to shape the outcomes of technological change. Subsequent chapters were intended to provide empirical evidence to support this view.

In the following five chapters we presented empirical material from our study of the process of TXE4 modernisation in eight BT exchanges in three telephone areas. Chapters 2 and 3 provided the background to our detailed analysis of the implementation process at workplace level by outlining the corporate strategy behind the TXE4 modernisation programme. We saw that TXE4 was introduced in order to improve the efficiency and reduce the cost of exchange maintenance. This reflected in part what Batstone, Ferner and Terry (1984) have referred to as the emergence of a new commercial paradigm at corporate level. However, although a clear corporate strategy to this effect existed it did not specify in detail how the new exchange system was to be implemented or how the maintenance labour force was to be organised in order to achieve these objectives. This, we suggested, left considerable scope for the attenuation of corporate strategy at local level, giving area managements considerable design space in devising sub-strategies for the implementation and operational control of TXE4 in the exchanges for which they were responsible.

In chapter 3 we noted the remarkable stability of the traditional internal labour market position of exchange maintenance technicians, as evidenced by their high degree of job security, relatively assured career progression and relatively high rates of pay and skilled status. Defence of this labour-market position proved to be the starting point for the maintenance technicians' union, the POEU, in national and local negotiations over TXE4 in the late 1970s. In the event the POEU was able to exercise a significant influence in setting the national industrial relations framework for certain aspects of TXE4 modernisation. These included agreements on staffing levels and job security, and across-the-board productivity increases in recognition of union and staff acceptance of modernisation more generally. The STE, on the other hand, was content to maintain its traditional view that modernisation was a matter of managerial prerogative and not something that it as a union should seek to subject to collective bargaining. The result of management and POEU negotiations was a national industrial relations framework for the introduction of TXE4 in which a balance was struck between the demands of the new commercial paradigm and the traditional paradigm which had preceded it. However, this national framework also left important elements of the implementation process to be determined at local level.

This again suggested considerable scope for discretion at telephone area and individual exchange level, emphasising the importance of local management sub-strategies to implement TXE4. It also raised the question as to how far existing collective bargaining arrangements at area level would and could be used to negotiate the introduction of the new exchanges. Significantly, in the two telephone areas where there were negotiations, it was over what are generally regarded as traditional collective bargaining issues, namely staffing levels and criteria and procedures for the selection and re-training of staff. Selection for re-training was based in these areas on the seniority principle. This meant in practice that only senior technician grades would be selected and that junior grades would therefore be excluded from the re-training programme. Consistent with other research we found no formal negotiations over the 'control' issues raised by technological change such as work tasks, skills and the organisation of work.

In chapters 4, 5 and 6 we presented the main body of the empirical data from our case-study exchanges. Our findings in chapter 4 considered the outcomes of change in TXE4 exchanges in relation to work tasks and skills. At the outset we distinguished between three main levels or dimensions of skill: skill in the task, skill in the person, and the political or occupational distribution of skill. In this chapter we were particularly concerned with changes in skills in the task (the skills required to accomplish work tasks) and the acquisition of skills in the person (the skills possessed by individuals). We found that TXE4 skills in the task differed from those required for Strowger maintenance in two important respects. First, the location and diagnosis of faults involved a strong emphasis on mental diagnostic skills, system knowledge and an ability to utilise a range of information provided by diagnostic aids. This indicated a qualitatively new kind of interpretive ability compared to Strowger. However, fault repair tasks required less skill than in Strowger. In particular the refined manual skills typical of many aspects of Strowger maintenance were no longer relevant.

The acquisition of skills in the person in order to carry out these new TXE4 maintenance tasks also differed in important ways from Strowger. Technicians in our Strowger exchanges tended to acquire such skills incrementally by a mixture of short training courses, trial and error, a 'dive-in' technique and learning by working alongside more experienced colleagues over a period of months, perhaps even years. In contrast, technicians tended to acquire TXE4 skills by a more extended programme of training courses, more intensive periods of familiarisation working alongside senior technicians, and informal advice and accumulated knowledge from senior technicians in other TXE4 units. When we looked at the attitudes and perceptions of technicians on these issues, we found that, while there was a general feeling that Strowger skills had been lost, these were more than compensated for by the new TXE4 skills acquired. Moreover, TXE4 maintenance work was more likely to be regarded by the technicians as highly skilled and more satisfying compared to Strowger.

In chapter 5 we noted that the introduction of TXE4 threw into sharp relief the problem of supervision. We concluded from an examination of national policy and our own empirical data that the role of the Strowger maintenance supervisor was essentially that of an administrative manager. Although the introduction of TXE4 opened up the possibility of new design choices, only one telephone area management used this opportunity to redefine the supervisory role as a system manager. In the other two areas the absence of any clear management policy on supervision reinforced the marginal and remote administrative manager role typical of the Strowger supervisor. For all the TXE4 supervisors, the absence of any initial re-training in the management of TXE4 maintenance contrasted strongly with the extended periods of training and increasing technical skill superiority of the maintenance technicians. Even the supervisors who had received full system-training were unable to become involved to any significant extent in solving technical problems in the exchange. For the non-system-trained supervisors, the technicians' new skill superiority eroded the traditional basis of their perceived authority, which lay in their accumulated experience of Strowger maintenance work. This new skill superiority had profound implications for the organisation of work.

In chapter 6 we examined the emergence of new forms of work

organisation in the TXE4 exchanges studied. Our broad conclusion was that team autonomy became the basic principle behind the organisation and control of maintenance work. This involved collective technician control over day-to-day maintenance work in the exchanges and a more flexible and collaborative approach to work execution. We also saw how flexible and collaborative approaches to work organisation were an emergent feature in each of our conversion exchanges during the initial operation of the new units.

The extent to which the forms of work organisation found in our TXE4 exchanges differed from the situation when they were Strowger exchanges depended to a significant extent on the size of the unit. In the larger TXE4 exchanges the extent of change was quite marked. The organisation and control of Strowger maintenance had been based on the load principle, involving a high degree of individual autonomy for the senior technicians in the day-to-day control of their work, combined with a rigid formal division of labour. In the smaller TXE4 exchanges the outcome was to some extent a development of the practice under Strowger. However, the degree of flexibility and collaboration in the execution of TXE4 maintenance tasks did mark a significant departure from Strowger practice.

Finally, as a result of the introduction of TXE4 we observed the emergence of a much more rigid division of labour in the occupational distribution of skill between senior and junior technicians. In Strowger units there had been a clear expectation that junior technicians would acquire the necessary experience and maintenance skills to progress to the more senior grade by working alongside senior technicians. However, this strong connection between the acquisition of skills and a clear and progressive career structure in exchange maintenance was broken in our TXE4 exchanges. By virtue of their exclusion from selection for re-training we found no evidence of junior technicians carrying out exchange system maintenance tasks. This rigid demarcation pointed towards an increasingly segmented and closed internal labour market, which had led already to low job satisfaction, de-skilling of the content of junior technicians' jobs and frustrated career expectations.

In our final chapter we related our findings on Strowger and TXE4 to some of the future implications of digital exchange modernisation in British Telecom. We noted that computer-controlled software technology lies at the heart of both control and switching functions in System X and that this has major implications for the size, processing power, flexibility and new facilities offered by the exchange network. System X is also capable of co-ordinating and integrating a whole range of computer-based customer service systems, including installation, maintenance and billing. Above all, it enables management to centralise the organisation of maintenance operations away from the individual exchange building, probably its most important potential influence on maintenance work.

At the centre of the new maintenance operations is likely to be a new type of first-line system manager. The occupants of this new role will be able to use the facilities of the new computer technology to make initial decisions about the nature of particular faults and also the maintenance tasks, amount of time and kind of staff needed to carry them out. System X's much enhanced automated diagnostic facilities may also lead to a restructuring of the occupational distribution of skill within the maintenance technician workforce, allowing junior technicians to carry out a significant amount of routine maintenance work. It appears likely, too, that the overall numbers of maintenance technicians required to carry out System X maintenance will be drastically cut compared with both Strowger and TXE4, possibly by as much as ninety per cent. When this is taken together with the growing influence of the commercial paradigm on BT's business, system modernisation and industrial relations strategies, this represents a substantially different framework for the implementation of new exchange technology compared to the introduction of TXE4.

8.3 Social choice and the outcomes of technological change

In chapter 1 we stressed the need to view technological change in the workplace as a process comprising a series of stages and 'critical junctures'. Critical junctures constitute the points at which choices concerning particular issues (skills, staffing levels, organisation of work, etc.) made by organisational actors can influence the eventual outcomes of change. How significant, then, was the influence exerted by the main organisational actors – area management, local trade union representatives, and workgroups of maintenance technicians and supervisors – at various critical junctures in the process of change?

Management

Our data revealed contrasting management responses to the implementation of TXE4 modernisation at telephone area level. In all cases responsibility for managing the introduction of TXE4 was delegated to junior middle-management. In Town Area one middle-manager was given overall responsibility for all aspects of modernisation and he developed a positive and coherent implementation sub-strategy. He was clearly identified as the promoter of change within the area and was thus able to create line-management continuity and consistency throughout the implementation process. In contrast, in neither of the other two areas was a promoter of change appointed. In consequence there was an absence of continuity, a less clear definition of management and supervisory responsibilities, and a relatively undeveloped implementation sub-strategy.

These differences in implementation sub-strategies had direct implications for the degree of management influence in establishing selection criteria for the re-training of maintenance technicians. However, their main significance was in shaping the role of the maintenance supervisor during and after the introduction of TXE4. On this question local area managements had considerable design space to devise their own policies. In Metro and Coast Areas, no clear policies were developed and as a result the maintenance supervisors were marginal actors in the conversion and operational management of the new exchanges. In contrast, Town Area management made a conscious decision to select and system-train a specialist maintenance supervisor to take responsibility for all TXE4 exchanges in the sub-area. Middle-management in Town Area was thereby able to exert a greater influence on both the process and outcomes of change.

If we relate these findings to those from other recent investigations of technological change, a number of wider implications emerge. First, our evidence underlines the important of viewing decisions and choices made by managers at operating levels as distinct and often divergent from those made by managers at more strategic levels within work organisations (see Buchanan and Boddy, 1983: 243–8). Second, we need to allow for the possibility of an attenuation (Child, 1985: 109) between corporate management decisions to introduce new technology and its implementation, in other words, a variability in the 'tightness of coupling' (*ibid.*: 112) between senior management intentions and their realisation in the workplace. The degree of tightness in this coupling is dependent to a significant extent upon the design space left by corporate strategies, either because of conscious decision or because of omission. This underlines a third point, the utility of conceptualising the range of management policies towards the implementation of technological change as 'implementation sub-strategies' (McLoughlin, Rose and Clark, 1985: 252) which have their own distinct determinants and dynamics. There is unlikely to be one coherent management strategy covering all stages of the introduction of new systems, rather a series of 'sub-strategies' relating to different stages in the process of change. Finally, our evidence shows that the role of operating managers (particularly at middle-management and supervisory level), both as promoters of change and as a focus for management continuity and authority, is crucial to the degree of overall influence exerted by management on the process and outcomes of technological change in the workplace (see Buchanan and Boddy, 1983: 24f; also the two case studies discussed in McLoughlin *et al.*, 1985: 261ff).

Trade unions

If we compare the influence of area management on TXE4 modernisation to the influence of trade unions at the same level, we find similarly contrasting outcomes. In the case of Metro Area, the local POEU branches were well co-ordinated and presented a unified response to management's TXE4 modernisation plans. After initial problems with the introduction of the first TXE4 exchange in the area, the branches reached agreement with management to form a joint modernisation committee to negotiate and monitor the introduction of TXE4. In Coast Area one POEU branch representative, a maintenance technician in one of the exchanges due for conversion to TXE4, was the prime mover in developing a positive union response to modernisation. In these two cases, and in the absence of clear management implementation substrategies, local union representatives were able to exert a significant influence on such issues as the criteria and procedures for selecting staff for re-training and the phasing of training courses and post-course experience.

In contrast, the local union organisation in Town Area was relatively weak and did not seek to become involved in discussions and negotiations over the introduction of TXE4. Moreover, Town Area management had a coherent and well co-ordinated implementation sub-strategy. The result was that it was management which exerted the stronger influence on such issues as selection for re-training. In all three areas, representatives of the STE, in line with its national policy, did not seek to enter into negotiations about the implications of TXE4 for the role of the maintenance supervisor.

Recent research has stressed that while managements tend to take decisions to adopt new technology unilaterally, these decisions and choices, once taken, can be subject to both formal and informal influence by trade unions at later stages (Rush and Williams, 1984; Benson and Lloyd, 1983; Moore and Levie, 1985). According to this research, however, formal involvement through various forms of joint consultation and collective bargaining rarely leads to trade unions achieving an influence over the 'control' issues raised by technological change in the workplace (see also Buchanan, 1983; Thompson and Bannon, 1985; Child *et al.*, 1984). Our findings confirm the view that it is normally traditional bargaining issues such as staffing levels, job security and selection for training that are subject to joint regulation, while issues such as skill and work organisation do not tend to appear on the collective bargaining agenda.

However, our evidence does not support the view that existing collective bargaining arrangements are in all circumstances unable to cope with technological change. Contrary to the rather pessimistic findings of Moore and Levie (1985), our data would suggest that it is possible for trade unions to exert a limited but important influence through joint negotiation and consultation, both at corporate and workplace levels. Whatever its weaknesses in the face of new technology and growing commercial pressures, the highly centralised national industrial relations framework in BT, combined with local union initiatives based on well organised co-ordinating committees and energetic individual officers, did provide the basis for important and lasting intervention by the POEU. However, as more recent events in BT have suggested (see chapter 7), it may be that in the future, commercial pressures and changes in management industrial relations strategy following privatisation may well pose a greater threat to the ability of the trade unions to influence the introduction of new technology than any inherent features of either technology, collective bargaining or consultative arrangements *per se*.

One final and important issue on which trade unions exerted an important influence should also be mentioned. The *de facto* acceptance of the seniority principle as a basis for selection for training in all three telephone areas had direct repercussions for the occupational distribution of skill between senior and junior technicians. The exclusion of junior technicians from access to TXE4 training in our case-study exchanges effectively reduced them to the most routine tasks and appeared to block off their expectations and possibilities of a career progression within exchange maintenance, at least for the foreseeable future. By giving priority in the allocation of scarce new technology jobs to the existing senior incumbents, the POEU representatives (and management, who were ultimately responsible for selection) inadvertently disadvantaged the younger and more inexperienced but not necessarily less able technicians.

This general question has been much discussed in recent research in terms of 'core' and 'peripheral' workers (see for example Friedman, 1977) or the creation of 'primary' and 'secondary' segments of internal labour markets (see for example Child, 1984: 254–5). In our TXE4 case-study exchanges the tendency towards a polarisation of the workforce into more rigidly distinct and segmented occupational sub-groups appeared to be confirmed. Whether this will hold true for System X exchange maintenance appears more doubtful in the light of recent management moves to adopt a more flexible re-training strategy.

Workgroups: maintenance technicians and supervisors

Recent research by Wilkinson has suggested that where their strategic position allows, particular occupational groups or workgroups are able to exert their most direct influence on the outcomes of technological change through informal or 'subterranean' means (see Wilkinson, 1983: 91–2, 94–8). His research revealed that it was during the installation and de-bugging of new technology, when new forms of work organisation and control were devised and chosen, that the influence of workgroups was most pronounced. On a related point, Child and colleagues have argued that the ability of particular occupational groups to influence the way new technological systems are used depends largely on 'the position they occupy in the decision-making structure of their organisations, and in particular the power they have to define "appropriate" working practices and job content' (1984: 181).

Our data largely confirmed these views. First, senior Strowger technicians occupied a powerful position as an elite and skilled occupational group within the internal labour market in British Telecom. This strategic position, plus the influence exerted by the POEU at national and local level, ensured that the status quo was broadly maintained with the introduction of TXE4. From this vantage point, the TXE4 technicians were able to take the initiative in developing new forms of work organisation at critical junctures during the installation, de-bugging and initial operation of their exchanges. In effect they filled the vacuum created by the introduction of TXE4 and designed alternative forms of work organisation in recognition of what they believed to be the inappropriateness of time-honoured Strowger custom and practice. This suggests that the workforce's own experience, skills and abilities can be a critical factor in successfully resolving practical problems raised by the introduction of new technology at workplace level. Indeed, the absence of clear management policies on work organisation, trade union preoccupation with traditional bargaining issues and, as we shall discuss below, the failure of maintenance supervisors in most cases to take a pro-active role, all contributed to the significance of the technician workgroup in shaping the organisation and control of work in the new exchanges.

Turning to the supervisors themselves, their capacity to influence the outcomes of technological change rested in the first instance on their strategic position within the organisation. We have already seen in chapter 3 how their position in the internal labour market owed more to the STE's strategy of maintaining differentials over the POEU than any strategic power that supervisory grades and the union had to wield in the organisation or workplace. Similarly, our data on the role of the Strowger supervisor suggested that even under existing exchange systems their position was sufficiently remote and reactive to mean that their capacity to influence change would be likely to be marginal. Against a background of the relative neglect of the problem of supervision in two of our three telephone areas, the capacity of individual maintenance supervisors to influence change was severely limited, whether during installation and de-bugging or after the exchanges had become operational. It was only in the cases of the system-trained supervisors that we found evidence of supervisory influence through their involvement in discussions about new forms of work organisation and in some technical problem-solving during the de-bugging of the exchanges. In summary, supervisors were, with notable exceptions, marginal actors in the implementation process.

8.4 Engineering systems and the outcomes of technological change

In order to bring together the various strands of the book and to develop further its wider implications, we wish to return to the question of the influence of technology on the outcomes of technological change. In chapter 1 we noted Wilkinson's observation that there was a particular sense in which technology can have an impact at workplace level. We quote the relevant passage again:

> Within adopting organisations . . . constraints on possible work organisations may already have been inbuilt during the design process . . . In this sense technology can have 'impacts' on work organisation and skills. (1983: 21)

Using our concept of engineering system, we will now review the ways in which the different exchange types, once chosen, had 'impacts' on work tasks and skill, the role of the supervisor, and the organisation and control of work at workplace level. We will conclude this section by drawing some more general conclusions from these findings.

Work tasks and skills

Our extensive comparative data on the influence of the Strowger and TXE4 maintenance work provided detailed evidence of the wide-ranging

215

influences of engineering systems on work tasks, 'the core of work' (Butera, 1984: 70). The variety of these influences has been examined in detail in chapter 4 and need not be repeated here. Suffice it to say that they ranged from direct links between exchange architecture and technology and particular aspects of fault location and repair tasks to less direct but still identifiable influences of the different exchange technologies on the overall balance between different types of maintenance (corrective and preventive). As far as skills were concerned, there were clear links between Strowger architecture, technology and appearance and certain aspects of skills in the task and skills in the person (manual dexterity, refined aural and visual abilities, incrementally acquired 'tacit' skills). Similarly, there were clear links between TXE4 architecture and technology and skills in the task and skills in the person (mental interpretive ability, system awareness). In general, the links between engineering systems and skills in the task were more direct than those between engineering systems and skills in the person and the occupational distribution of skill.

We also noted how the two exchange systems influenced the subjective experience of work for the maintenance technicians. On the one hand the aural and visual character of Strowger, its system appearance, enabled the technicians to see and hear the equipment working and, importantly from a maintenance viewpoint, those parts which were not working. In stark contrast the system appearance of TXE4 involved a more indirect relationship between the technicians and the equipment. There were no direct audible or visual clues to the workings of the system but, rather, indirect information provided by diagnostic aids. This different relationship underlined the essential contrast between the skills required to maintain the two types of exchange, the one emphasising manual dexterities and a direct physical content in the work task, the other, mental dexterities and a more abstract content in the work task.

This connection between technology and the subjective experience of work is also implied in the findings of Cynthia Cockburn's study of technological change in newspaper publishing. The move from hot-metal typesetting to computerised photocomposition apparently had a remarkably direct influence on the compositors' experience of work:

> The men also report a striking change in their relationship to the equipment on which they work. The linotype was large, its parts were visible and moved. As we've seen, the men knew the function of each component, they listened for changes in the sounds made by the machine and would respond to them . . . The new electronic keyboards however are small, smooth,

encased and unrevealing . . . Most of the men had had a glimpse inside the input unit. They saw an enigma. 'There's nothing moving in the damn thing. It's all chips and solder.' Men brought up in a mechanical era, used to cars as well as linotype feel helpless before computer technology . . . In such ways the men have moved from an active and interactive relationship to a passive and subordinate one. (1983: 102)

This is especially noteworthy, since the great bulk of existing commentary has gone to considerable lengths to deny any direct association between 'technology' and the attitudes and experience of workers (see Hill, 1981, for discussion). Our data suggests, however, that the experience of work under electronics-based systems is not necessarily a subordinate one. In fact the TXE4 maintenance technicians we studied were able to develop an interactive relationship with the new technology. What is significant in this context, though, is that important aspects of this relationship were influenced by the technical capabilities of the system. Compared to electro-mechanical systems we found that electronics-based systems involved a more indirect and abstract working relationship with the equipment. Whether this results in the subordination of workers is a matter of system design and the design of jobs and work organisation.

The organisation and control of work

How far can we trace an influence of the two exchange systems beyond the immediate work tasks and skills in the task? For example, did the nature of the exchange systems enhance or restrict the design space available to managers and workgroups in shaping the organisation and control of work? Our data suggests that the range of choices available to organisational actors was influenced in a number of ways by the nature of the two exchange systems. Concerning Strowger, although its step-by-step architecture did involve a technical inter-relation between the switching stages, each of the stages was nevertheless discrete. The functional configuration of the switching equipment thus enabled the division of work into discrete areas of maintenance responsibility. It was therefore possible in Strowger exchanges to adopt a highly formal division of labour with rigid demarcations between the jobs of individual technicians. The technology used to implement the Strowger step-by-step architecture, with its requirements for regular blocks of routine preventive maintenance, also acted as a strong imperative towards the allocation of maintenance responsibilities in the form of separate individual 'loads'.

Turning to the TXE4 exchange system, the common-control architecture showed a far greater functional interdependence of equipment parts than Strowger. In some cases the causes of equipment faults could be remote from the point at which the symptoms occurred. This required the technicians continually to bear in mind the potential effects of their work on the performance of the exchange system as a whole when carrying out maintenance tasks, whereas in Strowger faults could normally be treated in isolation. This also meant that a formal division of maintenance responsibilities into discrete jobs, so typical of medium and large Strowger exchanges, was generally inappropriate to TXE4 units. In other words, the choice of alternative forms of work organisation was more limited than in our Strowger exchanges and there was a strong technical imperative towards the adoption of a flexible approach in which maintenance responsibility for the whole exchange system was shared by the technician workgroup.

The intrinsic complexity of some TXE4 fault conditions also appeared to contribute to the greater tendency among TXE4 technicians to work collaboratively. More generally, the choice of a team-approach to the organisation of work was facilitated by the nature of the TXE4 technology, which required far less standardised and predictable routine maintenance effort than Strowger, shifting the emphasis of maintenance towards an absolute predominance of corrective activities. This lack of predictability of TXE4 maintenance tasks, together with the clear technical skill superiority of the technicians over their supervisors, also tended to enhance the autonomy and strategic position of the technician workgroups and to reduce the possibilities for direct supervisory control of work. Similar problems for management in controlling the work of maintenance groups following the introduction of electronics-based technologies have been identified by a number of other researchers, although they do not generally see the new technologies themselves as a significant explanatory variable (see Gallie, 1978: 82–4; Senker *et al.*, 1981; Senker, 1984; Scarbrough, 1984; Willman and Winch, 1985; Cross, 1985).

Our findings on the organisation and control of work both confirm and elaborate upon Gallie's conclusion that 'automated process technologies are conducive to a certain amount of team autonomy' (1978: 221). The elaboration comes from our use of the concept of engineering system and our multi-dimensional definition of team autonomy. The use of the concept of engineering system has allowed us to define more precisely which particular aspects of technologies (system principles, configuration, technology, dimensioning, appearance) are conducive to the adoption of team autonomy. Conversely, the differentiation between

218

different aspects of team autonomy (autonomy of the workgroup from the supervisor in determining the overall organisation of work, adoption of a flexible team approach to the overall division of labour between individual workers, 'team' or collaborative working, team autonomy in controlling day-to-day work operations) has enabled us to define more precisely how particular aspects of team autonomy can be shaped by technology as well as by other factors such as management strategy, union organisation and the strategic position of the workgroup.

Supervision

We have already noted the influence of the TXE4 exchange system on the team autonomy of the technician workgroup, including their relative autonomy from first-line supervision. However there are two further ways in which the nature of the Strowger and TXE4 systems influenced the role of the maintenance supervisor. First, both Strowger and TXE4 were automated exchange systems. Both had bolted on, or incorporated into them, fault-monitoring devices which provided exchange supervisors with a growing body of information about exchange performance. In fact the semi-electronic TXE4 exchange system had a greater inherent capacity than Strowger for allowing such automatic monitoring and interpretation of fault data, although specific software-controlled systems for the use of maintenance supervisors were only introduced towards the end of our project. In this connection we detected throughout our research an increasing emphasis within corporate management on the role of the supervisor as an 'information manager' (see below).

Second, the nature of the Strowger exchange system, particularly its electro-mechanical technology, was such that it required substantial amounts of routine preventive maintenance. This feature of the exchange system enabled national and local (supervisory) management to lay down in some detail the programme of activities to be carried out by the technicians over the course of a week or a year. The TXE4 exchange system, in contrast, did not require anywhere near as much routine maintenance and the type and nature of TXE4 faults were much less predictable in their maintenance requirements than Strowger. This feature of the TXE4 exchange system constrained the extent to which supervisors could lay down programmes of work for their staff and suggested the need for a more flexible system of work organisation.

As we saw in chapter 7, System X is likely to constrain even further the design space within which supervisors are able to establish patterned programmes of work for maintenance technicians. However, its enhanced information capabilities and its capacity for automating fault-diagnosis do open up the possibility of increased supervisory influence on the organisation and control of work. This could lead, as in other cases (see Dawson and McLoughlin, 1986), to the creation of a new type of first-line supervisor, a computer-based 'information' or 'system' manager. There were clear signs towards the end of our project that within BT corporate management were considering moving in that direction, both through the introduction of new exchange management training courses and by the proposal to create a new position of 'engineering manager' in charge of co-ordinating and monitoring System X maintenance operations. We would conclude from these recent developments that while technologies can have important enabling characteristics in the definition of supervisory roles these are more strongly shaped by management policy (or its absence) than by engineering systems *per se*.

General comments

It should be emphasised once again that we are not suggesting that the nature of work tasks and skills, forms of work organisation and supervisory roles found in our case-study exchanges can be explained entirely in terms of technical capabilities of the exchange systems. What we *are* saying is that the design space within which choices were made by organisational actors was influenced in important ways by their architecture, technology and appearance. The strongest links we found between engineering systems and work were in connection with work tasks, skills in the task and aspects of the experience of work. In areas such as job definitions and work organisation, however, we found a less strong but still identifiable enabling or constraining influence. The same was true for the overall balance between corrective and preventive maintenance in our two exchange types. We found a much weaker link between engineering systems and the division of labour between different groups within the workforce, the degree of autonomy of senior technicians from their supervisors and the definition of supervisory roles within the organisation. Our findings therefore identified the strongest influence of engineering systems on work tasks and skills in the task, and less powerful but still demonstrable influences as we moved further away from the 'core of work'.

Three final comments may be appropriate in concluding this section. First, our findings have certain affinities with those of researchers who have noted the strong determining influence of technology near the technical heart of organisations and in small businesses and a less determinate influence at higher levels and in large businesses (see on this

Dawson and Wedderburn, 1980: xxv; also Buchanan and Boddy, 1983: 17–18). This would clearly be a fruitful area for further investigation, as would studies of occupational groups whose work interfaces not so directly or extensively with new engineering systems as that of maintenance technicians.

Second, we recognise that our stress on the independent influence of technology is open to the criticism that we have ignored the social choices that occur prior to its introduction, particularly in the system selection (design) stage. Our answer to this criticism, outlined in chapter 1, was that it cannot be assumed that social choices made in the design process will inevitably be translated into particular outcomes, and that therefore the nature, extent and influence of particular design choices on forms of work and work organisation need to be specified empirically. However, this still leaves us with the legitimate question of how choices are made in the design process. This is a major area for research which requires investigation by engineers and social scientists. However, we believe that our concept of engineering system could represent a fruitful starting point, since it provides a framework for distinguishing between the design and choice of system architectures, technologies and appearances. It also directs our attention to the question of how far design choices are enabled and constrained by existing engineering knowledge and available technology.

We also believe that the concept of engineering system could be employed in further research on the 'impact' of microelectronics-based technologies in the workplace. While we have been able to conduct an in-depth analysis of technological change in the context of an already highly automated production system, the innovation concerned was not based on the use of software-driven control or the extensive use of microelectronics. As we saw in chapter 7, these developments have been incorporated in the architecture and technology of System X and other digital exchange systems. An investigation of the introduction of digital exchanges or other software-controlled systems would be able to test further the utility of the engineering system concept and also to document the changes in the nature of skills, work and organisation which staff and supervisors working with such systems are likely to experience.

8.5 The process of technological change in the workplace

Our aim in this book has been to show how managers, trade unionists and workgroups influenced the process of technological change in the workplace. We have suggested that, within a design space defined among other things by the capabilities of the technology being introduced, critical junctures arise at various stages during the process of change at which organisational actors may intervene to influence particular substantive issues. We have used this processual approach to explain the outcomes we have observed in our case-study exchanges.

Apart from its analytical and explanatory value in particular cases, the processual approach also sensitises us to the fact that there are no fixed outcomes of change under a given technological system, simply outcomes at particular moments in time. Our study of TXE4 modernisation in eight exchanges captured workplace realities over a period of three years. Soon after the end of our research, new faulting equipment became available capable of reducing significantly the amount of human interpretation (and skill in the person) required to locate and diagnose many TXE4 faults. Also, on return visits to our exchanges in 1985, we found that there had been modifications to the organisation and control of work since the conclusion of our main fieldwork. This did not involve a move away from team autonomy but we did find changes in the division of labour between particular technicians and the amount of collaborative working in particular units. In other words, processes of technological changes are best seen as part of a cycle which may last many years and even decades. Categorical statements about outcomes of technological change must therefore be tempered by an awareness that outcomes are sometimes themselves simply stages in an as yet incomplete cycle of change.

Adopting a processual approach also directs our attention to the wider development of new technologies – new system principles, architectures, technologies (particularly software technologies) and appearances. When looking at telephone exchange systems, therefore, it is particularly important to see the semi-electronic TXE range of exchanges as an intermediate step towards the fully electronic or digital exchange. So far, exchange modernisation within BT has involved a type of 'island automation', limited to discrete elements of the switching hierarchy within the overall telecommunications network. As we have seen in chapter 7, the adoption of digital exchange systems promises a qualitatively different type of automation, which will eventually involve the creation of an integrated telecommunications network transmitting both voice and non-voice data. Technological integration of this kind is likely to challenge fundamentally traditional forms of organisation, such as extended management hierarchies, departmental divisions, incremental career structures and occupational identities (see Partridge, Clark and Mucci, 1984; Rose and Smith, 1986). We cannot pretend that our study provides the answers to these challenges. We do believe it can give important clues to some of the directions this and similar kinds of technological change may take.

Appendix A Block diagram of the TXE4 exchange system

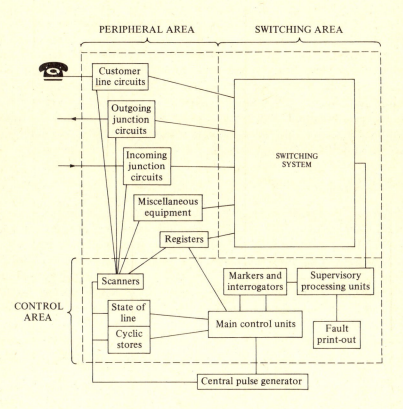

Appendix B Research methods

In a processual study of this kind, no one research method would have been sufficient to capture events and relationships as they unfolded. Accordingly, a variety of methods were used to collect data. These were: self-report diaries; interviews; questionnaires; observation; documentation; and informant interviews. The use of these methods, often in tandem, allowed us to gather a wide range of evidence on the changes that were occurring and also enabled us to cross-check and corroborate information from the same source. Each method and its particular use will be outlined in turn.

Self-report diary

Self-report diaries were completed by senior technicians in Strowger A and Strowger B, Conversions A to D (initial operation) and TXE4 A and Conversion A (routine operation) and by four junior technicians in Strowger A. These junior technicians were the only junior grades in our eight case-study exchanges who were carrying out exchange system maintenance at the time of our diary studies. The technicians were asked to complete a daily diary sheet for each working day over a four-week (i.e. twenty working days) period excluding overtime. Diary sheets were issued to them in a package at the start of the period of study and an explanation was given of how to complete them. During the period of study the technicians were consulted regularly by members of the NTRG to check that there were no difficulties in completing the diaries. It was stressed to respondents that, if they were unsure where to record the time on any particular activity, they should make an entry in a separate category marked 'other' and specify on the reverse of the sheet the nature of the task concerned. No technicians participating in the study declined to complete the self-report diaries, although pressure of work in some exchanges did affect response rates. The response rates for the exchanges expressed in 'technician diary days' (i.e. total number of diary sheets received divided by number of technicians completing diaries in the exchange) varied from 10.6 in Conversion B to 23 in Conversion A, but the majority were between 15 and 20.

The information collected from the diaries provided quantitative data on the balance between different types of work task, job content, collaborative working and the time taken to clear faults. Work task and job content data was analysed in terms of a scheme used in chapter 4. The purpose of this categorisation was to identify as far as possible those aspects of exchange work which could be directly related to the maintenance requirements of the specific exchange system. We called these *exchange system maintenance work tasks*, which comprised corrective maintenance (patrol/reported faults and night-routining) and preventive maintenance (block routines/dormant fault checks).[1] Work tasks common to both types of exchange system were categorised as 'other exchange work' and comprised activities such as miscellaneous engineering,[2] information handling, provision of service work, estate management, training, and other miscellaneous activities including interviews with the NTRG and unclassifiable time. Collaborative working data was computed on the basis of entries which indicated whether time spent on each of the three exchange system maintenance activities involved working with one or more senior technicians. Finally, the time taken to clear faults (or minutes per effective fault) was computed from technicians' diary records by dividing the time spent on patrol/reported faults by the number of effective faults. Frequency distributions were produced for each exchange and standard statistical formulae and techniques were used to calculate values for the mean, mean deviation and mode.

Interviews

Formal interviews were conducted with all fifty-one technicians and supervisors participating in the study (see table A, p. 7). Staff in the conversion exchanges were interviewed twice, at the beginning and end of the study period. The interviews lasted on average between three quarters and one and a half hours. With the permission of each interviewee the sessions were tape-recorded (only two respondents declined to be tape-recorded). Interviews were normally conducted by two members of the NTRG and were held in a suitable room in the exchange building during works time. Before conducting interviews an attempt was made wherever possible to make contact and have informal discussions with the respondent to answer any questions and allay any concerns they had about the research. This, coupled with our regular presence in the exchange during the periods of study, helped build a rapport with interviewees and overcome some of the impersonality that can be associated with formal interviews. This was especially the case in the three main conversion exchanges where an average of twenty-five visits (each lasting from between one and seven hours) was made to each exchange during the course of the research.

The precise format and questions asked in the interviews varied according to the grade of the interviewee, the type of exchange in which they were working (Strowger, TXE4 or Conversion) and whether it was their first or second interview.[3] However, the structure of the interviews followed a consistent overall pattern and covered the following areas: background of respondent; training and career; job content; work organisation; supervision; skill; job satisfaction; modernisation; and industrial relations. Once completed, the interview tapes were transcribed and in the two cases where tape recording was declined notes were written-up. Answers were then analysed, cross-referenced and coded, force-choice responses were aggregated as appropriate and verbatim quotations on particular questions and issues were grouped together and compared before being selected for inclusion in the report to BT (January 1985) or in this book.

Personal questionnaires

To support our interview data and to reduce the time required for interviews, a personal questionnaire was circulated to the technicians and supervisors in order to acquire general background data. This included personal details (e.g. age, place of birth, marital status, occupation of father, salary, distance of home from exchange or office); education and qualifications (i.e. secondary and further education); previous employment; career inside and outside BT; BT training courses attended (including TXE4); trade union membership (date joined/left); summary of exchanges and staff supervised (supervisors only).

Observation

Observation of the work of technicians and supervisors was conducted in the exchanges to familiarise ourselves with the overall nature of exchange work, to provide data on the nature of specific tasks and to monitor progress in the conversion exchanges. Whilst in some circumstances it was appropriate to observe work in a 'fly on the wall' fashion, in most cases the technical nature of the work or particular events required interaction with the maintenance staff to facilitate understanding. Thus our observation of work also included an important element of informal discussion with both technicians and supervisors. This provided us with a deeper understanding of the nature of exchange work and procedures. During the pilot study we carried out observation of the work of all the participating sample of senior technicians. We were thus able to build up a detailed picture of the general nature of exchange work prior to the main study. During the main study, the work of ten of the senior technicians was observed in detail for periods of between one and four hours. Observation of progress in the conversion exchanges also involved informal discussions with BT installation staff and Executive Engineers and general observation of exchange activities. In the months spanning de-bugging, changeover and initial operation, visits were made to the conversion exchanges approximately every four weeks. These visits were intensified in the days either side of changeover. Members of the NTRG were present at the 'pulling the wedges' of all four conversion exchanges, which in two cases took place at an hour rather too early for our comfort.[4]

Documentation and informant interviews

In order to provide an understanding of the context in which the modernisation of the exchanges was taking place, documentary data was collected in the local areas and interviews were held with 'key informants' (particularly Executive Engineers, Heads of Maintenance and trade union representatives) on the modernisation programme. Documentary data included exchange performance statistics, minutes of management/union meetings and area seminars, and copies of correspondence relating to formal and informal agreements between area management and the POEU.

Interviews with key informants from area management covered the following topics: general background to exchange maintenance and modernisation; selection and training staff for TXE4; TXE4 maintenance philosophy and practice; contacts with local trade unions on modernisation; and general industrial relations background to the local area. Topics covered with the local trade union representatives were: general background to local union organisation; policy on TXE4 modernisation; nature of discussions and agreements with management on TXE4 modernisation; influence of national-level union policy; the general area industrial relations background. These interviews varied in length and were usually tape recorded and transcribed in summary form.

In addition to this information collected at area level, interviews were held with members of various BTHQ departments, who also supplied documentary data on the national context in which exchange modernisation was taking place. Similarly, interviews and documentary data were provided by the national officers of the POEU and STE. Members of the NTRG attended the POEU and STE annual conferences each year from 1980–3 on the invitation of the respective National Executive Councils.

Notes

Introduction

1 For a discussion of the concept of technological determinism see chapter 1, section 1.2; also Wilkinson, 1983: chapters 1 and 2; Buchanan and Boddy, 1983: chapter 2.

2 It is now widely accepted that we need to distinguish between at least three main stages in the mechanisation of production processes: primary mechanisation, the use of power-driven machinery to transform raw materials into a product; secondary mechanisation, the use of machinery to accomplish transfer tasks, as in the continuous-flow production line; and tertiary mechanisation, the co-ordination and control of transformation and transfer tasks (see Gill, 1985: 63–4). This third stage of mechanisation is normally referred to as automation, since it is concerned not with the degree of sophistication or modernity of a technological process or device but with the way it is controlled (see Thurman, 1984: 27). Primary mechanisation is normally dated from the early to mid-nineteenth century and achieved an enormous impetus at the end of the century with the growing use of electrical power. The second and third stages date from the beginning of the twentieth century, although tertiary mechanisation is particularly identified with electronic-control technologies and the increasing application since the mid-1970s of microelectronics and micro-processor-controlled systems (see Forester, 1980: part 1; Forester, 1985: part 1; Gill, 1985: 1–35).

3 For further details on the NTRG see Annual Reports, University of Southampton.

4 Throughout this book TXE4 A refers to one particular exchange in the south of England which was investigated as part of our research. This should not be confused with TXE4A, which refers to a generic type of telephone exchange system (see below, section 2.4). The term TXE4A does not figure prominently in this book and as a result we hope that the use of the two terms will not cause confusion.

5 These three senior technicians comprised one from each of three exchanges, Strowger A, Conversion D and TXE4 A. However, we were able to gain a broad picture of their duties from interviews with the supervisors and the other senior technicians in these units and have incorporated this information into the text at appropriate points.

6 Initially we did not intend to study junior technicians in any detail, as none of them were eligible for TXE4 re-training. However, the very fact that they were being excluded from re-training meant that their jobs and career prospects were likely to change significantly as a result of TXE4 modernisation. We therefore conducted a small subsidiary study of junior technicians, concentrating mainly on two exchanges: Strowger A, where the five (out of a complement of seven) who participated in our study were engaged in traditional Strowger maintenance duties; and Conversion C, where we were able to study three junior technicians who experienced various aspects of the move from Strowger to TXE4. The findings of this subsidiary study are reported in chapter 4 and particularly in chapter 6.

1. Understanding technological change in the workplace

1 New technologies are thus, according to our definition, new engineering systems (see on this concept, Rose and Smith, 1986).

2 The concept has been used by Rice (1963) and Woodward (1980: 162), and adopted by Buchanan and Boddy (1983: 253). Buchanan and Boddy argue: 'If an organisation is in business to make biscuits, then a sequence of tasks, including mixing dough, baking and packing biscuits, must be carried out to achieve this overall objective (what Rice (1963) called the "primary task"). That objective and the technology used jointly determine the nature of tasks that organisation members have to perform.' The relation between primary task, technology (i.e. engineering system) and work tasks and skill will be one of the main focuses of our analysis below.

3 By 'proper' exchange we mean an exchange which can interconnect calls between any two of a large number of callers. The very early exchanges simply provided direct and fixed connections between a maximum of two or three callers.

4 The last manual exchange in Britain was closed in 1976. Subscriber Trunk Dialling (STD) – that is, the automatic connection of subscribers not connected to the same local exchange – was first introduced in 1958 and has since been extended to cover the whole country. International Subscriber Dialling (ISD) was first introduced in 1963. See chapter 2 for more details.

5 All post-Strowger exchange designs have common-control architecture, while the technology used in their switching and control functions has taken a variety of forms. The first common-control exchanges were implemented in electro-mechanical technology, with the control by means of relays and the switching matrix by electro-mechanical Crossbar switches (see chapter 2). A number of hybrid electronic/electro-mechanical common-control exchange designs, such as TXE4, have been developed in the past two decades, while the most recent exchanges use advanced electronic devices for switching and software programs for control. The development of the British System X exchange is described in chapter 7.

6 When a current is passed through a coil wound round the tube, a magnetic field is established along the axis of the tube and opposite polarity induced in

the overlapping free ends of the reeds. The reeds are therefore attracted together with a toggle or 'snap' action giving a high operating speed. When the current is disconnected, the magnetic field collapses and the flexure of the reed causes the contacts to separate. For further details see Ward, 1974: 25–6.

7 Unlike in Strowger, where the identity of the called party is not known until the connection is actually made (that is, at the point when the caller dials the final digit), for a call to be set up in TXE4 the complete identity of the called customer is required before switching can take place.

8 Each exchange has cleaning staff associated with it. One additional feature of the exchange appearance we identified during the research was a smell common to all the units studied. On investigation this was found to derive from the standard anti-static floor polish used by the cleaners!

9 It should be stressed, too, that the security of a particular unit also depends on the system dimensioning appropriate, amongst other things, to the number of customer connections and customer-calling rates (see Goodman and Phillips, 1976: 197). For example, TXE4 exchanges may contain anything between three and twenty Main Control Units, and in each case choices must be made by exchange planners as to how many MCUs to include in order to balance acceptable customer service with cost constraints (see Goodman and Phillips, 1976: 199; Huggins, Mills and Patel, 1977: 13). Apart from the enhancement of system security, another important implication of the modularity of TXE4 system configuration is that extensions, for example to the traffic-carrying capacity of an exchange, can be made by adding further standard modules (see Goodman and Phillips, 1976: 197).

10 Routiners can also be used by technicians under manual control, for example, to re-test equipment identified as busy by the night-routiner test program or more generally to put a particular item of equipment through a thorough test.

11 MAC does not, however, monitor live traffic. At the time of our project, this was carried out by Telephone Service Observations (TSOs) of a random number of calls by BT telephone operators. TSO was replaced in 1985 by TELCARE, the telephoning of customers by an independent survey company on behalf of BT in order to elicit their views and experiences of the telephone service.

12 A number of writers have made the important distinction between radical and incremental innovation, arguing that each has substantially different implications for the management and organisation of technological change. Among the features which distinguish a radical from an incremental innovation are the extent to which it is discontinuous with previous experience (in an organisation or industrial sector), its magnitude, and the degree of risk or uncertainty associated with it. For an influential exposition of the distinction between radical and incremental innovation, see Hage (1980). Hage's approach is discussed in Ettlie (1984) and Gerwin (1984).

2. Management strategies and the modernisation of the telephone exchange network

1 Our four Strowger–TXE4 Conversion case-study exchanges (11,000, 9,000, 12,000 and 15,000 lines) and two 'established' TXE4 case-study exchanges (12,000 and 11,000 lines) were therefore generally a little larger than the average.

2 The figure of 308 includes the 36 small TXE4 systems connected to direct dialling-in facilities. See the note and text to table 2.4.

3. Industrial relations and the negotiation of change

1 The term 'senior technician' is not a term used in BT to describe the job of Technical Officers engaged in exchange maintenance. It is used in this book, however, to distinguish the broad tasks and status of TO grades from those of 'junior technicians' or T2As. In exchanges where there were less than four resident TOs and no maintenance supervisor on-site, it was normal for area management to designate one TO as 'officer-in-charge' of the buildings. In cases where four or more TOs were resident, one was officially designated as Technical Officer with Allowance (TOA) under a national agreement with the POEU. TOAs were usually given some supervisory responsibilities in their exchanges and received in return a small additional payment. These supervisory roles are discussed further in chapter 5.

2 In Coast Area, for example, management agreed with the union to phase the training courses over a period of eighteen months to two years so as not to cause too much disruption to the personal lives of individuals and to enable them to acquire the new skills at a reasonable tempo. In Metro and Town areas, management generally aspired to a similar phasing of the training courses, although this was not always achieved in practice.

3 When interviewed, the middle-manager in Metro Area with responsibility for selection and training of staff stressed that selection had also been based on management's perception of the suitability of individual technicians. However, in the ten exchanges which had already been modernised in the area by 1983 only one resident technician had been rejected by management, with the acquiescence of the union, on grounds of non-suitability. In practice, therefore, the sitting-tenant principle predominated. In Coast Area, there were a number of additional criteria for selection including: no re-training for senior technicians over fifty-two years old; in cases of insufficient sitting tenants, re-training to be offered to other senior technicians in the telephone area on the basis of seniority as a maintenance technician; no re-training to be offered to senior technicians already possessing two maintenance skills, e.g. Strowger and Crossbar.

4 This is possibly a more general problem in the implementation of new technology or any large-scale re-training scheme, that initially there are only a limited number of re-training places available and that choices and prefer-

ences have to be made for logistical and financial reasons which may have unforeseen longer term implications.

5 'Strowger man' was a term used by management and technicians alike to refer to maintenance staff, at whatever level, who were imbued with the culture of Strowger maintenance. It was often mentioned with great pride ('I'm a Strowger man'), although the same phrase was also used, again by management and technicians alike, to denote staff who had got stuck in Strowger customs and practices and were held to be incapable of adapting to new systems. We should note that maintenance technicians were almost exclusively male. We did, however, encounter one or two female junior technicians during our research.

6 It should perhaps be noted that the interviews conducted at the end of our project (in the first half of 1984) showed a marked difference in this regard to interviews in 1982 and early and mid-1983. In the intervening period a number of technicians had attended presentations from management about the employment implications of System X and as a result were much more uncertain about their long-term future. This question will be taken up again in chapter 7.

7 Another factor which needs to be considered is that TXE4 replacement units were often equipped to cater for more exchange connections than the old Strowger units. This again makes direct comparisons of staffing levels more difficult.

4. Maintenance technicians: work tasks, skills and re-training

1 Certain block routine maintenance tasks had periodicities exceeding one month and in some cases up to twelve months. Some of these tasks will therefore not have been captured in our diaries. To this extent we have slightly under-estimated the proportion of time spent on block routine maintenance.

2 The length of time in live operation proved not to be a reliable guide to whether an exchange had settled down into routine operation or not. One of our exchanges (TXE4 B) had been operating for over five years but due to major technical problems was consistently failing to meet its performance targets. At the time of our study the maintenance staff were engaged in a systematic overhaul of the equipment supported by a specialist area faults team. In our view they were experiencing a 'non-routine' pattern of work and work organisation. For this reason we have not used our data from this exchange as a primary example of 'routine' operation. We should stress that these concepts of routine and non-routine operation are our own and not those of British Telecom.

3 The one area of 'other exchange work' on which TXE4 staff spent considerable more time was information handling. This accounted for seventeen per cent (TXE4 A) and sixteen per cent (Conversion A) of their total work time, compared with eleven per cent and ten per cent for Strowger A and Strowger B respectively.

4 The busying out of parts of TXE4 equipment was subject in all exchanges to an overriding maximum beyond which exchange system security, or quality of customer service, was deemed to be unacceptably prejudiced.

5 The use of the term 'appear' is important. As we show elsewhere in this chapter, whereas in Strowger the alarm identified the piece of equipment which had caused the fault, in TXE4 the cause of the fault could sometimes be remote from the symptom.

6 In fact some automatically identified faults proved to be false alarms. The first task of a technician responding to an automatic alarm in our TXE4 exchanges was to go straight to the area of equipment identified and flick a switch to return it to service. If the ringing stopped immediately, the technicians assumed either that the equipment was now functioning normally and thus took no further action, or that it was an intermittent fault which would have to be dealt with if it re-occurred. Some reported faults, too, were never proved to have been actual exchange faults and were recorded (as in Strowger) as either Fault Not Found (FNF) or Right When Tested (RWT). The cause of such reported faults may have been located outside the exchange, either in the external lines or, for example, in a customer not replacing a phone properly.

7 The figures in tables 4.2 and 4.3 are based on daily diary reports, so faults stretching over a number of days are counted separately for each day on which they occupied the maintenance staff. As a result, our method of data collection tends to under-estimate slightly the time per effective fault, particularly of course the more complex TXE4 faults.

8 The sample size for each question asked in the interviews varied according to its nature. For tables and diagrams presented in this book, the total number of responses received to a particular question is designated as 'n' followed by the relevant number. For questions asked of all engineering technicians the maximum possible sample size was forty-four; for those asked of all senior technicians, thirty-four; for all Strowger senior technicians, twenty-three; for all TXE4 senior technicians, eighteen; and for all senior technicians in conversion exchanges, sixteen.

9 The three categories of skill-type were constituted from the following responses, some of which are included in more than one category. Most technicians gave multiple answers and these have been aggregated:

> *Strowger mental skills:* electrical knowledge, circuit diagrams, fault diagnosis, logical mind, systems approach, deductive ability, mechanical engineering knowledge, college courses, ability to interpret information.
> *Strowger manual skills:* mechanical adjustments, routine cleaning, checking selectors and relays, soldering, wiring.
> *Strowger experiential and intuitive skills:* experience, fault diagnosis, visual abilities, aural abilities, checking selectors and relays, knack/feeling, knowledge of layout, patience, ability to interpret information.
> *TXE4 mental skills:* use of maintenance aids, logical mind,

awareness of system implications, deductive ability, ability to read diagrams, system knowledge, paperwork, courses, interpretation of information, fault finding.
TXE4 manual skills: mechanical adjustments, soldering.
TXE4 experiential and intuitive skills: fault finding, feel/intuition, mastery of documentation, ability to think before you act.

10 It is perhaps interesting to note that the technicians themselves referred to the systems generically as 'Strowger' and 'TXE4'.

11 Some of the technicians in our conversion exchanges appear in both columns. They were asked in their first interview (when they were still predominantly Strowger technicians) about Strowger maintenance, and in their second interview (when they were working in their new TXE4 units) about TXE4 maintenance. Interestingly, there were no significant differences in the responses between the technicians in Strowger A and B and those in the conversion exchanges prior to changeover, nor between the technicians in exchanges TXE4 A and B and those in the conversion exchanges after changeover. The responses have therefore been aggregated.

12 The conversion of an individual exchange from Strowger to TXE4 began, in fact, with a decision at regional level to select the particular unit for modernisation. Regional engineering planners were then responsible for adapting the basic TXE4 system design to the requirements of the particular installation, what we have called detail design or dimensioning (see section 1.3 above). This would take into account the existing and projected connection capacity of the unit, measured in terms of the number of exchange lines or customer connections, and the traffic-carrying or switching capacity, measured in 'erlangs' and reflecting customer-calling rates (see Goodman and Phillips, 1976: 196–7). In addition, account would also be taken of the availability of accommodation into which the new equipment would be installed. In most of the cases we studied the location of the new equipment was in the same building as the old Strowger unit, although it was sometimes situated in a purpose-built extension. Once the new exchange had been dimensioned in this way, regional engineering managers would then place a contract order with the equipment suppliers (at the time of our research, GEC, Plessey and STC) for the manufacture of the new unit. Since our main concern is with the implementation of change as it directly affected the exchange maintenance staff, our interest in this chapter is in the process of system implementation from the moment the exchange equipment arrived at the exchange building.

13 In Conversion A, the only unit for which we have detailed comparative diary data, the technicians spent sixty-one per cent of their total work time on patrol/reported faults during the initial operation of the exchange but only forty-one per cent of their time on the same tasks once the exchange and their working patterns had settled down.

14 The relatively high proportion of total work time spent on such tasks during the period of initial operation can be explained in part by the degree of

inexperience (lack of 'experiential' skills) of the technicians. Quantitative evidence of this is provided by data collected on the length of time it took the technicians to clear faults in Conversion A. During initial operation (data collected between two and three months after changeover), around fifty percent of faults took the technicians between one and three hours to clear. After nine months just under fifty per cent of faults were being cleared by the same technicians in between half an hour and two hours, a significant reduction.

15 It should be noted that large volumes of print-out can often result from a few repeated faults on the same piece of equipment and therefore do not necessarily entail a large amount of maintenance. Also, faults identified on the FPO are normally first-attempt failures and thus do not affect customer service. In the case of Conversion D, the large volume of print-out reflected a large amount of 'first-attempt' matrix-switching faults. We can only speculate on this question, but while the staff were working at fever pitch during the first two months of initial operation of Conversion D, it is unlikely that customer service was prejudiced to any great extent because of TXE4's second-attempt facility.

5. The problem of supervision

1 Our discussion of supervision in this chapter is based on our study of seven supervisors in three different telephone areas (see table A, p. 7). The limited nature of this sample should be borne in mind when considering the wider applicability of our findings to the rest of British Telecom. As with the other parts of our study, however, we believe that the limited nature of our sample is offset by the fullness of our data.

2 During the period of our study in this unit the exchange equipment was performing satisfactorily within its targets and there were no particular staffing problems. The only event affecting normal quality of service was a major cable fault. The local Gas Board had cut through a telephone cable and as a result taken a large number of customer lines out of service. In this case the maintenance supervisor took responsibility for liaison with the Gas Board and BT external staff repairing the cable, while the working supervisor (TOA) organised the temporary re-routing of customer lines within the exchange pending the repair of the cable. Within twenty-four hours the exchange returned to normal operation without any significant effect on customer service.

3 The staffing complement in our Strowger exchanges was decided by area managements against the background of many years 'custom and practice'. Amongst the main criteria were the number of exchange lines and level of traffic within an exchange.

4 Supervisory Processing Units (SPUs) and 'Markers' are two parts of the control area of the TXE4 exchange system. Interrogator/Markers operate under instructions from the Main Control Unit, identifying free paths available through the network and then setting up the chosen path. Once the path has been set up, the SPU, which obtains its information and instructions from the Interrogator/Markers via the MCU, takes control of the call and supervises a

number of operations including metering, call-timing and cleardown. For further details see Appendix A, TXE4 Block Diagram. Also Ward, 1974: 42; and POTTC, 1973: 9–10.

5 Interestingly, the 'TXE4 Exchange Management' course proved so successful that BTHQ subsequently introduced similar courses dealing with the technical management of exchange maintenance for supervisors of other non-digital exchange systems.

6. Work organisation and the emergence of team autonomy

1 Thompson and other writers have often underlined the fact that the dual labour market often coincides with the 'sexual divison of labour' (see Thompson, 1983: chapter 7; also Beechey, 1982). The existence of such gender-based labour market segmentation was confirmed by our study to the extent that around ninety-seven per cent of exchange maintenance technicians in BT in 1983 were male. However, as this was true for both Strowger and TXE4 exchange systems the introduction of new technology in this case simply reaffirmed the existing sexual division of labour.

2 Interestingly, when we returned to the exchange some eight months later, this technician had just returned from secondment to another TXE4 unit where he had been able to spend a number of weeks working alongside an experienced and patient senior technician. As a result of this experience he was now much more confident in his own abilities and was about to start taking on exchange system maintenance tasks in Conversion D. By the time we made our final visit to the exchange in 1985 to report on our findings, he had become a full member of the technician team and was able and willing to carry out all types of exchange system maintenance.

3 The degree of difficulty experienced by the technicians at this stage was indicated by the fact that the time taken to diagnose and clear 'effective' faults (see above, section 4.3) was a minimum of at least one hour. In fact half of the faults during the period of initial operation took the technicians three hours or more to clear.

4 The cyclic store is that part of the TXE4 system which stores information for each exchange line, for example the directory number and class of service (business, residential and so on). This data-store cycles through all terminal addresses at regular intervals in synchrony with the scanning equipment, determining whether the lines are free, busy or calling. The Main Control Unit is a special-purpose computer which lies at the heart of the TXE4 exchange. It controls the operation of the network (switching network) by collecting and processing information from other parts of the system. For further details, see Appendix A; also POTTC, 1973: 9–10; and Ward, 1974: 39–43.

7. System X: centralised maintenance and a new industrial relations?

1 Many of these new services, such as short-code dialling and repeat last call, can be offered before the network is fully converted to digital. Some new services

will also be available to customers connected to TXE4 and TXE4A exchanges (at the time of writing a number of these exchanges were being specially enhanced for this purpose).

2 According to the *Guardian* the software problems had been 'cracked' by late 1985. The System X modernisation programme was therefore to be accelerated so that the replacement of Strowger trunk and tandem exchanges could be targeted for 1988 (*Guardian*, 6.11.85).

3 Telephone operators remained outside the NCU in the Union of Communication Workers.

4 The stress on excellence was, of course, part of a wider vogue amongst British management in the 1980s, stimulated by Peters and Waterman's guide to America's 'best-run companies', *In Search of Excellence* (1982).

Appendix B. Research methods

1 In the TXE4 exchanges we have normally included time spent on Strowger-type routines (e.g. meter routines) as other exchange work. However, it is possible that a small proportion of time spent on dormant faults in the TXE4 exchanges included Strowger-type work.

2 In exchanges where individual technicians were allocated 'special faults' as a specialised duty and did not carry out corrective maintenance tasks on the exchange system equipment itself, this time was classified as other exchange work. In exchanges where special faults were not treated in this way, the time has been included in the patrol/reported fault category.

3 On one memorable occasion the researchers arrived at an exchange after a ninety-mile journey from Southampton without the appropriate standardised seven-page interview schedule. Fortunately one day's interviewing was saved by the innovative use of a telephone to dictate the questions to the interviewers as they were conducting the first interview!

4 Practice varied in our three telephone areas as to the timing and publicity of the changeover. In two cases, 1.30 p.m. on a Wednesday afternoon was the chosen time for 'pulling the wedges', since early closing of shops and the lunch-hour meant that business traffic was likely to be comparatively light. In these cases the local mayor, senior managers from the telephone area and the local press were invited to the changeover, which was observed by about twenty people in addition to those pulling the wedges. A rather more cautious practice was to change over exchanges at 7.00 a.m. on a Sunday morning, a more private affair involving mainly local BT staff and, usually, an excellent cooked breakfast. Perhaps the most striking aspects of pulling the wedges were its almost ceremonial and ritual status; the large number of people packed into the normally sparsely populated exchange; and the sprint down from the old exchange to the new to see if it was 'on the air' after the wedges had been pulled.

Bibliography

References to the following journals will be abbreviated as follows:
British Journal of Industrial Relations (*BJIR*)
British Telecommunications Engineering (*BTE*)
Industrial Relations Journal (*IRJ*)
Post Office Electrical Engineers Journal (*POEEJ*)
Post Office Telecommunications Journal (*POTJ*)

Albury, D. and Schwartz, J. 1982, *Partial Progress: The Politics of Science and Technology*, London: Pluto Press

Ashford, E. 1969, *The Aesthetics of Engineering Design*, London: Business Books

Atkinson, J. 1984, Manpower strategies for flexible organisations, *Personnel Management*, August: 28–9

Atkinson, J. and Meager, N. 1986, Flexibility – just a flash in the pan?, *Personnel Management*, September: 26–7

Bain, G. (ed.) 1983, *Industrial Relations in Britain*, Oxford: Basil Blackwell

Bamber, G. 1980, Microchips and industrial relations, *IRJ* 11(5): 7–19

Bamber, G. and Willman, P. 1983, Technological change and industrial relations in Britain, *Bulletin of Comparative Labour Relations*, Bulletin 12: 101–20

Batstone, E., Ferner, A. and Terry, M. 1984, *Consent and Efficiency – Labour Relations and Management Strategy in the State Enterprise*, Oxford: Basil Blackwell

Baty, R. and Sandum, K. 1985, System X: maintenance control sub-system, *BTE* 3(4): 277–83

Bealey, F. 1976, *The Post Office Engineering Union – The History of the Post Office Engineers (1870–1970)*, London: Bachmann and Turner

1977, The political system of the Post Office Engineering Union, *BJIR* xv(3): 374–95

Bedeian, A. 1980, *Organisations: Theory and Analysis*, Illinois: The Dryden Press

Beechey, V. 1982, The sexual division of labour and the labour process. In S. Wood (ed.), *The Degradation of Work?*, London: Hutchinson, 54–73

Benson, D. 1974, Local exchange renewal strategy: formulating a strategy, *POEEJ* 67(3): 130–5

Benson, I. and Lloyd, J. 1983, *New Technology and Industrial Change*, London: Kogan Page

Bibliography

Bessant, J. 1983, Management and manufacturing innovation: the case of information technology. In G. Winch (ed.), *Information Technology in Manufacturing Processes*, London: Rossendale

Blauner, R. 1964, *Alienation and Freeedom*, Chicago: University of Chicago Press

Boag, J. and Frame, P. 1985, Telecommunications – meeting the challenge, *BTE* 3(4): 277–83

Brander, R. and Burville, P. 1985, Evolution of System X – a review, *BTE* 3(4): 223–5

Braun, E. and MacDonald, S. 1978, *Revolution in Miniature*, Cambridge: Cambridge University Press

Braverman, H. 1974, *Labor and Monopoly Capital*, New York and London: Monthly Review Press

Bright, J. 1958, *Automation and Management*, Boston: Harvard University Press

British Telecom 1981, *Switching Maintenance: A Handbook for Supervisors*, London: British Telecom

  1982, *System X – The Way Ahead*, London: British Telecom

  1983a, *Area Re-organisation*, London: British Telecom Inland Division

  1983b, *Supervising Officer's Handbook: TXE4 Exchange Maintenance*, London: British Telecom LCS HQ

Broadhurst, S. 1963, The Highgate Wood electronic telephone exchange, *POEEJ* 55(4): 265–74

Brooks, J. 1975, *Telephone: The First Hundred Years*, New York: Harper and Row

Buchanan, D. 1983, Technological imperatives and strategic choice. In G. Winch (ed.), *Information Technology in Manufacturing Processes*, London: Rossendale

Buchanan, D. and Boddy, D. 1983, *Organisations in the Computer Age*, Aldershot: Gower

Burns, T. 1977, *The BBC*, London: Macmillan

Butera, F. 1984, Designing work in automated systems: a review of the case studies. In F. Butera and J. Thurman (eds.), *Automation and Work Design*, Amsterdam: Elsevier, 43–105

Butera, F. and Thurman, J. (eds.), *Automation and Work Design*, Amsterdam: Elsevier

Carter, C. 1977, *Post Office Review Committee Report*, Chairman: Charles Carter, Cmnd. 6850, London: HMSO

Child, J. 1972, Organisation structure, environment and performance: the role of strategic choice, *Sociology*, 6(1): 1–22

  1984, *Organisation*, 2nd edn, London: Harper and Row

  1985, Managerial strategies, new technology and the labour process. In D. Knights, H. Willmott and D. Collinson (eds.), *Job Redesign: Critical Perspectives on the Labour Process*, Aldershot: Gower, 107–41

Child, J. and Partridge, B. 1982, *Supervisors: The Lost Managers?* Cambridge: Cambridge University Press

Child, J., Loveridge, R., Harvey, J. and Spencer, A. 1984, Microelectronics and the quality of employment in services. In P. Marstrand (ed.), *New Technology and the Future of Work and Skill*, London: Frances Pinter, 163–90

Clark, J., Jacobs, A., King, R. and Rose, H. 1984, New technology, industrial relations and divisions within the workforce, *IRJ* 15(3): 36–44

Cockburn, C. 1983, *Brothers – Male Dominance and Technological Change*, London: Pluto Press

Coombs, R. 1985, Automation, management strategies and labour process change. In D. Knights, H. Willmott and D. Collinson (eds.), *Job Redesign: Critical Perspectives on the Labour Process*, Aldershot: Gower, 142–70

Crompton, R. and Jones, G. 1984, *White-Collar Proletariat – De-skilling and Gender in Clerical Work*, London: Macmillan

Crooks, K. 1974, Exchange modernisation – steering towards the decision, *POTJ*, Autumn, 24–7

1985, Local network strategy – today's plans for tomorrow's network, *BTE*, 3(4), 297–9

Cross, M. 1985, *Towards the Flexible Craftsman*, London: Technical Change Centre

CSE Microelectronics Group 1980, *Microelectronics: Capitalist Technology and the Working Class*, London: CSE Books

Davis, L. and Taylor, J. 1972, *The Design of Jobs*, Harmondsworth: Penguin

1976, Technology, organisation and job structure. In R. Dubin (ed.), *Handbook of Work, Organisation and Society*, Chicago: Rand–McNally

Dawson, P. 1986, *Computer Technology and the Redefinition of Supervision*, Ph.D., University of Southampton

Dawson, P. and McLoughlin, I. 1986, Computer technology and the redefinition of supervision, *Journal of Management Studies*, 23(1), January

Dawson, S. and Wedderburn, D. 1980, Introduction. In J. Woodward, *Industrial Organisation: Theory and Practice*, 2nd edn, Oxford: Oxford University Press

Edwards, R. 1979, *Contested Terrain: The Transformation of the Workplace in the Twentieth Century*, London: Heinemann

Ettlie, J. 1984, Implementation strategy for manufacturing innovations. In M. Warner (ed.), *Microprocessors, Manpower and Society*, Aldershot: Gower, 31–48

Forester, T. (ed.) 1980, *The Microelectronics Revolution*, Oxford: Basil Blackwell

1985, *The Information Technology Revolution*, Oxford: Basil Blackwell

Fox, A. 1985, *Man Mismanagement*, 2nd edn, London: Hutchinson

Friedman, A. 1977, *Industry and Labour*, London: Macmillan

Gallie, D. 1978, *In Search of the New Working Class*, Cambridge: Cambridge University Press

Gershuny, J. and Miles, I. 1983, *The New Economy: The Transformation of Employment in Industrial Societies*, London: Frances Pinter

Gerwin, D. 1984, Innovation, microelectronics and manufacturing technology. In M. Warner (ed.), *Microprocessors, Manpower and Society*, Aldershot: Gower, 66–83

Bibliography

Giddens, A. 1977, Functionalism: après la lutte. In A. Giddens, *Studies in Social and Political Theory*, London: Hutchinson

Gill, C. 1985, *Work, Unemployment and New Technology*, Cambridge: Polity Press

Goodman, J. and Phillips, J. 1976, TXE4 electronic exchange system: part 1 – overall description and general operation, *POEEJ*, 68, January: 196–203

Gruneberg, M. 1979, *Understanding Job Satisfaction*, London: Macmillan

Hage, J. 1980, *Theories of Organisation*, New York: John Wiley

Harlow, C. 1977, *Innovation and Productivity under Nationalisation: The First Thirty Years*, London: PEP

Harris, L. 1966, Electronic telephone exchanges: an introductory review of development, *POEEJ*, 59: 214–17

Harris, P. and Budgen, J. 1974, Exchange modernisation – the task ahead, *POEEJ*, Winter, 11–13

Hill, S. 1981, *Competition and Control at Work*, London: Heinemann

Huggins, G., Mills, W. and Patel, C. 1977, TXE4 electronic exchange systems: part 3 – system security and maintenance features, *POEEJ*, 70(1): 12–20

Jacobs, A. 1983, *Film and Electronic Technologies in the Production of Television News*, Ph.D., University of Southampton

Kerswell, G. and Kelly, A. 1983, Electronic exchange system TXE4A: part 2 – design and operation, *BTE*, 2, July: 101–10

Knights, D., Willmott, H. and Collinson, D. (eds.) 1985, *Job Redesign: Critical Perspectives on the Labour Process*, Aldershot: Gower

Lawrence, J. and Harris, L. 1966, A review of electronic switching developments in the UK, *IEEE Transactions (Communications Technology)*, 14, June: 208

Leggett, G. 1982, Electronic exchange system TXE4A: part 1 – background to the development, *BTE*, 2, July: 172–5

Lerner, S. 1961, *Breakaway Unions and the Small Trade Union*, London: Allen and Unwin

Mackenzie, D. and Wajcman, J. (eds.) 1985, *The Social Shaping of Technology*, Milton Keynes: Open University Press

Mallet, S. 1975, *The New Working Class*, Nottingham: Spokesman Books

Marstrand, P. (ed.) 1984, *New Technology and the Future of Work and Skill*, London: Frances Pinter

McLoughlin, I., Rose, H. and Clark, J. 1985, Managing the introduction of new technology, *Omega*, 13(4): 251–62

Merton, R. K. (1936), The unanticipated consequences of purposive social action, *American Sociological Review*, 1: 894–904

Moore, R. and Levie, H. 1985, New technology and the unions. In T. Forester, 1985, *The Microelectronics Revolution*, Oxford: Basil Blackwell, 511–27

Noble, D. 1979, Social choice in machine design: the case of automatically controlled machine tools. In A. Zimbalist (ed.), *Case Studies in the Labour Process*, London: Monthly Review Press

1984, *Forces of Production: A Social History of Industrial Automation*, New York: Alfred A. Knopf

Partridge, J., Clark, J. and Mucci, P. 1984, The integration of design and

242

manufacture through CAE systems? Theory and practice, *International Conference on Computer-Aided Engineering*, IEE Conference Publications no. 243, London: Institution of Electrical Engineers

Perrow, C. 1967, A framework for the comparative analysis of organisations, *American Sociological Review*, 32(2)

Peters, T. and Waterman, R. 1982, *In Search of Excellence – Lessons from America's Best-Run Companies*, New York: Harper and Row

Phillips, J. and Rowe, M. 1976, TXE4 electronic exchange system: part 2, *POEEJ*, July: 68–78

POEU 1979, *The Modernisation of Telecommunications*, London: POEU
　1981, *System X – An Information Document*, London: POEU
　1984, *Making the Future Work – The Broad Strategy*, London: POEU

Post Office Technical Training College 1973, *A Brief Review of Common Control Telephone Exchange Systems*, Issue 2, London: Post Office

Povey, P. 1979, *The Telephone and the Exchange*, London: Pitman

Price, C. and Boulter, R. 1985, Integrated Services Digital Network, *BTE*, 3(4): 311–17

Pryke, R. 1981, *The Nationalised Industries*, Oxford: Martin Robertson

Pugh, D. and Hickson, D. 1976, *Organisation Structure in its Context: The Aston Programme 1*, Farnborough: Saxon House/Lexington

Rice, A. 1958, *Productivity and Social Organisation*, London: Tavistock
　1963, *The Enterprise and its Environment*, London: Tavistock

Robbins, K. and Webster, F. 1982, New technology: a survey of trade union response in Britain, *IRJ*, 13(2): 7–26

Rolfe, H. 1986, 'Skill, de-skilling and new technology in the non-manual labour process, *New Technology, Work and Employment*, 1(1): 37–49

Rose, H., McLoughlin, I., King, R. and Clark, J. 1986, Opening the black box: the relation between technology and work, *New Technology, Work and Employment*, 1(1): 18–26

Rose, H. and Smith, J. 1986, The organisational challenge of new engineering systems: some themes for a research agenda. In C. Voss (ed.), *Managing Advanced Manufacturing Technology*, Bedford: IFS Publications

Rose, M. and Jones, B. 1985, Managerial strategy and trade union response in plant level re-organisation of work. In D. Knights, H. Willmott and D. Collinson (eds.), *Job Redesign: Critical Perspectives on the Labour Process*, Aldershot: Gower, 81–106

Rush, H. and Williams, R. 1984, Consultation and change: new technology and manpower in the electronics industry. In M. Warner (ed.), *Microprocessors, Manpower and Society*, Aldershot: Gower, 171–88

Scarbrough, H. 1984, Maintenance workers and new technology, *IRJ*, 15(4): 9–16

Senker, P. 1984, Training for Automation. In M. Warner (ed.), *Microprocessors, Manpower and Society*, Aldershot: Gower, 134–46

Senker, P. and Swords-Isherwood, N., Brady, T. and Huggett, C. 1981, *Maintenance Skills in the Engineering Industry: The Influence of Technological Change*, London: Engineering Industry Training Board

Strickland, L. and Hewitt, M. 1985, New operations and maintenance centres for second generation System X exchanges, *BTE*, 3(4): 286–9

Thompson, P. 1983, *The Nature of Work*, London: Macmillan

Thompson, P. and Bannon, E. 1985, *Working the System: The Shop Floor and New Technology*, London: Pluto Press

Thornby, A. 1983, TXE4 Configuration Control, *BTE*, 2: 43–9

Thurley, K. and Wirdenius, H. 1973, *Supervision: A Reappraisal*, London: Heinemann

Thurley, K. and Wood, S. (eds.) 1983, *Management Strategy and Industrial Relations*, Cambridge: Cambridge University Press

Thurman, J. 1984, Automation, work design and social policy. In F. Butera and J. Thurman (eds.), *Automation and Work Design*, Amsterdam: Elsevier, 23–42

Trist, E., Higgin, G., Murray, H. and Pollock, A. 1963, *Organisational Choice: Capabilities of Groups at the Coalface Under Changing Technologies*, London: Tavistock

TUC 1979, *Employment and Technology*, London: TUC

Vallance, I. 1985, Local Communications Services – shaping up for the future, *BTE*, 4(1): 2–8

Ward, K. 1974, *Modern Developments in Telephony: An Introduction to Electronic Switching and its Practical Applications*, London: British Telecom

Warner, M. (ed.) 1984, *Microprocessors, Manpower and Society*, Aldershot: Gower

Webb, T. 1979, The job security agreement, *POEU Journal*, May: 198–9

Whyte, J. 1974, Local exchange renewal strategy: foreword, *POEEJ*, 67(3): 130–5

Wilkinson, B. 1983, *The Shopfloor Politics of New Technology*, London: Heinemann

Williams, R. and Steward, F. 1985, New technology agreements: an assessment, *Industrial Relations Journal*, 16(3): 58–73

Willman, P. and Winch, G. 1985, *Innovation and Management Control: Labour Relations at BL Cars*, Cambridge: Cambridge University Press

Winch, G. (ed.) 1983, *Information Technology in Manufacturing Processes*, London: Rossendale

Winner, L. 1977, *Autonomous Technology*, Cambridge, Mass.: MIT Press
1985, Do artifacts have politics? In D. Mackenzie and J. Wajcman (eds.), *The Social Shaping of Technology*, Milton Keynes: Open University Press

Wood, S. (ed.) 1982, *The Degradation of Work?* London: Hutchinson

Wood, S. and Kelly, J. 1982, Taylorism, responsible autonomy and management strategy. In S. Wood (ed.), *The Degradation of Work?* London: Hutchinson, 74–89

Woodward, J. 1965, see Woodward (1980)
1980, *Industrial Organisation: Theory and Practice*, 2nd edn, Oxford: Oxford University Press

Index